WOMEN IN MEDIEVAL ENGLAND

WOMEN IN MEDIEVAL ENGLAND

LYNDA TELFORD

AMBERLEY

This book is dedicated to Dr John Ashdown-Hill
in appreciation of all his ground-breaking work
on the medieval period.

First published 2018

Amberley Publishing
The Hill, Stroud
Gloucestershire, GL5 4EP

www.amberley-books.com

Copyright © Lynda Telford, 2018

The right of Lynda Telford to be identified as
the Author of this work has been asserted in
accordance with the Copyrights, Designs and
Patents Act 1988.

ISBN 978 1 4456 6868 0 (hardback)
ISBN 978 1 4456 6869 7 (ebook)

British Library Cataloguing in Publication Data.
A catalogue record for this book is available
from the British Library.

Typesetting and Origination by Amberley
Publishing.
Printed in the UK.

CONTENTS

FOREWORD BY JOHN ASHDOWN-HILL

Inequality was a fact of life for medieval women. Generally the law was pro-male in every respect. That was consistent with the legal definition of a woman as written in 1180 – which stated that 'every married woman is a sort of infant'. For example, educational possibilities for medieval women were limited, and even a woman's personal possessions could not be bequeathed without specific permission from her husband. Many more aspects of medieval sexual inequality are presented here by Lynda Telford.

Nevertheless, it is perhaps worth observing that one very strange fact was that, at least in medieval *England*, women were apparently allowed to transmit rights to the throne! A number of people supported the claim to the English throne of King Henry I's daughter and heiress, Empress Matilda (or Maud), in the twelfth century. And although she never actually secured the English crown for herself, it did eventually pass to her son, King Henry II, on the basis of his descent from her. Moreover, ironically, Matilda's opponent, King Stephen, also based his claim to the English throne upon his mother, not upon his father. And of course, later, both the house of Lancaster and the house of York based their claims to the throne on key female ancestors. Finally Henry VII did the same. After he usurped the English throne, it would finally actually be sat upon by women (Mary I and Elizabeth I). Scotland was similar to England in that respect, though in other European lands, such as France, the Salic Law excluded women from the right of royal inheritance.

There was also one other way in which sexual inequality actually worked in favour of women prior to the sixteenth century. Men who committed (or were suspected of committing) treason found themselves put to death. However, women who committed (or were suspected of committing) treason were not executed. For example, in connection with the deposition of Edward II, Roger Mortimer was eventually hanged at Tyburn. However, his partner, Queen Isabel (the 'She-Wolf of France') was never executed. In fact, women were only given 'equality' in that respect by the new dynasty of King Henry VII, when the medieval period had ended!

Women in Medieval England does not confine itself to female influence on the struggle for the crown. In particular through her fascinating analysis of legal records, Lynda Telford makes a convincing argument that for ordinary women, the Conquest was in many ways a terrible step backwards in terms of their rights and position in society.

I

THE LOSS OF EQUALITY

The *Sarum Missal*[1] taught that the medieval wife should be 'bonair and buxom in bed and at board' and this promise was one of the vows taken by the woman on her marriage day. But bonair does not mean bonny and buxom does not mean cuddly. Together they mean courteous and obliging. In other words, they were vows of meekness and obedience, modesty and subservience towards the husband. That some women stoutly resisted the custom of being firmly controlled is understood, although open disobedience usually brought retribution in some form, sometimes severe. Since the Norman kings first established their rule over England in the middle of the eleventh century, every aspect of life had been irrevocably altered for the indigenous population. Life for women, including their duties and expectations within the marriage bond, were examples of a generally more restrictive trend.

It was not always so. The great Anglo-Saxon kingdom of the pre-Viking era was almost destroyed by Viking acts of aggression[2] but less than sixty years later, the heir to that ravaged kingdom was able to establish his claim to power. On that day in 937 CE, Æthelstan, the first real king of England, led his countrymen to a victory at Brunanburgh. This battle site has never been confidently identified and many claims have been made regarding its location, ranging from Axminster in Devon to Bumford in Northumberland. However, Simeon of Durham firmly stated that the Viking allies had travelled up the River Humber with 615 ships, which appears to make a case for Yorkshire. It must have been a very impressive sight for those inhabitants of East Yorkshire who were not already, sensibly, making themselves scarce.

Alfred had once been styled 'king of all England, except that under Danish domination'. Unfortunately that didn't amount to much at all, given that the Danelaw[3] covered all of Eastern England from Northumberland to East Anglia and in some areas stretched right across the country, to leave only the south and south west still able to consider themselves independent. Even after the Danelaw ceased to exist as a physical boundary, Danish influence continued. While the years of Danish domination had been relatively few, they left behind a firm legacy. Not only place names, many of which still endure in places such as the Yorkshire Dales, but also some very rare and strange Anglo-Danish burial goods such as the unique hogback tomb lids at Brompton near Northallerton in Yorkshire with their gripping bear ends. There are also a few enduring legends of feastings, battles, and great chiefs such as Erik Bloodaxe of York. He was a son of Harald Fairhair, who had been selected by the Northumbrians as their leader in 947 CE. But they also left behind a way of thinking and living, which would survive in people's minds as being fair and workable.

Æthelstan was to show, along with his religious piety, a great strength of leadership, which would quickly give him an international reputation. He would eventually be considered, both by his own people and outsiders, as having been a man of singular importance in his time. Yet so much of what was once known about this great lawmaker is now lost. William of Malmesbury, from the twelfth century, is still the most often quoted authority on the reign of Æthelstan, yet even William admitted that some of

his knowledge came from old songs and poems, and was therefore unreliable. What was to endure about Æthelstan was that essential Englishness, an idea of justice and fair play, the formulation of sensible laws that attempted to deal with any eventuality in an equable manner – a desire to give even the humblest person a position in law, and a set of rights and duties to be performed. These would even include that often to be disenfranchised section of the population, the females.

Whether the *Anglo-Saxon Chronicle* is to be considered as an historical work or merely as a popular fiction, it is, in its invasion scenes, entirely male. Nobody tells us whether the Vikings initially brought their own women with them. Ordericus Vitalis, the twelfth century historian who recounts the Norman invasion, at least informs us that the Norman women were afraid of the sea crossing and preferred to be left behind. This, of course, gave the Norman men the opportunity to intermarry with the females who were already in England. Did the Viking women stay at home, or were they made of sterner stuff? Did they make the crossing once their men had established some form of a system of survival and support for their occupation of the eastern part of England?

The native women there when the Vikings arrived were likely to have been initially enslaved, rather than killed – except, of course, for those unfortunates who became involved in the collateral damage that inevitably accompanies acts of war. This is also a form of conquest, the acts of intermarriage of the invading men and the surviving women once their own men were slaughtered or otherwise incapacitated by the invaders. The amount of slaughter among the 'native' men is now incalculable, but surely the surviving women of childbearing age were taken over by their captors, and whatever Anglo-Saxons had survived were in no position to prevent it. This scenario has been supported by evidence from Hampshire cemeteries, with taller men appearing in some numbers after the Roman period, while the stature of the local women remained much the same.⁴ The earliest of these graves bear witness to pagan beliefs, with bones and animals being buried with both men and women, suggesting the presence of meat offerings having been provided for the use of the dead. Some dogs are present within, usually, the female burials, but these were likely to have been sacrificed pets, whose deaths allowed them to follow their mistress into the afterlife.

The Anglo-Saxons, and their neighbours who lived within the Danelaw, had many laws covering marriage and the behaviour to be expected between man and wife. Life for them was always *public*, and it was in the interests of the whole community that a married pair could live together fairly amicably, as regular disturbances within one family group could affect all. The rights and duties of the pair were clearly defined, including the rights of the wife, whose likely compatibility with her husband was something her parents were expected to take into account. The married pair was not only expected to live in harmony domestically, but also within any business dealings they might undertake. The male and female roles were certainly different, but complementary, with both parties being considered equal. Higher status marriages would naturally have rather more parental input, and would probably also take place rather earlier in life, and this was a trend that tended to continue throughout the medieval period. People with more wealth and property would naturally wish to safeguard that inheritance, and arrangements would be made as soon as the parties were old enough to enter into a firm commitment. Poorer families would be limited to deciding upon the division of cattle or domestic possessions, but in either case the marital bond was considered to be both sacred and binding – the full consent of both the parties concerned had to be obtained and made clear, before the dowry or 'brydgifu' was arranged.

The Mundbara, or the woman's father or guardian, was obliged to take part to show his agreement, and he would also arrange for the 'faderfrum' or father's gift. This could take the form of land, cattle, money, or anything else of value, depending on the status of the families involved. His arrangement of this dowry payment signified his acceptance and his consent to the marriage of his daughter.

At the time of the wedding itself, the groom, after feasting with his friends, would go on horseback to the home of the bride, attended by his groomsmen. They would probably already be slightly the worse for wear after celebrating the nuptials in advance. Feasting was ferociously committed, and drunkenness was not in itself frowned upon. There were, in fact, many drinking games designed to test male superiority while inebriated, so it is quite likely that the wedding party was already very merry by the time it reached the home of the waiting bride. The bride was then led out to join her groom, accompanied by a brideswoman, her guardian and other male relatives. She would be handed over with the words 'I give her to thee, to be thy honour and thy wife. To keep thy keys, and to share with thee in bed and goods.' This ceremony would take place before a priest, standing under a cloth, held at its four corners by men, while the blessing was given and rings were exchanged. The new husband was also bound to 'use the wife well'. This was no empty promise, which could be ignored at the first sign of an argument, for if the wife was not perfectly satisfied with her treatment within the marriage, she was at liberty to leave it whenever she wished. Once the oaths were completed, the new wife was handed her husband's keys, to signify her new status as a housekeeper.[5]

Any bride who possessed a substantial dowry would naturally be in greater demand. This would allow her and her father or guardian a wider choice of prospective husbands and it would likely be made sooner. There was a real need for men of similar standing to find themselves brides with good dowries, and this must be done before anyone else had the chance to step in and snap up the more enticing and wealthy young women. A father's responsibility would be to ensure that his daughter was safe, both physically and financially, within the marriage, as well as any children born of the union. His choice was not only concerned with material comforts, but needed to take into consideration the probability of emotional contentment between the prospective pair. Both families would need to be able to rely on each other, and any discord between the young couple could jeopardise good relationships locally, particularly in a small community.

The morning after the wedding was the time for another important gift. This was the 'morgangifu', or morning gift. The husband gave it to his new wife and it represented her marriage portion. It was intended for her future security, and was entirely her own property, to sell or keep, or to bequeath to another person, exactly as she wished, without reference to the husband who had given it. This gift was often considerable. It could include land, property, livestock, rich clothing or jewels, or even valuable books. The wife at this time had the legal right to own land and other property quite independently of her husband or guardians. However, any finances that were to be earned within the marriage, for instance from some form of joint business, would then be equally owned between the husband and wife, and were not merely the property of the man. This gave the woman a genuine independence; her goods could be willed to her children, or used for her own comfort, as she saw fit. In effect, it was a dower, named thus in an ordinance of King Philip Augustus of France in 1214 and in the Magna Carta, not to be confused with a dowry.

A young woman named Eadgifu the Fair held, in her own right, estates in excess of 27,000 acres in eastern England, though such immense wealth was exceptional. She was the mistress of King Harald on the eve of the Norman Conquest, and was better known to history as Edith Swan-Neck.[6] Interestingly, Edith (or Edyth Swannesha) was considered by many to have been married to Harald Godwineson 'in the Danish style'. This presumably equates to a form of common law marriage, something that was recognised by the common law. Common law and religious law were often at odds, and certainly the clergy at that time considered that Edith was nothing but the mistress of Harald. However, during their twenty years together, they produced six children who were accepted as being fully legitimate.

Women of more modest means, though unable to personally own so much property, still benefited from the laws of equality. A substantial number of the grants of the period are made to husbands and wives jointly, and more than twenty-five per cent of surviving Anglo-Saxon wills were made by women, who were bequeathing their own property as they wished. There was no automatic right for any eldest son, or indeed any male relative, to inherit in preference to a female relative. Likewise, there was no particular bias in favour of the family of the father, regarding custody of any children of the marriage in the event of the death of the woman, or separation of the married couple.

The four weeks following the wedding was referred to as the 'hunigmonap' from which derives our own term honeymoon. The honey part of the name denotes the mead, made from honey, presumably drunk during the time of celebration. Once adult life started in earnest, the woman would have nothing to fear from her husband. It was customary to treat women with marked respect, and even the young girls of the family would be raised on a par with their brothers, expecting to eventually receive fair treatment from their own husband.[7] Naturally, working roles would be different, and lives would diverge, but the woman's role was never considered to be that of an inferior, despite both the Anglo-Saxons and the Danish descendants within the Danelaw being warrior-based societies. In time of war, if a man had the misfortune to be taken a prisoner, his wife would not only be expected to safeguard the home and any children of the family, but also to arrange and provide any ransom that might be required to secure her husband's freedom. In times of peace, they could work together fully, even in business, without the wife being considered a servant.

Later, when the Christian Church was attempting to dictate the terms of life for one and all, the Anglo-Saxon system still allowed for the expected influence of the wife over her husband. Many a husband would freely admit he had developed his own business or sphere of influence through that of his wife and her family in their support of him. Women seemed to accept the changes made when Christianity became popular, however, its apparently pacifist principles held some awkwardness for the men; for instance, what would be the use of a pacifist leader in wartime? The women were more easily assimilated and actually became saints at a tremendous rate, thereby exercising power over men even in the afterlife. Before death intervened, they had taken like ducks to water to positions such as abbess, which was merely a continuation of the organising and administrative position with which the aristocratic woman would already have been comfortably familiar.[8] Women would not at that time be confined purely to the domestic role, however much the clergy might have had the growing desire to confine women and allow them to exercise no authority at all over men. In the Church's estimation, only the occasional saintly abbess or prioress would be suitable to be given authority, even over other women. Even then, her role would need to be supervised by a priest, who conducted services and heard confessions, which, as a mere woman, she could never be allowed to do.

In the earliest mixed marriages, between part-Christian and part-Pagan couples, the Church had expected the Christian wife to have some influence for good over her Pagan husband. She would be assumed to be able to convert him to her faith, as when *Æthelburg* was married to King Edwin of Northumbria. In her case, her right to hold her own form of religious worship was a part of her marriage contract.

Although there was no allowance for actual divorce, except in cases of adultery, any woman was free to walk away from her marriage at any time if she was unhappy and the Church had no right to censure her for doing so. In fact, any woman deciding to take that course was also entitled to take her children with her, which was in contravention of all ancient practices that had all declared that any children of the marriage were the property of the husband. If the wife did leave, she was entitled to half the joint marital property, as well as keeping her morgangifu, which was still entirely her own. King *Æthelbert's* laws made the right of any woman clear: 'they have the right to leave any marriage which is displeasing.'[9]

However, the Church was even then beginning to interfere between man and wife, which seems to be contrary to its central task of promoting the sanctity of the marriage vow. There is a famous example of this, involving important and well-known people. In approximately 636 CE, Etheldreda, the daughter of King Anna of East Anglia, had wished to become a nun. She was, however, persuaded to make a marriage with one Tondbert, the king of South Gyrwe, which was an East Anglian sub-kingdom in the Fens. She received Ely (then known as Elge) as her marriage portion. During her three-year marriage, she had been constantly encouraged by St Wilfrid to retain her virginity and, to all intents and purposes, continue her life as if she had indeed been avowed religious. Her husband's opinion on this stance was not at that time recorded. It was only to be expected that he would at some point wish to become the father of an heir but in the circumstances he may well have made other arrangements. When he died, Etheldreda continued to live at Ely and once again made it clear she intended to take a life of retirement. By 660 CE, she was married again, albeit reluctantly, at the behest of her father – this time it was to a younger man, Ecgfrith, one of the sons of King Oswiu of Northumbria. The groom was described as having 'held her as a thing enskied (exalted) and sainted.' This may have been the case initially, but by the time he was in his early twenties he decided that he needed rather more from his wife than an object of adoration. For so young a man, such a celibate marriage was ridiculous, and he also would at least expect to be able to father children. St Wilfrid was still Etheldreda's advisor, which did nothing at all to help her marriage, and he still encouraged her celibacy. She asked to leave court, obtaining after some time a reluctant agreement from her husband, who was by then the King of Northumbria. No sooner had she left, than he changed his mind and demanded her return. She then fled to Coldingham Abbey, beyond the Tweed, to the protection of her husband's aunt, who was abbess there – but she was still pursued by the unhappy husband. During this flight, King Ecgfrith was said to have encountered an unusually high and dangerous tide, which lasted for seven days. This not only allowed her to escape but effectively dampened his ardour by convincing him that divine intervention must be at work. He gave up the chase, allowing her to retire to Ely, where she built a great double monastery. These were intended to house monks and nuns, although living entirely separately; they would meet only to worship in the central church, and were usually ruled by an abbess, who was a widow of eminent respectability. St Hilda of Whitby, who died in 680 CE, was the most well-known example of this type of religious leader. This was, of course, before monastic life was divided into the great religious orders, under the leadership of various charismatic and saintly men. In Hilda's day, Christian religious life was one entity, following the Celtic pattern of worship.

St Wilfrid is said to have obtained special privileges from the Pope for Queen Etheldreda and she was to rule Ely until her death in 679 CE, when she became one of the most popular of the Anglo-Saxon saints. Wilfrid went on to build Hexham Abbey on land that Etheldreda had given him.[10] The one continuing theme in her story is that despite being a Christian, and being subject to the increasingly influential Church, she still had a surprising amount of leeway to follow her own course in life. Eminent members of the Church hierarchy also supported her in her bid for freedom, despite her having taken marriage vows.

For the ordinary woman, once her marriage was established and her children began to arrive, her position was enhanced. She would be expected to play a substantial part in their upbringing and this would also give her added authority in the event of separation or widowhood. During any pregnancy, her condition would be carefully monitored. There are still references to the instructions that a pregnant woman should not eat salty pork, or drink alcohol, and should also avoid travelling on horseback. If a woman stopped menstruating, but was obviously not pregnant, or too old to bear children, she was advised to take hot baths, drink certain herbal preparations and dress warmly, in order to regain her health.[11] All very sensible and showing that she was considered to be still a person in her own right, not merely a disposable chattel.

Within the household, any Anglo-Saxon woman would be kept busy. There was a provision within their society for both male and female slaves, if they could be afforded, who would grind corn, act as servants, or be nurses for children. They also took over the weaving and sewing for the family. In any poorer household, all the work fell on the wife, until she had daughters old enough to be trained to take over some of her tasks. The housekeeper was also in charge of the essential dairy work, including cheese making, and the baking of bread. However, it would also seem that a certain amount of the cooking was done by men, and this is suggested by the old English word 'coc' which translates into cook, and has no obvious feminine equivalent.[12] Equally surprisingly, women are recorded as having then taken part in entertainments; not merely as observers, but also as singers or comedians. Storytelling and making music could be enjoyed by all, within the family or as a community, and there has always been a strong tradition of storytelling among Celtic-based societies that did not necessarily exclude females. These continue today among the many writers, historians and poets who have Celtic heritage and are the direct descendants of the original bard or seanchai, who kept the family or clan history intact and passed it on from one generation to another.

The children of the family were carefully protected by law, but only if they were legitimate. For the illegitimate child, life could be far harder and more insecure. Infidelity was difficult to hide in a close knit group, particularly when everyone took a close interest in the activities of their neighbours. Children were treated as miniature adults from an early age, though childhood was necessarily brief when there was much manual labour to be done and much to be learned in a relatively short lifetime. The Church also played its part in this enforced maturity, by accepting a male child as an oblate[13] as early as six or seven years old. Any youngster becoming a religious affiliate so young could not be expected to take vows, but they were still accorded the respect given to those who were chosen for the Church. The Tenth Council of Toledo in the seventh century forbade the acceptance of oblates before the age of ten years. Early commitment to the Church may well have served as a useful way to have a boy brought up and educated outside the home. This would be a forerunner of the later medieval practice of sending children to other houses to be trained,

usually in a household of slightly higher social status than their own. Fostering was also popular in Anglo-Saxon society, but was usually done by the family of the mother of the child concerned, presumably on the assumption that it was then easier to be sure that they were raising a child of their own blood.[14]

One of the greatest benefits afforded to women at that time was that they were considered to be full members of the State. Therefore, they were fully protected, as were their rights in law. Women could be referred to as being 'oath-worthy', which meant that they were fully competent and legally entitled to be called as a witness. They could act as grantees, or grantors, and were responsible for their own activities. After the Norman Conquest, even a noblewoman was often considered to be little more than an empty-headed brood mare. She was unable to bear witness, take an oath or administer one. Lesser women became nothing more than chattels, not even to be afforded the token courtesies extended to their social superiors. Not so the Anglo-Saxon woman. Even as an unmarried girl she could conduct business in her own right, and she retained that right after her marriage, with the added proviso that she and her husband could then do business either together or separately. One could not be blamed for the mistakes or shortcomings of the other, nor was the woman expected to pay any debts incurred by her husband if difficulties befell him. If the husband turned out to be a thief, his wife was considered innocent of any crime that he committed, unless stolen goods were found 'under lock and key' in which case, as the housekeeper and holder of the family keys, she could be regarded as an accomplice. If a woman met with abuse, she could claim compensation for any injury to her person, in just the same way as a man. The clergy, unfortunately often all too willing to condone or turn a blind eye to the beating of recalcitrant wives, tended to be at odds with the law in this matter. The law clearly stated that any abuse was not to be tolerated or excused, whether it was towards 'maiden, wife, or widow'. With regard to sexual abuse, the Church tended to believe that all sex was sinful, therefore the only true and holy life involved a vow of celibacy. Women, designed by nature to be child-bearers, were in essence sinful in themselves, and therefore a temptation. The only way for them to redeem themselves was to remain virgin or eventually to become a respectable widow. The clerical horror of what might be termed 'normal' women, fulfilling the function nature intended them for, says rather more about frustrated abstinence than any imagined sinfulness on the part of most ordinary women, particularly those with any claim at all to physical attraction. Women in general would come to be censured for not being able to achieve a level of supposedly saintly behaviour that would be practically impossible to emulate in everyday life. Even sanctified nuns were not considered capable of living within their own rule, without the supervision and guidance of men. The mere presence of a woman was considered by some to be polluting, and blame was quickly attached to any woman suspected of using her wiles to attract or control men.

In comparison, the fortunate Anglo-Saxon woman seems to have been living in a social environment of downright common sense, in a time when sexual crimes were generally regarded with horror and rape was severely punished. In Anglo-Saxon society it was more expensive to pay for the rape of a slave woman than to have seduced a freedwoman, the onus being on the degree of unwillingness about the act of the woman concerned.[15]

If a woman was widowed young, particularly if she were childless, she could reasonably be expected to remarry, though she could not be forced to do so; nor could she be pressured into marriage by a third party, whether from a member of her own family or otherwise. Æthelred's Code of 1008 CE stated clearly that any widow should remain single for twelve months after the death of her husband, but she may then choose any other husband she wished. If she was left childless, she was still able to claim one third of the marital land, or other property, as well as keeping her morgangifu. A law of Cnut states 'neither widow nor maiden is to be forced to marry any man she dislikes, nor should she be given in marriage for money.'

It might be worthwhile at this point to take a brief look at those laws that were fundamental to the daily living of all classes of people. Bede, in his *Ecclesiastical History*, considered Æthelbert of Kent[16] to have been 'the first English king to enter the kingdom of Heaven'. Whether or not he was holy beyond the norm, he was famed for his law-making and Bede writes of him:

> Among other benefits which he conferred upon the race under his care, he established with the help of his counsellors a code of laws after the Roman manner. These were written in English and are still kept by the people.

These are famed as being the earliest set of written laws of any of the kingdoms of post-Roman Europe, and are the first such documents written in the Anglo-Saxon language. They are, however, rather confusing and do not make the position of the women of their society as clear as could be wished.[17]

Æthelbert's Code contained ninety clauses, only the first of which referred to the Church, regarding penalties for disturbing the peace or damaging church property. The remaining laws give what amounts to a tariff of compensations, intent on itemising the cost of reparations for physical injuries or affronts to personal honour. These did not imply that rights were actually equal, for they were not. The life of a king was vastly more important than that of an ordinary person, and therefore more valuable financially. The value of an ordinary person would also depend on whether he was free, partly free, or a slave. This wergeld was understood by every man and woman, who were all well aware of their own standing within the system.

The clauses relating to women exist on the same principle, and Christian teaching or values do not figure largely. For example, a woman might be abducted, which did not seem to be in itself a problem. The problem arose in deciding what recompense should be awarded to settle the outcome. If she were a slave, then fifty shillings would adequately repay her owner. If a woman were betrothed 'at a price' to another man, then twenty shillings would be compensation enough. However, if she is then returned, the abductor is fined thirty-five shillings with fifteen shillings owed to the king. Separate tariffs applied to assaulted or abducted widows, dependent as always upon their class. Casual sexual acts were not condemned, but were priced pragmatically, again with an eye to the status of the woman concerned. This of course, also derived from her official 'owner'. A fine of fifty shillings would be enforced for the crime of 'sleeping with a maiden belonging to the king '– but only twenty-five shillings for sleeping with one of the domestics. But was the compensation to be paid to the woman or to her 'owner'?[18] 'If a freeman lies with the wife of another freeman, he shall pay his wergeld and get another wife with his own money and take her to the other man's home.'[19] In essence, in this case, the offender was obliged to replace the dishonoured wife with a new one. Despite the confusion over which of the injured parties the money should be paid to, it still seems a more enlightened system than the one of torture and death facing adulterous wives in Germany. The details of that form of punishment were unfortunately recounted with some approval by St Boniface, in a letter to King *Æthelbald* of Mercia.

Property was the decider, as in so many other forms of law. Clause 37 of Æthelbert's Code says 'If a freeborn lock-bearing woman misconducts herself, she shall pay thirty shillings compensation.'

This reflects the level of betrayal of her husband, who had entrusted her with the family locks and keys.

It is intriguing to see that Christian ideas among the Anglo-Saxons, who were only newly converted, had surprisingly little influence at this time. The Anglo-Saxon word 'haemaed' is used for any sexual intercourse, whatever its context, and only some time later did separate words become common, which would denote unlawful 'unrihthaemed' or wrongful 'wohhaemed' intercourse.[20] Even when Christianity was well established, it took a long time for its sexual teaching to be heeded by people who still preferred the old ways, with several Anglo-Saxon kings cheerfully continuing to have more than one wife. King Cnut, who ruled both Denmark and England after 1016, had his recognised queen, Emma, but also his recognised concubine Ælfgifu of Northampton. This lady occupied a place that was far higher than merely being a mistress. It was clear that she was also Cnut's wife 'according to the Danish custom'. This habit was not restricted only to Denmark. In seventh-century Northumbria, King Oswiu was succeeded by Ældfrith, who was his son by his official Irish concubine. In fact, in seventh-century Ireland, lawyers accepted the practice of primary and secondary wives. As with English law, their main concern was with property, and the rights of any heirs to the various unions. In England, there was no polygamy, but the practice of having a wife and a concubine was hardly likely to be restricted only to royalty. As has already been mentioned, a marriage was not necessarily intended to be for a lifetime, and if the couple separated it was not automatically the female of the pair who was discarded. As shown in Æthelbert's Code, any woman wishing to end a relationship could do so, taking with her not only half of the joint goods, but all the mutual children. If the children for any reason stayed with the father, the wife received an extra child's share of the property.

Later seventh-century Kentish laws would make provision for mothers, specifically widows, left to raise their children alone, saying: 'If a man dies leaving wife and child, it is right that the child shall accompany the mother. One of the child's paternal relatives, who is willing, shall act as a guardian for that child until he is ten years old.' King Ine of Wessex's laws, also seventh-century, made similar arrangements. Clause 38 of his code states: 'If a man and his wife have a child, and the husband dies, the mother keeps the child and brings it up. She shall have six shillings for its care, with a cow in the summer and an ox in the winter, and the kinsmen are to look after the property until the child is grown up.' With reference to these laws, respecting the rights of both the children and their mothers, Christine Fell[21] makes it clear that the original wording used is 'bearn', which is similar to the northern 'bairn' and does not specifically refer to the sex of the child; this may be either a boy or a girl, and therefore shows that the female child is equally protected.

A century or so after Æthelbert, King Wihtred of Kent (690–725) became the first ruler to insist that his subjects became Christians. This was to mean the enforcement of Christian marriage laws, which banned all of the 'illicit cohabitations' or 'irregular marriages'. Existing unions of that kind were then punishable by fines, excommunication, or expulsion from the kingdom, if the parties concerned should be foreigners. Later clauses would, interestingly, mention the worship of devils, though even here women were not expected to do exactly as their husbands decreed. 'If a husband sacrifices to devils, without his wife's knowledge, he is liable to pay all his goods … If they both sacrifice to devils, then they are both liable to forfeit all their goods...'

Even the new Christianised code of ethics could not entirely prevent people from taking the law into their own hands, and the old ideas of vengeance still held.

> He who finds another man with his wedded wife, within
> closed doors, or under the same blanket, or if he finds another
> man with his legitimate daughter, his sister, or with his
> mother, if she is given in wedlock to his father, he can fight
> the intruder with impunity. If he kills him, the man's kin will
> not be allowed to avenge him.[22]

Perhaps it might depend on whether he looked bigger and stronger,
or seemed likely to be able to kill the offended party instead.
In which case, perhaps creeping away and pretending to have
seen nothing might be more sensible. However, the laws of Cnut
were far stricter and more severe on the subject of punishment
for female adultery, and were also concerned with the monetary
compensation to be paid.

> If a woman during her husband's life commits adultery with
> another man ... her legal husband is to have all her property
> and she is to also lose her nose and her ears.[23]

The Christian 'Penitentials' would emphasise the gravity of sins,
and the penances which would be imposed in order to atone for
them. One proscribed all sexual activity during Lent, for three days
before taking Holy Communion, and also forbade any man from
seeing his wife naked.

The eighth Archbishop of York, Egbert, claimed that laymen
'with their wives and families' were eager to be freed from 'carnal
concupiscence before receiving communion at Christmas'. It
sounds rather as though he is convincing himself, and perhaps the
laity were not quite so enthusiastic about the ban as he imagined.

The development of the Christian mind-set was a long time
in transition, and the Council of Hertford in 673 shows, in
the *Penitential of Theodore*, just how many concessions had
to be made; the hardships being caused by the new rules were

even acknowledged by Pope Gregory. A hundred years later, compromise was still necessary. For example, if a woman left her husband and after five years had not returned to him, he could, with the bishop's permission, then remarry. If either husband or wife were captured in war, the remaining party could also remarry after five years had passed. An adulterous woman, who had been rejected by her lawful husband, could remarry after five years after performing a penance. The *Penitential of Theodore* is often unsympathetic towards women. The menstruating woman was considered to be unclean. Adultery by the woman was grounds for a separation, but not in the case of adultery by the husband. Should the husband decide to take back the erring wife, it was entirely on his terms. Yet there is still leniency in other areas, sometimes where it might be least expected. For example, if a poor woman should kill her baby, she should not be heavily punished; and there was understanding and some leniency for daughters if they wished to reject the husbands chosen for them. The *Penitential* was concerned not so much with the rights of individuals, but with the proper and right organisation of society, with 'the security of the kingdom and the salvation of souls'.

On 5 January 1066, Edward I of England (known as Edward the Confessor) died at Westminster. He was of the ancient Saxon house of Cerdic and his marriage to Edith, the daughter of Earl Godwine of Essex, had been childless. The chosen successor to the throne was Harald Godwineson. He was chosen not merely by Edward himself, but also by the Witanagemot, the king's council of earls, magnates and advisors.[24] However, at the death of Edward there was a problem, as there were conditions governing the selection of a king. He needed to be of the royal blood. If he had already been named as the successor to the previous king then he was in a favourable position with regard to possible succession. He needed to be possessed of both physical strength and strength of character to help him rule the kingdom both wisely and justly. These conditions were intended to ensure that the best man available was chosen in times when there was no obvious direct successor. In January of 1066 there was no one man who seemed to fit all the requirements – but there were several claimants. The rulers of England, when they were from time to time threatened by the Danes, had frequently looked to the Normans for support and they had also consequently inter-married with Norman aristocracy. By 1042, Edward the Confessor was the only remaining offspring of these Anglo-Norman alliances, carrying royal blood from both sides. He had been accepted, even welcomed, as ruler, both by the Saxon and the Scandinavian factions in England. He had kept the kingdom together by diplomacy and compromise, in an era when either, let alone both, of those skills were highly unusual. Over in Normandy, Duke William was achieving stature and many leading magnates gave him their support. It would be logical if Edward were to assume that this cousin of his might be the man capable of uniting the two lands and preventing any possibility of another unfortunate Scandinavian takeover of England. T.J. Oleson suggests that Edward had already promised the throne to Duke William – possibly even openly, at the March Witanagemot of 1051.[25] If Edward had actually promised the throne of England to William, an embassy would have been sent to formally acknowledge such an important development. The 'E' version of the *Anglo-Saxon Chronicle*[26] tells us that Count Eustace of Boulogne (brother-in-law to Edward I) visited the king at Gloucester, and then embarked at Dover for Normandy in that year. Thus, when Edward I died in January 1066 and Harald Godwineson stepped forward to take the throne, justified though he was by the approval of the Witenagemot, there was over in Normandy another man who considered himself to be the rightful heir. Duke William believed that the promise made to him by Edward back in 1051 should hold.

The struggle for the throne would not only involve England in the catastrophic battle of Senlac Field, that determined conflict of 14 October 1066 which ended with the death of Harald Godwineson, but also effectively brought with it the death of English freedom. It should have taught the Normans something about English determination, for had the forces led by Harald Godwineson not had to see off an attempted invasion by Harald Hardrada the month before, then return to tackle the Normans immediately, the result might have been different. The victory of the Normans was not due to any lack of skill on the part of the English. In fact, the warfare would extend over the following three-and-a-half years, so strong was the English desire to be freed of the Norman yoke. However, the continuing struggle would prove a tragedy and a waste, not only in manpower, but also for any possibility of real settlement in the foreseeable future. The carnage which was to follow the Conquest, shown most starkly in the 'harrying of the north' was a portent of the fear, anguish and sheer hatred which the subjection of the people and the imposition of an alien feudal society was to create.

This feudal system, at its height, would consist of three broad classes, consisting of men of prayer, men of the sword, and men of the countryside. In none of these was womanhood initially of any importance, certainly not politically. The chief beneficiaries of the new system would, naturally, be the conqueror's Norman followers, and when the lands changed hands, with French-speaking Normans replacing Anglo-Saxon landholders, it was only one of the many changes the people would have to endure. Latinate clergy would impose a new liturgy, extinguishing the old English literary traditions, and in the courts oath-taking and fines would be replaced by the brutality of trial by combat, blinding, or castration.[27] The most obvious symbols of the new subjection were to be the defensive castles that sprang up across the country, at all strategic points. In fact, a mere twenty years after the Conquest, only two major estates in England had remained in English hands, so complete was the takeover.[28] The feudal system, in the medieval context, worked by an arrangement of land holdings, or fiefs, given in return for military service. A tenant did homage to the landholder, became his 'vassal' and the holding he received was complete with its workers, upon whose labour all depended. The vassal undertook to serve his lord, with horse and arms, and in return the lord gave him a certain amount of protection. This was the practical response to the collapse of a genuine central authority after the tenth-century Viking attacks, the breakdown of urban communication, and the disappearance of cash money.[29] Women were to find themselves devalued. Their future position would depend not upon a set of laws, which clearly defined their rights, but upon the whims of a husband whose complete authority over them would in future be supported by the clergy.[30] The clergy would enjoy a moral superiority, as representing the only social hierarchy to survive the breakup of the Roman Empire. Unable to bear arms themselves, they would compensate by monopolising the mysteries of the sacraments, and learning of all kinds.[31]

For the women who had experienced both ways of living, before and after the Conquest, it must have been a frightening and confusing time. Their menfolk would be either dead or fled, or if still at home, would be just as subject to the new masters as the women themselves. The casual equalities of living were completely gone, and it must have seemed as if justice had also gone. People had become like animals, to be passed from hand to hand alongside the land on which they lived. Their masters now spoke a language they largely could not understand, yet punishments would be inflicted for all apparent acts of disobedience, or any infractions of the new rules. The lady of status who found herself widowed and remarried to a Norman, might at least have understood some of his speech, and also understood what had happened to change life so dramatically. For the field worker, it must have seemed that they were better off under the Vikings, with whom at least they had some ideas in common. The Normans, in general, had scant sympathy for their new subjects and future prospects were not good, and for women they were particularly bad. The worries about the fate of their children would have become nightmarish had they known that it would be centuries before women would once again control their own property, or be able to inherit it for their own use.[32] The women of the mid-eleventh century, seeing their homeland devastated by war, would have been astonished to learn that it would take another 800 years before they could regain the rights that they had taken for granted, and which the Conquest had taken away.

2

THE NECESSITY OF MARRIAGE

Perhaps the best place to begin, when looking at the upbringing of any child, is to examine the standard of living of the family concerned. This defines not only the quality and quantity of the food, clothing and housing of that child, but the aspirations of the family with regard to their offspring, given their social level and their income. It is a given that the enormous changes due to the Conquest affected the lives of the English women as much as the lives of their men. Farm workers were obliged to do a certain amount of work on the demesne of their lord, as a labour payment for their own holdings. This had a domino effect on the work patterns of the women also, as they then would have to make up the shortfall of labour on their own lands, while the men worked elsewhere. This was, naturally, in addition to the domestic duties expected of them, which included the bearing and rearing of their children, which could not be allowed to interfere with the requirements of physical labour. The main focus of control, however, showed itself in their villein status, to which these previously free people had been reduced. Later generations of medieval peasants, who would grow up knowing little or nothing of the Conquest itself, would still have to live with the system which had been imposed.

This initially dictated that the family, as a unit or individually, would be quite unable to leave the manor to which they belonged to seek better conditions elsewhere. They would need their lord's permission for everything, even the right to marry, and this could be given or refused entirely at his whim. They would also be subjected to a system of payments, from the cradle to the grave, which helped to keep many of the common people from achieving any real prosperity and which would eventually come to be deeply resented.[1] It must not, however, be assumed that every peasant family lived in dire conditions, though unfortunately many did live in filth and squalor. Within the peasant communities there were different levels, ranging from the desperately poor to those who might be considered to be comparatively wealthy, who would, in time, be able to afford small luxuries of the kind way beyond the expectations of their more unlucky neighbours.[2]

In consideration of the desperate poverty of many of the villein class of tenants, the lord would commonly provide many items on loan to a family newly taking over a tenement. These items were listed in the Court Rolls in an inventory similar to that commonly used in modern times when a tenant takes on a lease. The items provided were to be returned, or otherwise accounted for, on the removal or death of the tenant concerned. Interestingly, the records show that this did not always happen. The people who spent their lives working on another man's land, rather more for his benefit than their own, were just as likely to become resentful as today's labourers. Quite often, lacking the necessary permission to make a change, they simply did a moonlight flit, taking with them whatever could easily be carried from the property provided by their landlord. Field equipment, such as beasts of burden, wagons, and large implements could not usually be removed without difficulty, but smaller items such as pots and pans, shovels, axes, other working tools and household essentials were commonly filched, going missing at an alarming rate. Many peasants believed that if they could make their way to a walled town and remain undetected there for a year and a day, then they would be free of their landlord and he would be unable to reclaim them, or demand their return. This probably stems from the important 'year and a day' used in 'handfasting' in Saxon times. This had been intended to give a young couple a taste of marriage, for that requisite year and a day, after which they would be permitted to either make their union permanent, or go their separate ways.

Whether or not the landlord usually thought it worth his while to pursue a small group of fleeing tenants is debatable, but he would certainly be concerned for his property, not to mention the financial loss involved and the lessening of manpower on his estate. Other items commonly provided by the landlord might include tables of the trestle type, chests, large brass pots, coffers in which things would be stored, and perhaps a lamp or even a spinning wheel. Sometimes a cupboard would be allowed, or even an oven or a kiln. These may well not represent the whole of any family's possessions. Their prosperity or otherwise would depend not only on their ability, or inclination, to be industrious, but their ability to produce a saleable surplus – to have those essential extra pairs of hands to help provide the necessary food, clothing, essential household goods, or even those decorative items so dear to the heart, in imitation of their social superiors. There was often a wide variation in any such collection of treasured possessions, which would not necessarily be subject to the generosity or otherwise of the landlord.

Archaeological evidence shows that pottery brought in from regional centres was common, and these items could have travelled as far as 100 miles from their sources, and often included some fine, highly glazed items that would have been much prized.[3] A family, depending on the number of members and on their diligence, and consequently their earning power, might expect eventually to increase their status, along with their possessions, which could then include sheets, mattresses, blankets and other comforts, as well as baskets, bowls, towels, changes of clothing, and other easements. The most prosperous peasant families could own items such as silver spoons and small pieces of jewellery, which were used not only for personal display but as a form of family savings. Small items of jewellery and various coins still turn up on village sites, and they now have a rarity which demonstrates how valued they once were. They would have been carefully preserved within the family, and hidden away. A fourteenth-century silver spoon was found hidden in a thatched roof in the 1980s and the high price it was to subsequently bring at auction testified to its extreme rarity for collectors.[4] It was a delightful survival, though its discovery in an unusual position poses unanswerable questions. Was it so carefully hidden by its rightful owner, or perhaps secreted as a stolen item, squirrelled away by a thief for later sale but never recovered?

At the opposite end of the spectrum, the manorial courts describe people with appallingly little in the way of material possessions, particularly in the late thirteenth and early fourteenth centuries. In 1279, on Chalgrave Manor in Bedfordshire, a bondsman died leaving behind only his surcoat, which he requested should be given to the church. A cow was his only other possession and that was intended for his sister, who was a leper.[5] Unfortunately the woman, who might have seemed unlucky enough already, never received the beast, for the bondsman's lord demanded it be given to him, as a heriot payment.[6]

Such wide variations in the standard of living would result in vastly different prospects and expectations for any offspring. For many families mere survival was enough of a struggle, and even the monastery or nunnery would not be willing to accept any child who could not be provided for, except as a servant. To become a religious it was necessary not only to be of a certain status but also required the provision of a dowry, sometimes impossible to find, even if the child concerned was deemed to have an inclination towards religion. Therefore, the standard of recruits into the Church was often dictated more by one's financial standing than by any real vocation.

At whatever level the family lived, their household tended to consist of the parents and their own children only. This is a more compact family unit than is often realised. It certainly contrasts with the more sprawling family groupings of the traditional Saxon or Anglo-Danish longhouse arrangement, where extended family and/or friends might live together.

Ideally, as children grew to adulthood, they would expect to be able to claim either a part-share in the family possessions, or a stake in the family holding. Daughters would need a dowry with which to attract a husband. If material possessions were lacking, then some skill or ability would need to be cultivated in order to earn a living. It must, however, be understood that for poorer people this would not entail being apprenticed to a formal trade. Such training would again be available only to those who could afford a premium, which was intended to cover the costs of the years of training as an apprentice, and the keep of the young person in the meantime.

For daughters, domestic skills would be a part of life from earliest days. Even the smallest girl could collect eggs or feed poultry, and her work would increase in scope and responsibility as she grew. She would eventually be required to be competent to run her own household, having spent her childhood learning not only cookery, basic perhaps but still essential, and the care of smaller siblings. Everything else from spinning, weaving and sewing to farm and field work would be necessary to provide for her own future family, and in order to be able to help out at busy times. If the mother of the family had any particular skill, such as midwifery, this would be passed on, and the daughter would be grateful that it would give her an edge over other village women. They would from time to time need her services and help provide her with a useful recompense, even if her clients were unable to repay her with anything other than food and drink.[7]

It is futile to nurse a romanticised view of the cottagers' lives, with a house by the village green, and a gaggle of children playing happily outside surrounded by chickens. The cottagers' lives were difficult and their diet was terrible, particularly if they remained poor or had too many children to feed. Scurvy is usually considered to be a disease of sailors who spent too long away from fresh food while afloat, but it was also rife among the medieval poor, especially during the winter. It tends to be first noticeable as a lack of energy, but quickly leads to spongy gums, loss of teeth, haemorrhages beneath the skin and even blindness. The cure was known and in the first spring days, people would be seen gathering the first green shoots of newly sprouted plants. Scurvygrass (*cochlearia officinalis*) is a member of the cabbage family, and often used as a cure, though young nettle tops, hawthorn shoots, or chickweed were almost as good, with the latter also being useful for skin ailments, which were another product of a poor diet and unhygienic living conditions.[8] Rickets was another problem, being caused by a vitamin D or calcium deficiency. Sunlight is the main vitamin D provider in northern Europe, unfortunate if there is a series of poor summers. Fish, dairy food, eggs and green vegetables are the answer, the lack of which causes softening of the bones over time.

A long hard winter would mean that many a peasant family, subsisting on pottage, bread and any meat that may have been salted away, usually pork, suffered from a diet that was not only boring but also unhealthy. Even the salting down of a pig, or part of one, could present problems. Firstly, a pig needed to be fed, usually on scraps or the acorns in the local wood. This would depend on whether the family had the right of acornage, which gave them permission to graze their pig there. Secondly, the vital salt, used liberally in the preserving process or to prevent excess meat being wasted, was one thing that a poor family would be unable to provide for itself. It came from the coast, where seawater was evaporated, or from a few places where it could be mined. That made it expensive, and it must have been heartbreaking to realise that the meat of the family pig, fattened with difficulty and then killed to keep the family alive during the winter, had gone bad due to the lack of salt used. The Domesday Book describes how fines were levied in Cheshire, which was one of the places where salt could be mined, intended to prevent carriers overloading either horses or wagons.[9] Salt was an important source of local revenue, with streets or marketplaces being named after it. Its importance had yet another significance for the rich, as the salt cellar itself was often a valuable piece of plate. One's status at table was defined by the salt cellar, as one would be placed either above or below the salt. Only when the summer season was fully established could a peasant family enjoy the benefits of whatever vegetables might be available, such as cabbages, leeks, onions, peas and beans, eked out with wild garlic, wild sorrel, dandelions and any other edible greenery. These could be added to the usual oatmeal gruel to make the 'mess of pottage' so often referred to. The word 'mess' eventually came to mean the place where a group of people ate together, and is a term still used by the armed forces.[10]

Eventually, a family would be raised – with almost inevitable losses over the years. The estimates of infant mortality at this time are unreliable. Some court records provide data concerning the number of children dying from accidents, or in suspicious circumstances, but there is no accurate or even satisfactory record of the number of children lost. The highest estimate of infant mortality is fifty per cent but the most common one is around thirty per cent, which is perhaps a more realistic figure. Accidental deaths included being overlaid in bed, either by parents or siblings, and difficulties experienced during feeding. If the mother's milk was unavailable or insufficient, then the child's chances of contracting illness were greatly increased; other methods of supplying a child with milk tended to be highly insanitary. Accidents also accounted for a large number of deaths once the child became mobile. Falling into the fire or the village pond was quite common. Small children were often looked after by only slightly older ones, while the mother worked or was occupied with the new baby. The little child-minder, easily distracted, was often barely able to look after him or herself, with unfortunate results.

Even for gently-born women, infant mortality was common. A woman might then be expected to attempt another pregnancy far too soon, hence the use of wet nurses for those who could afford them – not to preserve the figure as is sometimes believed, but because it was known that breast feeding a child tends to have a contraceptive effect. Falling pregnant soon after a miscarriage would lead to repeated losses if the woman did not have time to recover from the previous pregnancy before entering into another one. Being given the necessary time may have resulted in fewer but probably healthier births for the woman concerned. Even queens, such as Katherine of Aragon, wife of Henry VIII, or Margaret of York, the wife of Henry VII, lost children. At the most exalted level in society, the survival rate was roughly three out of five.[11]

However many children were reared, their future needed some consideration. For many, having to follow in the footsteps of their parents was a depressingly regular outcome. For the girls, marriage and motherhood would be expected, though some women found the single life had to be faced and then had to find some way of supporting themselves. This often led them into taking care of parents, or becoming someone else's servant. For boys, the examples of the relatively few humbly born men who made good, usually through the Church, would have seemed merely a dream. Without money, education or sponsorship from some person of standing, rising into a higher level would be impossible – even being able to become a successful farmer or tradesman was beyond what was likely to happen.

This brings us to the question of the age of young people at their marriage. Because royal or noble betrothals, even marriages, tended to take place while the couple were very young, it is often believed that all medieval marriages were contracted in the early teens. Certainly the suggested 'fourteen years old for boys and twelve years old for girls' is regularly quoted, but this tended to be the case in families where extensive estates, titles, or substantial dowries were at stake. Naturally, if great estates needed to be secured, there would be a scramble to confirm a betrothal, or better still an actual marriage, as a way of securing future prosperity. For peasant families, there was also the necessity of finding a suitable partner to marry, though the requirements would be different. Not for the peasant farmer the worry about wealth and position, he would require a woman who was strong enough to work, and capable of raising a family. It was necessary to ensure that the couple were not too closely related to one another, always a problem when people did not tend to move far away from the villages they were born in. The penalties of too much inbreeding were known and feared. The next problem would be a financial one, as a tax would have to be paid on marriage. This was the 'merchet', a payment for the licence to marry. These taxes were at the discretion of the lord, or other landowner, and might be applied erratically or regularly, or only when the lord was in some financial difficulty of his own. The lord of the manor of Wakefield in West Yorkshire found himself in need of cash in 1316 and instituted an unprecedented collecting of lapsed 'fines', both for 'legerwite' (the fine for indulging in illicit sex) and for merchet. It is sometimes unclear whether the 'legerwite' fines were levied on the people or on the property itself. However, the result was the same, money or goods had to be found. Some manors levied such fines only on their better-off tenants, but others were indiscriminate. In Lincolnshire, at Spalding, the fines tended to be imposed regularly, though in one recorded case, only a few herrings were demanded.[12] This was a level of fine which a woman would be capable of paying for herself, though demands were often far higher. Sometimes a woman had to pay both the legerwite and the merchet together.

The main concern for the medieval prospective husband was that the woman he intended to marry could conceive a child. It was often necessary to have some evidence of this before the man would commit himself to matrimony from which there was no escape. The old Anglo-Saxon 'childwite' tax could still be imposed if a woman actually produced a child without first managing to get the man to the altar. This was the fine for producing an illegitimate child. Sometimes both that and the legerwite tax could be used as a successful method of taxing brothels, even those run on an 'amateur' basis.

Despite the apparently firm control of sexual matters by the Church, nature will out. Although fines were imposed and people presumably shamed in front of their friends and family, they continued to behave in a casual way towards fornication, while the Church fumed at its inability to stop it and the lord of the manor pragmatically made money out of it.

At Wakefield Manor Court in 1316, no fewer than seven female villeins were fined for lechery. To be fair, no such fines had been demanded in the area for some time, and it would seem that the numbers involved are more in the nature of the lord of the manor clearing up several outstanding cases all at once. In the Manor Court Rolls for Walsham le Willows in Suffolk, in 1340, one Alice Fitte was fined two shillings and eight pence for 'giving birth outside of wedlock'. Downham in Cambridgeshire in 1311 had tried to enforce morality when twelve jurors stated that Alys, the daughter of Amicia, had committed adultery and was therefore 'in mercy'. The phrase 'in mercy' is a common abbreviation for amercement and merely means that she was fined.

Local people were expected to do their bit in keeping sexual dalliance within bounds. In 1316, at Ossett near Wakefield, the whole community was fined forty pence for having concealed the conduct of three local sisters, Eva, Alice and Annabel, who had all been deflowered outside marriage and were therefore all fined as lecherwites.

This all seems to be quite bucolic and cheerful, with lovers carrying on in the woods, but there was of course another side to it. Perhaps the generally easy-going attitude towards fornication could be attributed to so many people being obliged to marry someone they did not actually choose for themselves. It is, however, reassuring to learn that so many women were in a position to pay their own fines. They were also sufficiently in control of their own sexuality to defy the rules, choosing their own sexual partners, at least for temporary liaisons. There was unfortunately still a good deal of pressure on them not only to marry legally, but very often to marry somebody chosen on their behalf. This was by no means confined to the noble lady, betrothed in childhood to the son of another noble. Village girls often found their life partners chosen by their fathers, brothers, uncles, or even their lord of the manor. Not only might a low-born girl, with a minimal dowry or no dowry at all, be obliged to accept the only man who offered for her, if the local landowner needed to keep up the manpower on his estate, he could force all available women of child-bearing age to marry. This could happen even without some catastrophe, such as the plague, having decimated the numbers of labouring men in the area. One woman complained that the males of her family took staves to the marriage contract ceremony, all the better to frighten the bridegroom with, if he turned out to be reluctant. When questioned about the staves, they claimed that they had brought them merely to help them get over the muddy ditches on the way. It is unlikely that the intimidated groom was reassured by this excuse.[13]

There are a great many letters extant, from the Pastons, the Stonors, the Lisles, the Plumptons, the Cely Papers and the papers of John Shillingford, which give glimpses into the personal lives of these people, often describing severe marital difficulties or reluctance to wed on the part of their offspring. However, these people were all relatively privileged and the problems encountered by peasant women, finding themselves in a similar situation but without money or support or any network of powerful friends, are often distressing to read about. In 1289, in Cambridgeshire, one Agnes Seynpel was fined twelve shillings by her overlord. She had refused to marry his choice of a husband for her, and the fine she had to pay was to give her a few months further freedom in which to find some husband of her own choosing, before being obliged to accept the man offered. The poor woman must have been desperate not to be forced into a lifetime with someone she disliked, or perhaps had never met. The records are unfortunately silent on whether she was able to find someone more to her liking or not. Despite the power held by local lords, this is not the only instance of a woman refusing to marry a man chosen for her in this way. It is encouraging that some did still dare to defy those in authority over them, but it must have been a stressful time, and it is always possible that there were later repercussions.

The Prior of Norwich, in 1308, granted twenty-four acres of land to a man and his wife, on condition that within eighteen months they married one of their daughters to the prior's bondsman. If the marriage failed to take place, not only would the land revert to the prior, but the couple would also face a fine of forty shillings.

At Horsham St Faith, in Norfolk, where the Prior of St Faith also happened to be the lord of the manor, between 1284 and 1290 nineteen men and twenty-nine women were summoned and told that they were expected to marry. The proposed spouses were in that case chosen by a jury of local men, and heavy fines were to be imposed if the marriages did not take place, the fines being the equivalent of twelve days' wages for a labourer. If they did refuse, they could choose their partners for themselves, though they would still be obliged to pay the fines. There is evidence that the local men and women much preferred to pay up and be allowed to choose for themselves rather than to submit to the arrangements made for them.[14] Also at Horsham St Faith, in 1291, a mother was fined six pence for impeding the marriage of her daughter to a man chosen by the jurors. The girl was fined three pence and the man was also fined three pence. He had apparently already refused other brides who had been chosen for him in this arbitrary fashion so the mother was probably correct in assuming that he was unlikely to make her daughter a good husband.

Ecclesiastical court cases suggest that while marriage itself was a serious and permanent business, premarital sex was taken far more casually by both sexes. It could still cause problems with ordinary marriages, due to resulting pre-contractual difficulties, which could nullify any subsequent marriage. The complex nature of the rules of consanguinity could be a minefield, even for someone such as Henry VIII, and could be guaranteed to ring alarm bells at local level when a previous sexual relationship caused later problems.[15] One enquiry found that Stephen Gobat had agreed to marry Juliana Bigod, but later claimed that he could not marry her due to an affinity arising from her earlier sexual relationship with William Attemore. Stephen claimed he was related to the said William by a prohibited degree of consanguinity. Almost a year later, another man, Stephen Pertefeu, claimed that he also had a contract of marriage with Juliana. In the meantime Gobat had decided that his contract with her was legal after all, that he was not related to William Attemore at all, and also that his agreement to marry Juliana predated her contract with Pertefeu. However, Juliana's contract of marriage was nullified with regard to Gobat on the grounds of his affinity with Attemore, which was just the opposite of what he wanted. It was finally decided that Pertefeu was her legal husband. The problems of a sexual relationship with one man causing legal affinities preventing her marrying another were confusing at best.

There was often confusion about what constituted legal marriage and what did not. In 1422 John Astlott and Agnes Louth were before the York Courts. John was a merchant and at one time, when he was due to go abroad on business, Agnes begged him to propose to her. She said that her father was nagging her to find a husband. John subsequently exchanged vows with Agnes, after taking a goose to her father's house as a gift. John went off on business but lost a great deal of money, after which Agnes decided that she didn't want to marry him after all. John believed that owing to the vows they had taken, they were already married, despite having no formal church ceremony, and took her to court.

In York, a case before the courts from 1351 to 1355 caused dissention even among the judges. John Bullock was alleged to have vowed to Isabelle Roll, 'If I take any woman as my wife, then I will take you.' They had then slept together. However, John then went on to marry someone else, and the case was brought to court by Isabelle, who claimed that John had a pre-contract with her.[16] Much of the confusion was due to the nature of the vows themselves. It mattered whether the intended was actually saying 'I will take you now, as my spouse' or whether it was the rather more open promise of 'I will probably marry you in the future.' These were known as *verba di presenti* or *verba di futura*.[17] Unfortunately, far too many women were beguiled by the second, rather than holding out for the first. It was better if vows were said before witnesses, which could save many future problems.

It was not, in fact, uncommon for two women to claim consummation of a marriage with the same man, when a promise between a couple, followed by sexual union, could constitute the legal tie. Many a local charmer with ready promises could have found himself in trouble with the courts when the local girls gave in to him after listening to his declarations of love (and commitment). Although virginity was often made much of, lack of it did not necessarily create a barrier to the serious marital intent of future husbands in the real world.[18] Such pragmatism on the part of prospective husbands may well have reflected their own pre-marital adventures.

There must have been some people to whom religious instruction meant more, and various ballads told of the feelings of guilt in brides for not retaining their virginity, even if it had been surrendered after some persuasion. For them all, the relatively free love of their adolescence had to be put aside once a serious marriage proposal was accepted and arrangements began to be made.

The *Liber Gersumarum* of Ramsey Abbey gives some detail about marriage arrangements. Out of 194 cases where the husband was known, forty-one per cent were outsiders. However, the ecclesiastical courts, which listed both names in cases where marital disputes were heard, indicate that perhaps as many as two-thirds of marriage partners came from the same village.[19] However, popular fifteenth-century poetry was very much against any real freedom of choice in marriage partners. The *Mutatis Mutandis* says 'self will is taken for reason, true love for fancy chooseth, and no man thinketh shame.'[20] Such was the general distaste at the idea of young people having a choice in their life partner. Although there was a fair amount of freedom before actual marriage in the choosing of a sexual partner, the long haul usually turned out to be a rather different matter. Distance and family concerns would always play their part in limiting choice.

The Church, ever equivocal, argued that both partners to any marriage had freely to consent to it. Yet it was at the same time concerned that young people accept their family's choice for them without any real protest. The Church was offering a theory that was difficult to put into practice. Certainly, any marriage could only be canonically valid if both parties consented freely, yet there were still cases where a bride was literally forced to the altar and forced to agree, which duress must have been obvious to the officiating priest. So where would such a situation leave the consent requirement, and what of the priest who was prepared to conduct a ceremony with an evidently unwilling bride? These cases of abuse must have not only probably led to a later failure of the marriage itself, but must also have raised serious legal questions about its validity. Technically, any marriage performed under duress was indeed invalid. Unfortunately, any girl wishing to make a case for separation, citing force as her cause, had to be pretty quick off the mark, as once the marriage had been consummated, with her consent or otherwise, then the union was deemed to have been rendered legitimate. The solution was to have the parish priest 'read the banns' for three weeks prior to the actual marriage, to give time for any interested party to raise objections. The usual objections that were considered acceptable were consanguinity, a prior contract, or a previous marriage by one of the parties concerned. It still did not give any protection or support to any young person being forced into an unwanted life union by family pressure. The fact of simply not wanting to go ahead with it was not considered to be sufficient reason to cancel the nuptials. If nobody spoke up during the reading of the banns, then the marriage took place at the church door, which was originally intended to curb abuses such as bigamy, by making clandestine marriages less easy. In theory, anyone could watch the proceedings as a witness. The general horror at the idea of a clandestine marriage was that it was one sure way of circumventing an arranged one. It was a way of jumping the gun and securing the preferred partner, if there was one. It would certainly muddy the waters of legality with respect to any future attempts to force one of the couple into marriage elsewhere.

For a couple considering themselves in love, and preparing to have a clandestine wedding, the great attraction was that such marriages, even without parental consent, and in the early days even sometimes without the presence of a priest, were still canonically valid. All that the law required was that the couple should declare themselves before witnesses, which was to be followed by consummation. Sometimes just the betrothal was considered bond enough, and sex then took place before any formal vows at all were exchanged. By about 1500, the Church had changed things by its preference for the legitimate union to begin only after solemnisation of vows in front of a priest. This not only made the role of the Church central to the proceedings, but also meant that the ceremony surrounding the event became more complex. This had the effect of reducing the number of clandestine marriages. Unfortunately, it also raised general marital expectations to a pitch that was difficult to live up to in everyday life – rather like the modern-day bride who becomes obsessed with the gown, the reception and the honeymoon, so that what comes after is something of a let-down.

Sometimes, naturally, passion overcame common sense, and a couple who had made a romantic but hasty marriage, clandestine or otherwise, later realised that they had made a mistake. This could then lead to bigamy if the couple finally parted (unofficially) and found someone else they wanted to marry. They had, of course, no way of legally freeing themselves from their first legal partner.

There were, however, some cases where bigamy was entered into deliberately in order to try for a better deal. One such case, in 1290, was taken as far as the King's Court. Edmund de Nastok and Elizabeth Ludehale wanted to marry, but were both poor. They did marry secretly, but then Edmund negotiated with Richard de Brok for the hand of his daughter Agnes. The reason was easy to see, for Agnes had a very good dowry: six horses, ten oxen, twelve cows with calves, twelve steers and heifers, eighty ewes with lambs, twelve rams, thirteen pigs, various quantities of oats, rye and salt, and some items of rich clothing. The list ended with various cloths, towels and no less than 100 shillings in cash. Edmund de Nastok may have been handsome, he was certainly possessed of some charm and the ability to persuade in order to get the father of such a well-heeled daughter to even consider him as a prospective son-in-law. Perhaps Agnes was impressed by him and added her pleas to persuade her father to allow the marriage. They did eventually marry and Edmund became the proud owner of all the goods Agnes had brought with her. Shortly afterwards, Elizabeth, Edmund's original wife, turned up. She pleaded her prior contract with him and the plea was originally heard in the Church courts. It soon became clear that Edmund had hoped that if he married Agnes, albeit bigamously, he might somehow be allowed to keep some part of that substantial dowry, but the plot misfired. Edmund had to return the full value of the dowry he had obtained by deception to Agnes, and their union was declared to be invalid. He also had to pay to her £16 in damages.[21]

It would seem that rural and urban marriages tended to follow slightly different patterns with regard to the age of the partners at first marriage. One must be careful not to confuse later remarriages with the original ones, but there is evidence that people who moved into the towns to find work, which included many young unmarried women, tended to marry rather later. They also often gravitated back to the country to find their partners, possibly because their work restrictions meant they were not free to do so while living with their employers.[22] Living as a part of someone else's household, even as a domestic servant, meant that any young woman would be likely to be kept not only very busy, but also under supervision. Therefore she would have little or no free time and would be discouraged from gadding about and forming undesirable or unsuitable relationships during the term of her service.

The York Cause Papers depositions suggest that child marriages, except among the landed gentry, were not usual and by the late fourteenth century were rare.[23] The fourteenth century saw a general movement towards the towns so it was not unusual for women to be still unmarried in their twenties, even if they were not actually employed as household servants. This pushes back the age of first marriages to a surprising degree, if we are only familiar with gentry marriages with their usually young brides. There was a feeling, unfortunately often ignored by noble families to their own detriment, that any girl bearing children too young was likely not only to endanger her own health, but would probably produce inferior offspring. This goes back to the Ancient Roman ideal, which preferred a girl to marry at around eighteen or twenty years old, when she was more mature and certainly stronger and less likely to produce sickly or otherwise deficient children.[24] There was also the universal, ageless block of poverty, which had to influence the moment at which humbly born couples were able to set up some sort of a home together. This would be subject to work, and often to whether a cottage could be made available for their use, as well as how generous a landowner might be in his loans of essentials. There was the hope that the families might be able to provide some support in that direction. Consequently, the twenties seemed to be the optimum time for the first marriage in the majority of cases at that time. Of course it wasn't simply one's overlord who had a vested interest in a marriage, so did one's family, with members looking out for suitable partners for their relatives – suitable meaning being able to bring some benefit to the family in general, rather than a purely romantic attachment.

Alwin of High Easter in Essex did very well on behalf of his five sons. He was a half-virgater, which meant that he held approximately fifteen acres of land.[25] He managed to marry two of his sons to women who were due to inherit a half-virgate each, while another son married a widow who also had a dower of half a virgate. The fourth son would take over the family holding so only the fifth son would need to be provided with a bought parcel of land. Although Alwin paid the merchet fee on all the marriages, he had still done exceedingly well for his family, and the sons were unlikely to protest at marrying women who brought them land as a marriage portion.[26]

Fathers of girls who were likely to inherit useful parcels of land were surely very circumspect about future sons-in-law. They would not only take over the land by right of their marriage, but would also be responsible for the care of their parents-in-law in their old age. Even where the available acres were poor, or few, families would make the best deals they could, and if the parents of the prospective bride had already died, then the inheriting son would arrange marriages for his siblings. The same arrangements were also made in urban areas, with no actual land involved.[27]

Marriage contracts, wherever they took place, required careful planning, sometimes over a long period. There might even be a form of deposit paid, as an indicator of good faith. Even then, matters did not always work out as intended. In any small area it was possible there was a degree of consanguinity, often due to the groom having had a sexual relationship with some woman related to his future wife. This brought them within the bounds of affinity and might be deeply regretted, as it would cause not only embarrassment but potential financial loss. John Love wished to take up a vacant holding, but could not afford the fee of £3. Agnes Bentley offered to pay it for him, if he married her daughter Alice. Unfortunately, he had to admit to Agnes that he could not afford to take up the offer, as he had in the past had sexual intercourse with one of her kinswomen. In another case, Agnes Smith was so much desired by John Tolle that he gave her twenty-four shillings as a bond to 'reserve' herself for him. He claimed that if there should turn out to be some impediment to their eventual marriage, she should return the money to him. However, she then found out that he had had a relationship with one of her kinswomen, so not only was the marriage no longer possible, but Agnes refused to give John his money back.

While some people fought over money, others had little or nothing at all to bring to the bargaining table. Marriage for love has often been assumed to be the privilege only of those unfortunates who had nothing else to offer, though even with the poorest people some little ceremony was preferred. In the clandestine marriage made between Alexander Wright and Isabel, daughter of Joan of Wisbech, the court was told that the pair had managed to have one such small ceremony. Alexander had asked

Isabel, before witnesses, to be his wife, and she had agreed to marry him. He had given her a kerchief and a small chest, and they had held hands while he pledged himself to be her husband. As this simple agreement was witnessed, the couple were confirmed by the courts to be legally united in marriage. A more regular form of marriage, blessed by the Church, would be preceded by a betrothal. This would give the families time to make their financial arrangements for the couple's future. Then the banns would be read in the local church. After the three weeks' delay, which allowed for objections, the wedding party would go to the church door, where the financial details such as the dower would be announced to the assembled villagers. As mentioned earlier, the dower usually guaranteed the wife a right to a portion of her husband's property if he should pre-decease her, while the dowry was the portion which the woman took into the marriage with her. After these formalities, the vows would be declared in public, still at the church door, to make witnesses not only of the wedding party itself, but anyone who happened to loiter outside. The vows were similar to those still in use:

> Man: I take thee … to my wedded wife, to have and to hold, from this day forward, for better for worse, for richer for poorer, in sickness and in health, until death us depart, if holy church it will ordain, and thereto I plight thee my troth.
> Woman: I take thee … to my wedded husband, to have and to hold, from this day forward, for better for worse, for richer for poorer, in sickness and in health, to be bonair and buxom in bed and at board, until death us depart, if holy church it will ordain, and thereto I plight thee my troth.

The rings would then be blessed and exchanged and the words 'with this ring I thee wed, and with my body I thee honour' were spoken. If the priest could persuade the wedding party to delay their celebrations a little longer, they would then all go into the church itself to hear Mass. However, priests often complained that peasant families were unwilling to take the time to indulge in more religious ritual, being eager to get on with the more entertaining part of the day.[28] Marriages were, of course, festive, with feasts and revels provided as far as the families could afford. For many people, it would be the only real celebration in their lives, until their own children were of marriageable age. Village people generally led hard lives, often living on the breadline, particularly if there was a large family to feed. Sometimes the proceedings got out of hand, and drunken brawls and inter-family arguments were a result. However, that is no different from many of today's celebrations, when family members of widely differing views are flung together in close proximity, with the fuel of alcohol releasing inhibitions making the atmosphere incendiary. Drunkenness may be considered reprehensible, but when the people were normally faced with a punishing daily routine, lightened only by church rituals and the occasional family gathering, it seems a pity to judge them on that one rare day of relaxation, which they would remember all their lives when the bad times came. There were always moralists who wished to dampen the pleasures of other people.

> Further we enjoin, that marriage be decently celebrated with reverence, not with laughter and ribaldry, not in taverns or with public drinkings and feastings. Let no man place a ring made of rushes, or any worthless or precious material, on the hand of any woman in jest, in order that he may more easily gain her favours, lest in thinking only to jest, the bond of marriage may actually be tied. Henceforth, let no pledge of contracting marriage be given save in the presence of a priest, and three or four respectable persons, summoned for that purpose.[29]

It is, or should be, perfectly understandable if people at a wedding feast, who often had so little, should over-indulge and become a little boisterous. Indeed, boisterousness was the very nature of the day, with its sexual content being, for once, encouraged. It must not be assumed that the young people concerned were innocent of physical matters; they would more than likely have had sexual encounters before committing themselves to a marriage. These adventures might be only with each other, but they were equally likely to have been with other people, and they may have already been expecting a child when they married. This was no less usual then than now. In fact, in medieval times it was more understandable, when a man would need to ensure that the future marriage partner was fertile. So much was this accepted and allowed for, that the lord of the manor would turn a blind eye to the sowing of wild oats, providing the appropriate fines were paid. The Church might frown on such practices, but people in the real world had to be more realistic.[30]

The priests had already had their way in the Church's restrictions on the times when a marriage could take place. Lent was, of course, prohibited, as was Rogationtide (25 April and the Monday, Tuesday and Wednesday before Ascension Day.) These were days of supplication and prayer, in addition to Advent and Christmas. Just under a third of the year consisted of banned days, about eighteen to twenty weeks in all, which were largely still being observed in the sixteenth century, when both marriages and conceptions fell in number around those times.

The bawdy nature of the proceedings increased as night approached, when the groom might be encouraged with exclamations such as 'Go to it, and remember God made man before he made woman.' These would not have caused offence, any more than the public escorting to bed, or tearing of 'favours' from the couple's clothing, if love knots, ribbons and other small tokens could be afforded. The tradition of throwing the bride's stocking into the assembled crowd was another habit designed to break down inhibitions, when the object of the wedding night was not so much romantic love, as the conception of a child.

3

BE YE FRUITFUL AND MULTIPLY

Taking it as a given that the main reason for any medieval marriage union was the production of children, the advancement of the family played a large part in future considerations once that family was raised above bare subsistence level. Prosperity without children to pass it onto was pointless. No sensible person wished to devote a lifetime's hard work to the probable benefit of someone else, so producing heirs to whom to leave whatever one had managed to acquire was paramount.

The Church, of course omnipresent, still considered sex of any kind to be a necessary evil, but evil nonetheless. The clergy spent a great deal of time wriggling on the double hook of admitting that children needed to be born, yet hoping that people would generally consider using sex merely as a duty towards such procreation, and that they would certainly not enjoy it, as therein lay sin. Much had already been done towards taking all the pleasure out of physical intimacy: the idea of marriage itself being a duty, the production of any children also a duty and with little regard to natural affection, let alone natural desires. Yet people did still manage to find pleasure in their relationships with each other – from young people choosing sexual partners before marriage, to married couples who grew fond of each other and were able to work together, eventually handing on an ethic of shared work and loyalty to their children and grandchildren. So, for better or worse, the couples were married and, in theory at least, paired for life. The bride may well have been already pregnant and if she were not, then conceiving a child would be one of her first concerns.

Medieval gynaecology was very basic, and it was not really possible to know whether or not a woman was with child, until the child began to move in the womb. This was known as being 'quick' with child. The menses may stop for several reasons other than pregnancy. Shock, overwork or poor diet may all result in the loss of the monthly period, so it could not be taken as a definite indicator, although for most women it is usually the first clue than conception has taken place. The womb itself, and its method of working, was a fearful mystery, with all kinds of fantastical explanations of how a child came to be born. In fact, until the Renaissance and the anatomical drawings of men such as Leonardo da Vinci, even the position of the womb was debated. Galen of Pergamon[1] worked in the arena, formulating his theories of medicine from the mangled bodies of gladiators, which unfortunately did not allow him much experience with the anatomy of female cadavers. There were some female gladiators, but they were considered something of a comedy act, like dwarves, and Galen's subjects were certainly predominantly male. He did refute Plato's idea that the womb was an independent creature, living inside a woman's body, loose and floating, changing its position at will. Galen considered it to be something like an inverted scrotum, with its own seed, which, if left unused, would cause hysteria. Unfulfilled sexual desire in women was believed to account for all manner of ailments, generally under the name of 'green sickness' and this was popularly supposed to account for any oddness in single women or young widows. Leonardo da Vinci was able to dissect human corpses in Florence and his anatomical drawings, wonderfully realistic, were the first real attempts to explain the workings of the womb, and the process of childbirth itself.[2] But he lived in the sixteenth century, and for those people who lived before him and later people for whom his knowledge remained unavailable, the womb was still believed to be a mysterious organ, usually depicted as being filled with many miniature men and women. Some medieval drawings of the womb showed it to have seven separate chambers, the three on the left were for the production of girls, the three on the right produced boys, while the odd one out, as one might expect, produced hermaphrodites. Some people, right up to the nineteenth century, believed that the testicles contained *homunculi* or very tiny people, who lived there until they were implanted in a womb. In the womb they then remained until they had grown and acquired sufficient size and strength to enable them to climb out.

Of course, the first duty of any husband was to ensure that his wife conceived. It has always been a sad fact that the woman carried the blame if the couple produced no children at all, as men have always liked to imagine that they were possessed of great virility even if the evidence showed otherwise.[3] They certainly have always had a greater ego to protect in sexual matters. This was not, thankfully, a legal ruling, and the courts showed themselves to be reassuringly even-handed about infertility problems in matrimonial cases. However, on a more personal level, women still tended to be blamed, unless there was positive proof otherwise, such as children from a previous relationship.

Infertility was not considered grounds for dissolution of marriage, which is probably why so many men were eager to father a child before their wedding, to make sure the chosen woman could actually manage to become a mother. However, impotence was another problem altogether, and did provide firm grounds for the separation of the married pair. Before going to the extreme lengths of attempting to end the marriage, it was usual to try one or two remedies, in the hope that the embarrassing and demeaning problem might be dealt with, or prove to be only a temporary one. Eating mint, or chewing the seeds of the ash tree, were considered helpful in overcoming the problem; but if frigidity was present, then mandrake root or sage were supposed to incite passion in women.[4] Mixtures such as cinnamon, ginger and cloves could be tried but were merely heating rather than aphrodisiac.

Was it possible that a man's natural potency could have been stolen by some malicious witch? If so, how did one go about making her give it back? At least these hypothetical questions might succeed in distracting attention from the poor man's real problem, even if it caused worse ones for the nearest old woman, living innocently alone with her cat, who might well then be blamed. If there was no possible witch living locally, then one might try mixing bran with pig's liver, stirred in well with a good dose of urine. It was not quite clear whether the man was expected to use his own. There was always massaging, to improve the circulation. But presumably, that would have been one of the first things the man's own wife would have tried?

Albertus Magnus, in the thirteenth century, had applied his intellect to the problem, and came up with a recipe. 'If a wolf's penis is roasted in an oven, then cut into pieces and chewed, the man who consumes it will experience an immediate desire to have intercourse.' All very reassuring, except for the part he apparently missed at the beginning of the recipe, 'first catch a wolf...' This solution is in line with perceived thinking over the centuries, which has always assumed that any part of an animal remotely resembling the male genitals is likely to prove itself a good cure for all their ailments. Thus horns, bones, animal genitals, have all been hopefully – if not successfully – used, until several species have been hunted to extinction or near-extinction due belief in the cures of sympathetic magic. The tiger disappears today, as does the rhino, in a part because of such ridiculous theories.

There was a school of thought that insisted that flagellation could be used to stimulate the man. It is not suggested that this be done as a form of punishment, the recommendation being that it 'be used lightly to stimulate, until the penis and the insides of the thighs are red and smarting.' It is not clear what one is meant to use to achieve this, though anything from hazel rods to nettles have been described at one time or another. If a good bunch of nettles was the source of stimulation, it certainly would be 'red and smarting' particularly if the victim thought of taking a bath afterwards. It might work on a certain level, but there was always the possibility of problems in the future, if the result was actually enjoyable and thereby created dependence in the subject.

There are a few less painful or potentially harmful ideas, such as putting six large cloves of garlic into a cup of boiled milk, to be drunk from at least twice daily. Whether this was likely to make the subject feel any friskier is debatable, but his wife was likely to object to him getting close to her for some time in protest at the terrible smell, so perhaps he would be unlikely to find out whether it actually worked or not. Crab apple was said to 'promote a healthy attitude towards sex' although Culpeper, who might at least have been expected to suggest some pleasant herbal cure, could only come up with the idea that a man should 'piss through his wife's wedding ring', presumably not to be attempted while she was still wearing it. One midwife thought that a good impotence cure would be to 'drink water from the mouth of a stoned horse'.[5] In this instance the 'stoned' horse is not one that has been fed some chemical hallucinogen, but an 'entire' horse or stallion, one still retaining his stones.[6] This would seem to be yet another attempt at sympathetic magic, in hoping that the virility of the stallion would pass into the man. Stallions are known to be unpredictable creatures, and the man would be very lucky not to find himself kicked across the yard.

The only idea upon which the so-called experts all agreed, was that worrying about the problem would certainly not improve it. Indeed, it was likely to make it worse. Unfortunately, the sufferer might then also be struggling with a severe case of indigestion after a diet of garlic milk and pig's liver in urine. He was probably wearing various amulets of dried dog's penis, or fake unicorn horn, and with his wife refusing to sleep with him until the garlic fumes had abated, there would be little else he could do but worry. He would be well aware that his wife had a legal right to have a sex life, and also to expect children from her marriage. If he failed to provide these, she would be entitled, after three years of the unsatisfactory situation, to have her case brought before the courts with the intention of having the marriage dissolved – enough to cause him many a sleepless night, whether or not he was actually fond of his wife, as he would have to undergo humiliation and the real possibility that no other woman would care to risk marriage with him, for fear of a similar outcome.

However, if things did go according to plan, the wife would in due time be able to announce that she believed herself to be with child. Any certainty on that point would have to wait, of course, as would the outcome. Many women claimed to be able to know the sex of the unborn child, either by the way the pregnant woman carried the growing bump, the state of her general health, or the use of various further charms or potions. If their prognosis proved to be correct they could claim great success and perhaps make a living from such prophesying. But they were just as likely to be wrong, and often this would cause problems if the putative father was promised a son and then found himself with a daughter. Some men were famously peevish about such things; Henry VIII in the sixteenth century was a case in point, so it was a dangerous to make promises to a man if the result could not be guaranteed.[7]

As a pregnancy progressed, the mother would expect to have her 'gossips' around her (originally in Old English 'godsibb' meaning 'sponsor' or 'godparent'), that is her village friends and family, women who would give her support along with a good dash of folklore, superstition and probably also a fund of stories of other pregnancies that ended well or badly. These would sometimes be enough to scare a young woman and make her wish it all safely over. Safety could not be guaranteed. One woman in three might expect to die during her childbearing years, from birth complications, a haemorrhage, or from infection contracted during or shortly after parturition. Many women also suffered dreadfully in later life from prolapse of the womb, as a direct result of giving birth to several children. While preparations were being made for her child to be born, the woman would also be advised to make her confession and receive the blessings of the church, just in case things did not end happily. Similarly, the midwife was empowered to personally perform a hasty baptism, in case of need, provided that there were witnesses present. It was important that any child appearing likely to die was baptised. If a priest could not be quickly found, it was necessary to prevent the soul being lost and ending up in Limbo, that place for unbaptised infants, who were not to be allowed into Heaven to join the company of the blessed.[8] As well as prayer, with St Margaret usually being invoked, nobody thought it did any harm to hedge one's bets a little, with lucky charms, and perhaps a piece of coral about the mother-to-be, to ward off the evil eye.

Before labour was due to start, the room would be prepared with coverings over windows and doors, shutting out most of the light and air and with a roaring fire raising the temperature. The women would await the onset of labour proper and all men would be excluded. No doctor, priest, or male sibling, not even the woman's husband, would be allowed back into the room until all was over. Likewise, the mother would not be allowed out. This is the origin of the term 'confinement', when the prospective mother was confined to her room to give birth. The actual birth process could take place in bed, on a low truckle bed brought in for the purpose, or on a birthing stool – on which the mother sat upright, supported by another woman. There was a gap in the seat of the stool, to enable the midwife to check on proceedings and have the child directed into her hands once labour was completed. The great advantage of a birthing stool, as opposed to any kind of bed, was that gravity was able to greatly aid the birth, with the child easing down more normally. These items of furniture were used from earliest times, and there are several pictures extant of women in ancient Rome being supported during childbirth on a similar item. This contraption would be the property of the midwife, if one was used, though as always the woman's own family would provide what they could for the confinement.[9]

If the mother lived in an area where a large church, or an abbey, was in possession of a holy relic applicable to childbirth, this could be used as a focus of prayer. Some items could even be borrowed, such as birthing girdles, attributed to the influence of one saint or another. There was no suggestion that the saint in question had actually used it, of course, but some of these items became quite famous in their locality. One such was kept at Reivaulx Abbey in Yorkshire, under the name, and presumably also the protection, of St Aelred. This could be wrapped around the woman in her travail in the hope that the blessings of the saint would help her to achieve a safe and speedy delivery.[10] Other places are known to have cherished similar relics, which might be sent for in case of difficulties. Other treatments, both physical and spiritual, might be tried in attempts to aid the mother. Sweet oils were often rubbed onto her stomach and thighs, which may well have had a relaxing effect. Herbal drinks were often made, and there are certain herbs that have for centuries have been associated with childbirth, particularly raspberry. The leaves of the common raspberry (*rubus ideaus*) infused into a drink, tone the tissues if taken throughout the pregnancy, but are particularly effective if used during the final months. Common nettle (*urtica dioica*) is also useful, being a good source of iron.[11] Other cures, more superstitious than efficacious, might be tried. These included letting down the mother's hair, or untying all knotted items that were close to or in contact with her. Sometimes a knife would be laid on the floor under the bed in the hope of 'cutting' the pains. If the birth appeared to be proceeding normally, i.e. the child was presenting in the correct position, but the birth was otherwise delayed, a good handful of pepper, held under the woman's nose, causing an enormous sneeze, had apparently been known to bring about the desired result.[12] If, however, the child was presenting wrongly, in the breech position, any competent midwife should be able to turn the child, after oiling or soaping her hands. If a child were definitely stuck, having gone over its time and becoming too big, being unfortunately trapped by a too-small pelvis, or having already died, or being a fallopian pregnancy, there was not a great deal to be done. It is a fallacy to imagine that any form of Caesarean operation could then be performed, as might be expected in modern times. Such an invasive operation was allowable by the Church but only in the case of a mother who was already moribund and beyond saving. If there was any hope of saving a full-term child, then it was permissible to cut into the body of the woman in the hope of drawing the child out, but it was well known that any such intervention would certainly kill the mother, if she was not already dead. In fact, it was not until the 1880s, when simple anaesthetics had been produced, and a basic hygiene level had become established, that any woman survived a Caesarean at all. It was recognised in medieval times to be a last-resort, which would take the life of the mother, only in an effort to save that of a viable child. It is also incorrect to assume that Gaius Julius Caesar was delivered in this manner. It would certainly have killed his mother, and it is well known that the mother of Caesar, Aurelia Cotta, lived to a ripe old age. The *Lex Caesaria*, established in the time of Numa Pompilius (715–673 BCE, well before Caesar's time), stated that if a pregnant woman died, the baby had to be taken from her womb. The Lex *Julia* was the one carried down to the Christian church, which recommended that the body of a woman in extremity might be opened in an effort to save her child.[13]

So, assuming that our hypothetical mother had survived with her child, both would have been thoroughly cleansed by the attendant women. The child would then have been warmly wrapped. In many cases it would have actually been 'swaddled', which meant being encased in almost mummy-like wrappings to prevent unnecessary movement. It was believed that this would encourage the limbs to grow straight. The wrappings would have to be removed at intervals, to clean the child, but the free movement of limbs, so important for development of the muscles, would have been lacking in the earliest days. Breastfeeding was important, as any other method of feeding the child was unsatisfactory, if not downright unhygienic. Wet-nursing was common, and some friend or relative might be in a position to help with that, if the mother proved to have insufficient milk of her own. The mother might hope to be able to have four weeks' rest after the birth, to regain strength and form a bond with her child. This was, of course, the ideal scenario but many mothers with little or no help and other children to care for would be unable to lie abed for so long. She would not, however, be expected to regain her full life out of doors. Until she had been 'churched' she was considered to be unclean from the childbirth, and the simple ceremony of churching was usually performed around the fourth or sixth week after the birth. Only when that had been done, could she fully return to normal life.

Baptism was too vital to be delayed until the mother was on her feet and in the world again. It would be done as soon as possible, to ensure the safety of the soul of the child, if any mischance should befall it. Because of the constraints of time and the churching, the mother would usually be left at home while the godparents took the child to the church. Once the baptism was completed, a celebration would be in order, with such gifts for mother and child as could be afforded.

The description of childbirth in the sources tend to show the ideal, and cannot usually convey to the reader the horrors of childbirth in a dark and grimy room, perhaps with a child whose birth is delayed, a midwife helpless, a mother either screaming in pain or haemorrhaging into a torpor. Nor can it adequately describe the eventual loss of a much-wanted child after months of hopes, or the loss of the mother. Her death could perhaps leave a house full of other children, who would then necessarily be dispersed between whatever relatives could take them in, if the father found he could not cope. Such an unfortunate outcome was common enough for many second marriages to be entered into purely to ensure that there was someone available to raise a brood of motherless children, rather than for any more sentimental reason.[14]

Although the problems of infertility and impotence have been touched upon, what of the family whose very abundance of children was in itself a problem? Too many children allied with too little money have been the reasons for more misery within any family than just about anything else. They forced the family group into a level of poverty it has little chance of ever getting out of and meant that with each successive pregnancy the existing children had to share what little there was with yet another mouth to feed, yet another body to clothe, yet another human to take up space and need attention. Added to this, there was the very real problem of a mother growing weaker with each pregnancy, more likely each time to lose her own health, or even her life. The belief was that she was obliged to continue to do her duty. To allow her husband to have sexual relations with her, take the risk of another pregnancy, and yet another, until her health may have been forfeit. Her survival, or otherwise, was in God's hands.

The Church had long considered that this was not only the woman's duty but the price she had to pay for protection within marriage. Many marriages may well have been fond, even happy, and mutual dependence either developed into mutual affection, or a reasonable facsimile of it, over the years. But there must have been an equal number of unions in which the woman was a drudge, working in the home as well as the farmyard, dairy or fields, bearing and rearing children with regularity. She may well have done this without the mutual tenderness and support that was popularly supposed to have been one of the chief consolations of marriage.

For every woman who grieved over a miscarriage, or was deprived of her child by its death, there must have been another who realised with growing dismay that she was pregnant yet again. Husbands may well have desired children too, certainly sons, who would carry on the family name, inherit whatever there was to pass on, and be able to help with the workload. However, children became more of a burden than a joy when their numbers exceeded the ability of the family to provide for them. And while carrying a child, the woman's own ability to work hard became curtailed, at least towards the end of her term. She would be largely expected to continue with her normal routine as long as possible, with the added weight of a big belly and the other inconveniences of pregnancy. The swollen legs and feet, the tiredness that could not be eased, the hunger that perhaps could not be filled would have to be ignored. Not for the poorer woman the pampered period of waiting, choice foods, a family rushing to help when she tired. For the poor woman, however much she and her husband desired and indeed loved the children they had produced, after the first few years it could easily prove to be a famished, exhausting process, taking from her body's reserves without hope of replenishment. For too many women, this would lead to the signs of old age while they were still young. Was it then any wonder that some women, realising with dismay that another child was on the way, were desperate to find some way out?

Although most women were not stupid enough to lay open claim to possessing any occult powers, given the Church's views on the subject and the obvious dangers should things go wrong, most villagers would know of a wise woman. These were sometimes known as 'cunning women' and they might have enough knowledge to be able to provide something that would end an unwanted pregnancy. Even now, in the ordinary herb garden, there are several plants that would have then been used regularly as simples, and whose usefulness is now either unknown or neglected. Many herbal remedies are surprisingly effective, provided that the plants have been picked, dried, stored and used properly and these remedies have been known and valued for centuries. Although, just like their counterparts in modern medicine, they cannot be a hundred per cent guaranteed to provide a solution, they were certainly better in many cases than the more intrusive 'physical' methods sometimes used. Attempting to procure an abortion in that way of course risked damage to the mother, caused by the attempted insertion of some foreign body.[15] Today, people remain largely ignorant of the strength of popular herbs. For example, sage, used in too large a quantity, is capable of causing a miscarriage. This is not intended to frighten any pregnant woman who is preparing the Sunday dinner – the amounts are impressively large – but in nineteenth-century Italy it was customary for women to regularly wash their hair in a strong infusion of sage leaves, when its more unfortunate results began to be noted.[16]

One of the most valuable herbs easily available is garlic, which is a wonderfully effective antibiotic. Though slower to respond within the body than chemical medicines, such natural remedies are usually kinder and less liable to side-effects. Modern antibiotics may take as long as six weeks to completely leave the system and, particularly with broad-spectrum antibiotics, some of the contra-indications can be quite terrifying.[17] They have also been blamed for the rise of 'superbugs' and the return of the original complaint in a more aggressive form due to immunity. Penicillin was not discovered until 1928 and during the First World War the European supplies of garlic were commandeered for use at the front. Many lives were saved due to the plant's ability to fight wound infection.[18] The original version of penicillin had been around since ancient times and in the medieval period it was common for any sensible housewife, nurse, or midwife to keep a lump of bread in a container, which was allowed to become mouldy. This was an effective dressing for wounds. The blue-mould cure was not fully understood, but it was known to work well. Other things also worked, such as the herbs rue, pennyroyal, tansy, wormwood, southernwood and mandrake.[19] Any or all of these remedies may have been tried by the woman desperate to limit her family, with variable results, but often with a return of the menstrual period, making the experiment worthwhile for her.

Any 'cunning woman' would make most of her living from such preparations, along with their antithesis, which were the potions intended to restore potency. This contradiction is, of course, part of life's pattern. There must have been a great deal of sowing of wild oats, while at the same time praying for crop failure.'[20]

Trying to end a pregnancy is not only inconvenient, or expensive, but positively dangerous. Women have tried many methods, including jumping off high places, enduring hot baths, drinking vile potions, or inserting various damaging implements, in attempts to dislodge the foetus. This is often far more firmly attached to the mother, and to life, than anyone would give it credit for. But desperate people are driven to have faith in whatever they think may help them in their crisis. Such belief is shown by Queen Katheryn Howard (the fifth wife of Henry VIII) when she said 'a woman may meddle with a man and have no outcome from it, unless she would'[21] – or perhaps, like many young people, she was convinced of her own invincibility.

Any preparation capable of ending a pregnancy might also be expected to prevent one from occurring in the first place. Women who attempted to protect themselves in advance might be very willing to pay for similar potions as their pregnant neighbours. There has, from ancient times, been a firm belief that pregnancy can be avoided, and this has resulted in the use of many imaginative devices, including reliance on the ubiquitous vinegar-soaked sponge. Pliny recorded that wearing something like a lead corset would likely be a powerful check on the aphrodisiac tendencies of men, having noted the effects on lead workers, although this remedy does seem rather extreme for general domestic purposes.[22] The usual *coitus interruptus* is often recommended but can prove highly unsuitable. However, this did become the method of choice for many people for centuries. Though the Roman writers talk a great deal about sexual relationships, even going so far as to admit that knowledge of the contraceptive arts are necessary for courtesans, it was considered far less so for the ordinary wife to understand such mysteries.[23] The ancient writers also, unfortunately, give very few details of what actually was tried at the time.

In the medieval period, much of the contraceptive knowledge was a mixture of charms, prayers and hope. The Church, unsurprisingly, believed that any attempt to thwart nature's processes was not only wrong but sinful – after all, what were sex and marriage for? Families desperate to keep their number of children down to a sustainable level received little or no help from that quarter. All that could be suggested was abstinence, but that in turn not only prevented the conception of new souls, but also interfered with the marriage debt, which could become a legal matter. Any man doing his best to restrain his attention towards his wife by indulging in masturbation was again in trouble. Male seed was considered very precious indeed, and must not be wasted, therefore masturbation was also sinful. The Church actually preferred that a man went for relief to a prostitute, but then he would be committing adultery – and what of the soul of the lady of negotiable affection, or her body, if she became pregnant? You couldn't do right for doing wrong.

There were attempts, some from surprising authors, to give advice. Pope John XXI (1276–1277) wrote a best-selling book called *The Treasure of the Poor,* though it is highly unlikely that any poor people would see it and benefit from its doubtful counsel. They could not afford to buy books and probably couldn't read anyway, so its suggestions were aimed at the wrong audience. One of the suggestions made in the book was that the man should put a plaster made of hemlock on his testicles before having sex with his wife. This was supposed to prevent conception. One assumes that His Holiness had not actually personally tried the remedy. Hemlock (*conium maculatum*) is a member of the carrot family, as is the pretty flowering cow parsley, growing in the hedgerows, which is also known as Queen Anne's Lace. It does, however, possess very different properties. It is deadly poisonous, with the active ingredient of coniine, which disrupts the peripheral nervous system, and causes paralysis and asphyxia.[24]

For anything at all to work, a far better understanding of anatomy was required. Galen's view that women were merely a 'reversed' version of men, that is having inside them pretty much what men have outside, did women a great disservice for centuries. This was particularly in the belief, prevalent into the nineteenth century, that in order to conceive at all a woman needed to release a seed in her climax. This made things very difficult indeed for any woman who conceived a child as a result of being raped, as the fact of a conception was taken to mean that she had enjoyed the experience, and that it was, therefore, consensual. Women were generally believed to be colder and damper than men, whose warm and dry heat accounted for their physiological and moral superiority. A woman's lack of heat gave her a slippery and untrustworthy nature and also explained why women were sexually greedier than men, needing intercourse with men to warm them up. Such misogynistic explanations of the nature of the female sex did lead men down some very thorny paths, with questions arising such as whether or not the Blessed Virgin Mary had menstruated like other women. Several eminent gentlemen decided, after much discussion, that she probably had.[25] Such esoteric concerns were far beyond the range of most women anyway, and merely give the impression that those who spent their time on such obscure questions would have greatly benefited from getting out more in the fresh air.

This leaves us with a list, ranging from the sublime to the ridiculous, of some of the methods resorted to over the centuries in an effort to be able to have sex without pregnancy. From ancient times we have the use of a pessary of dried elephant dung, or from Egypt the animal of choice tended to be the crocodile. As neither of these creatures was commonly found in medieval England, the problem of collecting their dung, let alone using it, did not arise. Also from Egypt, there was the use of onion juice, to be applied to the penis just before sex. It was probably guaranteed to sting like mad, as well as making the eyes water. A genital bath of water, ginger and vinegar sounds more pleasant, with the added attraction of giving the gentleman a good wash before he climbed into one's bed. A recommended medieval remedy was for the woman to hold her breath during sex. Then she had to sit with her knees apart and sneeze. The sneezing may well have expelled some, if not all, of the semen, but the holding of the breath could be awkward if the act was much prolonged. Another trick was to drink fresh sheep's urine, perhaps the blood of a rabbit; or wear a pair of weasel testicles tied to the thigh during intercourse. A rather more sensible idea was to use the scooped-out shell of half a lemon, inserted into the vagina prior to having sex, to act in much the same way as a cap. Not only was the cap-shaped shell useful, any remaining lemon juice was likely to act as a spermicide. Even simpler, if lemons were unavailable, it was common to insert a wad of sheep's wool to catch the sperm. One oral contraceptive used over a long period in certain areas was to collect the seeds of Queen Anne's Lace (cow parsley or *anthriscus sylvestris*), chop them into small pieces and drink them in a cup of water. Cutting these seeds releases terpenoids, which block the production of progesterone.[26] This brings us back to the simplest of all, if not the most regularly successful, good old *coitus interruptus*, or perhaps the use of *coitus obstructus*, which involves pressing the forepart of the testicle to block ejaculation. This one appears in Sanskrit texts, and is recommended there, though the medieval Church would have taken a dim view of it, as they did of most things that were intended to allow the pleasure of sex without the accompanying pains of pregnancy. It is to be hoped that at least some of the more sensible ideas were tried with happy results.

That attempts at contraception were not usually successful is indicated by the existence of the foundling hospitals. There, women, married or otherwise, who found themselves expecting a child that for one reason or another they could not cope with, would be able to leave it in the hope that it might be cared for by others. The subject of romantic songs and stories has often been the foundling child, left by its parents at some place where its later confirmation of identity was made by some keepsake left with it. Even in Victorian workhouses there were pathetic scraps of clothing, often stitched by the mother, left with or on the child, in the hope that at some time in the future she would be in a better position and be able to reclaim the child. But what of the anonymous child left in a blanket outside the local convent, or left at the foundling hospital without any means of identification? The reception of foundlings, or children exposed (that is left for the public to find and hopefully save), was in the hands of the Church.

The foundling hospitals were never as numerous in England as in other countries, notably Italy, but they were not intended to be medical hospitals, more like a modern day children's home or orphanage. By some church doors was a shelter, into which a baby or small child could be laid to await retrieval.

In the days of ancient Rome, any unwanted child could be exposed at the whim of the paterfamilias, and the baby could then be taken by anyone who found it, sometimes to be brought up as a slave or a prostitute. Italian foundling hospitals cared for both orphaned children and abandoned ones, albeit separately. The abandonment of a small child is largely the same as infant exposure. Anyone may take it, whether to raise it carefully or to use as they wish, but the main reason for the difference in treatment between the recognised orphan and the unidentifiable foundling is that the unknown child carries with it the stain of probable illegitimacy. That some perfectly decent women, even married ones, must at one time or another be reduced to hiding their state and then disposing of the resulting child when it was born, is undeniable. It must have been a heartbreaking decision to have to make, even if the circumstances made the decision perfectly reasonable. To leave one's child in the hope that it might be saved by kind people who would raise it carefully, but to never know whether that had in fact happened, or even whether the child had lived and later, to wonder whether it was grown with children of its own, or had a life full of misery and abuse, must have been a torment. Unmarried women would sometimes be driven by circumstances into abandoning unwanted children as a last resort, in the hope of being able to forget past mistakes and regain respectability. Many others would have been the children of prostitutes, an undesirable side-effect of the way of life, preventing the mother from making her living. However, it is known that such women were less likely to abandon female children, who might one day be able to support the mother, presumably from work in the same profession.

Tertullian[27] in his *Apology* says, 'it is certainly the more cruel way to kill, by exposure to cold, hunger and dogs...' This was his protest against the common Roman practice of exposure of unwanted infants, which were not always illegitimate but merely superfluous to the requirements of the family, or financially unaffordable. Certainly in the medieval period, there was not always a convent of caring nuns handy, or anyone prepared to take the child home with them and bear the expense of raising it, even as a future servant. There must have been many infant deaths, even within a country that had a strong Christian ethic about the sacredness of human life.

Modern day evidence has shown that women who give up their children for adoption usually continue to worry about them. Attempts to find the child or children sometimes take place in later years with variable results, but the pain of separation and loss often continues. It must have been much the same for the medieval woman who was forced into a similar situation. Despite the passing of centuries, people's motives then were no different, nor the people themselves any better or worse, than we are.

4

RESPECTABILITY

Wifehood, and 'respectable' motherhood were the only acceptable alternative to virginity in the eyes of the medieval Church. That the woman may well have been pregnant at her marriage could be ignored, such things happened, then as now, and at least the man could have been sure that his wife was not barren, which for many would have been disastrous. As has already been discussed, though impotency was a reason for annulment of the marriage, barrenness was not. A man with a farm to work, or a business to bequeath, and no prospect of a son to leave it to, was in a pitiable situation. The passing on of the family name, with whatever there was to leave, was to ensure one's own small slice of immortality.[1] With this in mind, the average man would be pleased, rather than otherwise, at proof of fertility, seeing in it a form of insurance for the family future – not only as hope for sons to carry on after him, but strong hands to work, and healthy offspring who could eventually father sons of their own.

Daughters also had their place, to take up the burden of endless work as they grew to maturity – to help the mother, to learn all they needed in order to assist with the upbringing of younger brothers and sisters, who became the living dolls upon whom they could practise the skills they would eventually use in earnest. In some rural areas it was long a tradition for one daughter, if the family was prolific, to be assigned the role of future carer for the parents. She would not necessarily be expected to marry, but to spend her life looking after them as they aged and grew feeble. Her position was doubly unenviable, as her brother would presumably marry and have his own family, to which she would inevitably become a general helper and yet remain subservient to the brother's wife, once the parents were dead.

If the family had no sons, this could be dealt with by finding a suitable husband for the eldest daughter, with the intention that the son-in-law would then be the heir to the holding. If so, that daughter would be a good prospect for a man without resources of his own and if he were already provided for, then his land or business could be joined to that of his wife's family. Many a woman found herself matched to the son of a neighbouring farmer who could, through marriage, join two holdings together to mutual advantage, and hopefully also provide grandsons to deal with both. Such essentially pragmatic, if unromantic, matches often did well enough. Country people are usually sensible and realistic and in the medieval period most people still had some tie to the countryside. They were just as matter-of-fact about marriage as their social superiors were and as likely to deal with the choice of a life partner rationally. Romance was certainly best left behind as a memory of the wilder, earlier years. The thrill of romantic attachments was something that tended to walk hand-in-hand with youth; for the years of maturity and for actual marriage, common sense was a far better indicator of suitability.

A hard-working, amiable, and fertile spouse became the aim, far preferable to some wayward charmer whose unreliability, however enticing, made for an uncertain and even precarious future. Security needed to be supplied with the marriage vows. For the medieval woman, life was defined by status. This was not merely social status, but most definitely the marital tie gave the woman her assured position, recognisable to others. Women were categorised as maidens, wives, and then widows (except for nuns) and anything interfering with that natural progression was best avoided.[2] That any woman might find herself living outside of these strict categories is undeniable. Any unmarried woman, even a nun, could not be guaranteed to be still a maiden, and many a woman might have the misfortune to suffer a drop in status, which might in its turn drive her into prostitution in order to survive. The wheel of fortune could be particularly ruthless for women, dependent as they often were on the prosperity of others, and without real independence or rights. They lived from birth to widowhood under the control of another person, usually a man.[3] Girls were under the control either of their fathers, or elder brothers. Married women were expected to defer to their husbands. That many a woman was perfectly capable in her own right, and often also able to give her menfolk the sharp end of her tongue, is a fact; but even then she could only go so far. She was, in essence, subject to the authority of her husband, and if he turned out to be lazy, profligate, a drunk, or violent, she was stuck with him. Only in the most extreme cases could she hope to end her union with an unsuitable spouse, and even then it would take recourse to the courts, the assistance of many witnesses, and the likelihood that any complaint against him would be dismissed. If that should happen, she would be forced back into proximity with him, with an ongoing resentment that could prove a spur for further marital discord. There are cases in which the wife, even with witnesses to speak for her, could not expect a fair hearing, and she would then be ordered to pray for marital harmony, while her husband would be merely warned to treat her with 'kindly affection'. Such an admonition might be expected only to be effective as far as the next incident[4] and that could be exacerbated by the well-meant interference of friends and neighbours. Despite the fact that many women were quite capable of giving as good as they got in the domestic situation, the law supported the man. This inequality often could, and would, be brought home to any recalcitrant wife in unpleasant ways, from a beating at the hands of her husband, to a highly unpleasant and often dangerous ride on the local ducking stool, if she acquired a reputation as a scold.

The law drew a line at the man actually endangering the life of his wife (and many people are familiar with the proviso that he could legally beat her with a stick 'no thicker than his thumb'). However, that did not take into account being attacked with fists, feet, or even teeth. If a man completely lost his temper with his wife, he was unlikely to bother to take into account whether whatever he hit her with was the legally approved diameter.

On the other hand, if a wife was able to hold her own with her husband, as some strong-minded and possibly also strong-armed matrons no doubt did, the husband would receive scant sympathy. He would then be far more likely to keep his indignities to himself, knowing that no other man would respect him for being so feeble as to let his wife get the better of him. Such cases, though widely quoted in a humorous context, were very much in the minority. The level of institutionalised sexual prejudice against women was not only in the domestic context, where any woman was officially unable to refuse her husband sexually, and must be prepared to put up with his choices for her and her children. She could own nothing, and could not even leave a few personal possessions to her friends without his permission, as these would be considered to belong to him.

In the wider world, women were considered to be to blame for the sin of Eve. This had resulted in mankind being evicted from Paradise, due to Eve's disobedience of God's command. As a mere female, any woman was considered to be potentially lazy, lustful, unreliable, and responsible for all the physical, intellectual and moral weaknesses of society in general. Therefore, the happiness or otherwise of any woman depended all too obviously on whether the husband she drew in the lottery of life was reasonable or not. Some men did care deeply for their wives, and others were able to respect theirs, being able to appreciate their contribution to the wellbeing of the family. Chaucer wrote: 'What is better than wisdom? Woman! And what is better than a good woman? Nothing!'[5] However, unfortunate women lived out their married lives just as subject to the authority of their husbands as any creatures who were obliged to endure the tempers of a bully. It all depended on the nature of the man and whether he was likely to use force to impose his will.

The extent of the husband's power is shown through the bequests husbands made in their wills, which leave to the wife, as a gift or favour, items that might otherwise be thought to be hers already, and were indeed essentials. Such bequests prove that the women, even within a happy marriage, were not actually considered to be the owners of their possessions, apart from the very clothing they stood up in. The law, incidentally, meant that literally – it did not refer to changes of garments, jewellery or any personal trinkets, which were legally referred to as 'paraphernalia'.[6] Not even the common law of England could allow any woman to be sent out into the street naked, though even the clothes she stood up in were still the legal property of the husband, not her own; he merely had to allow her to retain the bare minimum for decency's sake. When making his will, the cautious husband would necessarily spell out that his wife should be allowed to keep her personal clothing, to make it perfectly clear that such items were his gift to her.[7] In the Logge will No. 169, John Twynho[8] left to his wife Alianora 'all the bodily ornaments belonging to her, given by me'. In the Logge will No. 245, John Fyssher left his wife Margaret 'all her array, apparaill, girdels, ringes, bedis, and broches, to her body belongyng, for her owne propre wering…' Such bequests were a confirmation of the wife's possession of her personal items, necessary to her as those goods might be, only as far as they counted as part of her husband's estate. They could, if necessary, be disposed of as an intrinsic part of that estate. If the husband left debts owing, and there was insufficient money to pay them, then all such items belonging to the wife could go into the general pot to service the debts. The husband could not bequeath his wife's personal items to someone else during her lifetime, but they could be taken towards payment of debts unless her ownership of them was clearly established by him.[9] At least five of the Logge testators made this point when making their wills, in order to guarantee that the wife's personal items would stay with her without argument.

Agnes, the wife of John Blacston of Tring in Hertfordshire, was apparently seized by force by one Richard Holte. Indeed, force of arms was said to have been used, namely swords, and bows and arrows. It was said that he had taken and abducted her '*cepit at abduxit*' along with certain goods and chattels belonging to her husband John, namely wool and linen to the value of ten shillings. However, the charge against Richard Holte did not include the words '*contra voluntatum eius*' (against her will). This was therefore classed as a trespass and not a felony, which a rape and abduction would have been. It appears that the mention of swords and other weaponry was a bit of a legal fiction, which allowed the case to be heard by the king's justices, and do not imply that Richard had actually used any force at all. What had actually happened was that Agnes Blacston had run away with Richard Holte, and the so-called theft of wool and linen cloth referred to in the indictment was in fact the clothing she was wearing at the time, which still legally belonged to her husband. By running off with Agnes, Richard had technically stolen the items of clothing she was wearing at the time, from John.[10]

Matrimony has attracted more stories, misogyny and old wives' tales than any other social arrangement.[11] Men held a great fund of stories about the wickedness, shrewishness, temper and even lust of their women, and each other's. The war of the sexes was in full swing just as much then as at any other time. Women had the ability to beguile with sweetness and tears, intimidate or manipulate through scolding or pleading, and even the withholding of sexual favours, despite the legal right of the husband in accordance with the 'marriage debt'. His only recourse was to turn to violence if she drove him too far. The local priest would probably be the last resort when a couple found that they could not reasonably get on together. Unfortunately, he would only be likely to try to promote peace and wish that the pair would 'treat each other gently'. He would have been instructed in the appropriate response to marital discord within his parishioners families and he would ask in confession if the husband had helped his 'wife and meyne' when necessary, and had refrained from causing any strife with her.[12] That was his function, though how much actual influence he would have on what went on behind closed doors was debatable. There were instructional works, such as the poem 'How the wise man taught his son',[13] which were supposed to supply good advice on the best way to treat one's wife, in order to have a peaceful marriage:

And son, thy tempre thou kepe also and tell not all thyngs that you may, for thy tonge may be thy foe. Therefor son, thinke what I say...

Son, thy wife thou shall not chyde nor call her by no vylons name. For sche that shall lie by thy side, to call her wicked is a shame.

Unfortunately, these favourable precepts were spoiled by others, which required the necessary obedience from the wife.

> With love and awe thy wife thou chastys and late feyre words be thy yerd.
> For awe it is the best gyse, for to make thy wife afeared.

There was a companion poem, named 'How the good wife taught her daughter', which provided the necessary advice for a woman to treat her husband with reverence and respect. This made clear that the key to a happy and successful marriage was to love and honour the husband above all earthly things and to deal with his inevitable moods by using only 'fair and meek' words. It was another impossible standard which women were expected to keep, with no recognition of basic human frailties. No doubt some men did make excellent husbands, fair and reasonable, and were fond of their wives. But being treated constantly with awe and respect does not improve character, nor can it guarantee that meekness and cheerfulness will be forthcoming from the woman. Obviously, the writers were merely trying to record their ideas of another romanticised ideal, a roseate view of what marriage was all about. The constant and often very heavy work facing ordinary women, the bearing and rearing of the children, the requirements to be always amenable to the husband's sexual demands, can be very tiring and wear out any natural response, let alone natural affection. The idea of the 'marriage debt' was intended to work both ways, with the wife, as well as the husband, being able to demand a satisfactory sex life from their spouse. However, despite the regular warnings about the lustfulness of women, the strong likelihood is that it was the woman who was most often expected to comply. Many men still grumbled that their wives too often refused them, which was probably true. There were many dates in the annual calendar when any woman could reasonably and legally refuse sex without attracting any censure.

Menstrual periods were the obvious times, but holy days proliferated, and these were also times when sexual congress was discouraged. If any woman was reasonably clever, and presumably not blessed with a delightful dote of a husband,[14] she might want to take advantage of the leeway the Church gave her. By professing religious devotion, she could cut down by about half the times when she might be expected to agree to sex with her spouse. In that way the Church, with its plethora of saints' days, could in some ways become a woman's best friend, even an unwitting accomplice in contraception by default. Perhaps some women might have taken to religion for that reason, rather than any genuinely deep piety. If the woman decided to keep to the dates referring to the holy martyrs as well as the saints, she could probably manage to keep her husband at bay indefinitely.

The cause of this avoidance and reluctance quite probably lay not so much with the act itself, as with the fact that such acceptance was not only expected but also required by law. This alone is likely to have made the prospect less enticing; it turns what should be a pleasure into merely a duty and then the request becomes a demand, an imposition. This is all the more likely to be the outcome if trust between the married pair was lost, or never established in the first place. A violent husband is unlikely to be viewed as desirable, nor is the man who is openly an adulterer. Any local community might attempt to exert its own form of pressure on a violent abuser, if only because his behaviour was likely to disturb the peacefulness of the neighbours. In Wakefield, in 1332, a jury directed Richard Childe to pledge that he would 'receive his wife into his home and treat her agreeably, and provide for her faithfully and courteously, to the best of his ability'.[15] Sometimes the family of the beaten wife decided to intervene, as in the case of one Ellen Assholff. Ellen's father, Thomas Assholff, sued John de Scholes saying that they had agreed for half a mark of silver that John would provide Ellen with necessary food and clothing. But John apparently did not keep his word. Instead he beat her and drove her out of the house. John actually counter-sued and claimed that she had taken goods and chattels with her.[16] These inter-family arguments could lead to real tragedy in extreme cases. In a coroner's case, a battered wife called on her brother for help against her husband, who beat her regularly. Alerted that the abuse had again been taking place, the woman's brother burst into his sister's home and, seeing his brother-in-law's raised fist, he hit him with a hatchet and killed him. But for many poorer women, no help at all could be expected. One man beat his wife severely on the arms, back, legs and head with a heavy wooden staff, then hung around long enough only to see if she would die. When she finally did die, he absconded to his father's house in Salisbury.[17]

Jealousy was just as likely to cause marital friction. The Wakefield Manor Court Rolls summoned one John Kenwood of Hepworth for living in adultery with Alice, the daughter of Simon de Hepworth. In the process of this affair he had driven his lawful wife from the house. He did not appear to answer the summons but was fined six shillings and eight pence in his absence. Another man, accused of living in adultery with a harlot, was fined forty shillings for his scandalous behaviour. The wife of one Thomas de Langsfield not only committed adultery with John de Risseleye, but went so far as to run away with him, adding insult to injury by taking some of her husband's goods with her.[18] There was a proverb suggesting that the jealousy of the husband was likely to drive a wife into adultery, but it was often far from being a laughing matter, or a minor titillation for the neighbours. Serious incompatibility could lead to homicide, as happened in 1271. Walter de Bedel of Renholde went to the house where his estranged wife was then living, and asked her to go with him to get a bushel of wheat to give to their sons. The wife, Isabel the daughter of Reynold, agreed to go with her husband, intending to collect the wheat for their children, but on the journey he struck her with a knife above the left ear, giving her a severe wound, 'to the brain'. He then threw her body into a ditch.[19]

The unfortunate fact was that there were few ways in which a couple could part from each other if the marriage was unsatisfactory. This is the real reason behind the acts of violence, the attempts at running away, or the falling in love with someone else. One risked not only the fines for committing breaches of order, but the contempt of one's neighbours, but many considered that preferable to spending a lifetime with someone they disliked, despised, or feared, or having to give up someone preferred. In the present day divorce might sometimes be considered too easy, and marriage entered into without due thought of the outcome, but perhaps it is marriage itself that is too easy, and always has been. The swiftness of marriage often gives no time for reflection, or really getting to know the person one imagines oneself to be in love with for all time. If marriage were less easy to undertake, if expectations were not so unrealistically high, and the demands within it were not so pressing or so binding, then perhaps the trauma of divorce would even now become less necessary.

Some people certainly seem to be able to get along, raise their children and live together in long-term harmony although perhaps a cynic might say that their expectations are lower. However, the 'goodwife,' that archetypal woman of the peasant class in medieval England was human too, and not always the meek and mild, obediently pious wife and mother that the Church, or perhaps even her spouse, wanted and preferred her to be. Women have always had the knack of falling out with other women, and woe betide the men, in their attempts to ever have total control of her. The *Ancrene Rule*,[20] written by a Dominican friar, was probably intended for the use of anchoresses, or women who gave themselves up to a life of holiness, solitude and prayer, but its precepts were also intended to be useful for ordinary women. The female ideal, the Virgin Mary, was always taken as the model for this, being the idealised figure of womanhood. She was reputed to have spoken so little that her words are quoted only four times in the Bible. Many men would have been delighted to have a wife who only spoke when absolutely necessary, but it has never been easy to control the tongues of women, which can be their greatest weapon. It is therefore very interesting to see in the Manor Court Rolls just how many times women were fined for having 'scolded and quarrelled' with each other. The records of Yeadon, in Yorkshire, in 1449 show that one Joanna, the wife of Richard Couper, was fined for quarrelling with Margaret Piper 'in contravention of a fine already imposed'. This suggests that the arguments between the two women were long standing. Sibyll, the wife of John Watson, was also fined for arguing with Margaret, but then Joanna was fined again, because she had 'equally scolded and argued with Sibyll'. The court declared that the 'good order of the manor' had been disturbed by the women being unable to get on, as no doubt it had. Also there is little doubt that the husbands of the women concerned would have had a good deal to say about it when they returned home, after paying the fines for their wives, for of course the women had no money![21] John Packard was fined a second time as he had not paid, or had been unable to pay, a previous fine of thirteen shillings and four pence, which he owed on account of his wife Alice having struck Margery, the wife of William Wodebite, which blow actually 'drew blood'. Some of the husbands, made even poorer by fines imposed for the misbehaviour of their wives, must have felt that their nominal superiority over their women was often a heavy responsibility.

Women's actions in law were limited to the prosecution of the murderer of a husband. The Magna Carta in 1215 (Article 54) states firmly that, 'no one shall be arrested or imprisoned on the appeal of a woman for the death of any person, except her husband.' On the other hand, if she were the perpetrator of the fatal attack on her spouse, she would be accused of petty treason, and could well be burnt at the stake. Petty treason was a vicious law that aimed to protect persons, from the king downwards, from attack by their social inferiors. This applied not only to those who were at a better level in society itself, but also to anyone who might be considered to be in authority over another. For a woman, it meant her husband, though it could also mean an attack by a person upon his or her employer who might also be considered to have authority. What this meant, in reality, was that the law fell very cruelly on any person who had killed another in self-defence.

Many women were obliged to take on a good deal of fieldwork, to help the family make ends meet. Much of the work they did, and the medieval drawings which illustrate their lives, show them undertaking tasks that we would not necessarily consider to be women's work, and which rather dents our image of the medieval woman as being the weaker sex. For many centuries, keeping poultry or milking cows was the farm wife's prerogative, but she might also be required to work at stone breaking, for use in the mending of roads; thatching roofs; haymaking, or mowing the fields. The *Luttrell Psalter*, that wonderfully illustrated book, gives an insight into the hard lives of humble people. They are usually wearing rather dashing and brilliantly coloured clothing, rather than the drab garb we might expect, but artistic licence does not blunt the reality of their work. It shows women carrying sacks of grain to the miller, harrowing the fields, weeding, cutting the standing corn with a hand sickle, and numerous other backbreaking jobs. The dainty ladies of the upper classes might be seen riding their palfreys or reading books, or being entertained in gardens of lush grass starred with flowers. Work for the peasant woman was the antithesis of this, hard and heavy, and any woman would need to be able to turn her hand to almost anything. Very few, if any, of these women would be paid anything like the same rate as a man, as they were used by employers as cheap labour. The husbandry manual of Walter of Henley[22] suggests that a woman who could read and count should be used for stocktaking, 'for much less money than any man would take'. It is clear that women were expected to work in any area where a spare pair of hands was needed, but also in positions of some responsibility; even then, the employer would take advantage of her if he could, in paying her far less than her work was worth.

Working with one's own family might suggest that a woman's contribution would be more valued, and many women worked with their husbands in the urban environment, as towns rapidly expanded. A woman could often trade quite freely in the towns, although that required either capital to set up some form of business, or a family business already established in which she could take part. This takes us rather above the level of the poor rural fieldworker.

In Exeter, Lincoln, London, or Worcester, it was not unusual for a woman to take on an apprentice in her own right, and female apprentices were common in the silk trade. In early fifteenth-century York one Alice Hecche was apprenticed to her father, who was an armour maker. This is a rather rare example of a father's faith in his daughter's abilities.

For most women, it was still the traditionally 'female' jobs of cooking, laundering, minding children, domestic service, or becoming nurses or midwives. It was also common for women to be used in the wool trade, picking over fleeces, as their nimble fingers were believed to be suitable for the work – or perhaps it was more a case of men considering that such greasy, dirty and humble work was beneath them, or that the employers refused to pay a decent wage for the tiring but low-status manual work involved.[23]

In London, in 1422, the women who sold fish were not allowed to oversee the trading in oysters at Queenhithe. Nor were women allowed to study medicine in any form. They could not act as reeves, or become jurors, nor could they take any part in local government. The accepted, and most acceptable, image of any married woman was still that of the wife and mother. The woman still drew her status and respectability from her state of marriage, rather than from any work she did outside the home, however useful or indeed essential that work might be.

Many women had found opportunities for paid work after the Black Death in the late 1340s owing to the severe lack of manpower. There had been a partial emancipation of the male workforce. The men suddenly found themselves more in demand, and that they were slightly more able to dictate the terms of their employment. This had rubbed off on the women, who found themselves more necessary, although for the females it did not, unfortunately, lead to any permanent improvement in their situation and certainly did not give them any greater power over themselves. This was the case even though they would certainly have found themselves burdened with more work. They would also have found themselves burdened with more insistence that they marry, or remarry, in an attempt to replenish the manpower that had become seriously depleted. It was a cruel system that could force any bondswoman to marry, against her will, because her overlord required her to do so. There was nothing at all she could do to improve her situation if the man chosen for her beat or raped her, spent what little money she may have had, or they had managed to earn, or forced her into drudgery. This was in addition to the constant risk of childbirth, which so many women did not survive.[24]

Although the marriage vows included the promise that she would be faithful to her husband, in a sexual sense, however unpleasant or abusive he may have been, the same fidelity was not required from him. He could have affairs all over the village if he chose to do so, and expect to be punished only by a fine.

If the woman ran away from a wife-beating husband, she risked being caught and returned to him, when she would likely be beaten for daring to leave. Small wonder then, that women had a special saint who was supposed to help those who were forced to suffer living with a bad husband. St Wylgeforte was supposed to help those women who had nobody else to turn to; but as this saint does not appear in the *Oxford Dictionary of Saints*,[25] he or she was probably ineffectual. The desperate, following having recourse to prayers to the saint, were then left without any assistance at all. The legal definition of a woman outlined in 1180 was that 'every married woman is a sort of infant' and this was not to change in the immediate future. It betrayed the general belief that, despite maturity and motherhood, or any other capability, most women were still considered infantile, and quite unfit to have charge of themselves or anything else.[26] In view of this belief, it is surprising how many husbands were able to rely on, and trust, their wives as they undoubtedly did, the women having proved their worth.

The few women who seemed almost to live on the outskirts of the normal world were those to whom the average woman might at some time in her life have reason to visit, but certainly not socially. Visits to these singular people would only be made at a time of stress, and the reason for the visit would need to be kept quiet as far as possible. These were the local 'wise' women. They occupied an anomalous position depending on whether the Church or the local lord turned a blind eye to their activities. They may have gained their dubious position by accident or design, but despite the Church's stranglehold on spiritual matters, the medieval mind could always find room for marvels or a touch of mystery. Therefore these women were often tolerated, at least until the next purge, or when something went wrong, when they would likely be blamed for the local troubles. This was not only a distinct possibility, but could be said to be an occupational hazard, and a very dangerous one. Some of these women certainly believed in their own powers, and thought that they had a gift, whether of divining the future, or making some herbal preparation that might be intended to do anything from attracting a preferred lover to obtaining an abortion. Some were out-and-out charlatans, using the credulity of their clients to fund a living for themselves, however precarious. However, they also risked being discredited and even their health and lives. Despite official opinions on anything appertaining to the occult, interest in such things was widespread and belief was often firm. Despite previous failures, the wise woman would still be consulted as a last resort, when life went wrong. The most bizarre and unhealthy stories were eagerly passed on as being gospel truths, and natural phenomena were regularly interpreted as being signs or portents. This gave the charlatan a very fertile ground on which to work. Convincing the locals must have been far easier without general scepticism. A few examples will serve to illustrate the general willingness to accept that supernatural forces were at work in everyday life.

The sky, the location of Heaven, was naturally the focus for strange events and many were recorded throughout the medieval period. The *Anglo-Saxon Chronicle* for the year 685 said: 'In this year in Britain it rained blood.' These signs were usually to be interpreted as warnings of dire happenings to come, such as the entry for 793, again from the *Anglo-Saxon Chronicle*. 'In this year, terrible portents appeared over Northumbria and miserably frightened the inhabitants. There were exceptional flashes of lightning (manuscript 'D' of the *Chronicle* records 'exceptional high winds and flashes of lightning')[27] and fiery dragons were seen flying through the air. A great famine soon followed these signs, and a little time after, in that same year on 8 January, 'the harrying of the heathen miserably destroyed God's church in Lindisfarne.' It is easy to see how a severe storm and the sudden appearance of the Viking invaders and their subsequent destruction of the abbey became linked, though it is rather harder to believe that 'fiery dragons' could have also been witnessed.

Other stories centred on actual marvels and show the medieval desire for miracles and wonders to enliven existence. John of Worcester claimed that in 1130 a bright light was seen moving in and out of a cloud. 'In shape and size it was like a small pyramid, broad at the bottom and narrow at the top.' He further claimed that 'this was seen by the clerks of St Guthlac in Hereford Castle and also by the watchmen in Brecon Castle as well as in Herefordshire by shepherds watching their flocks that same night.' He ends his account with a very heartfelt 'May Christ's mercy save us!' This phenomenon, supposedly witnessed by many, might have been of interest to later Ufologists.

Signs and bizarre happenings seem also to have been of particular interest to William of Newburgh, who recorded several.[28] One of his accounts refers to two dogs, discovered 'on the splitting of a vast rock, with wedges, in a quarry'. He claimed that the animals were found inside this rock and that although one of them then died, the other was 'for many days fondled by the Bishop of Winchester' (Henry of Blois, 1129–1171). Again from a quarry, William of Newburgh claimed that a 'very beautiful double stone was found, composed of two stones, joined together by some adhesive matter.' Inside this stone, when broken open, was found 'a toad, with a small golden chain around its neck'. On the bishop's order, both stone and toad were then reburied, and William speculated that 'they had been made by evil angels' to capture the attentions of mankind.

Matthew Paris[29] wrote that in 1236 at Roche Abbey in Yorkshire 'bands of well-armed knights, riding on valuable horses, with both standards and shields, coats of mail and helmets decorated with other military equipments' had appeared out of the ground and then vanished back into it again. This continues a tradition of belief of other worlds existing below the ground, and also touches on the belief in the fairy world, which was very strong in Anglo-Saxon times. There were several tales of fairy women and fairy children, who somehow entered the normal world. There they lived on sufferance and after a period of time usually disappeared again. This also leads us to a belief in 'changeling' children, where a normal child was taken away by the fairies and replaced with another child, similar in appearance but with a totally different character. Many areas had their fairy hill or fairy glade, where these beings were supposed to appear and it was considered dangerous to watch them or be befriended by them. The eating of their food, or taking any of the fairy drink, could be expected to cause one to lose all memory and become a stranger when returned to the real world. This belief in fairy folk is still given lip service in many areas even now.

In Ireland in 1895 it led to the horrific death by burning of a young woman named Bridget Cleary[30] whose husband said he believed that she had been taken away by fairies and replaced by another lookalike wife. Unfortunately, the sufferings of this young woman may well be more attributable to the fact that she had stepped out of the mould, tried to improve her life, and set herself up as a dressmaker. In effect, she was trying to move away from the habits of her time and place, and marginally away from the control of her husband. This was the reason why she was murdered by him, rather than his declared belief that killing the fairy woman would bring back his own more docile wife. It was,

in fact, a medieval attitude that had lingered almost to the present day, with tragic results.

The examples, and there are many, prove that the mind-set was always ready to accept the idea of supernatural occurrence. If these strange happenings were not validated by the evidence of one's own eyes, then there was often someone else living locally who could claim to be a witness to them and that was just as good. Occult belief was made all the more attractive due to a general helplessness about one's own condition in life. It gave the appearance of having somewhere to turn when the ability or authority of the Church and law had failed to satisfy. This could range from quite sensible and perfectly acceptable medical help, with the use of herbs, say, pennyroyal and rue to 'heal' the problem of an unwanted pregnancy, but spiralled down to the folk belief that being able to spit three times into a frog's mouth would protect a girl from pregnancy in the first place. The very difficulty of performing the ritual should have warned anyone that it was highly unlikely to have been effective.

Although serious witch hunting did not become organised until the late sixteenth and early seventeenth centuries, there was an awareness of the dangers of witches long before then. Pope Innocent VIII, on 5 December 1484, produced the Bull of *Summis desiderantes* in which he both blessed and encouraged those people who were engaged in witch hunting. It was, of course, only too easy to accuse any woman of witchcraft. St Joan of Arc had been burned at the stake as a witch as well as a heretic, after having admitted that she had seen saintly visions.

Mother Shipton was a Yorkshire witch, famed as a prophetess.[32] She was born Ursula Sontheil in 1488 to a fifteen-year-old mother named Agatha. The father was unknown, or Agatha refused to name him. She was befriended by the Abbot of Beverley, and may have stayed in that town, but Ursula grew up in and around Knaresborough, making potions, remedies and studying

herbal lore. At the age of twenty-four she married Tobias Shipton and after his early death, appeared to have developed the power of foretelling the future. She lived until 1561, dying at Knaresborough aged seventy-three.

The famous case of Dr John Dee,[33] at the court of Elizabeth I, shows that witches did not necessarily have to be women. The queen had great trust in him, and he is said to have foretold the best date for her coronation (15 January), promising her great success and a long reign so long as she was crowned on that date. She did as he asked, being crowned in the snow on a cold winter's day, but the results of her exemplary reign would appear to show that her faith in him was not misplaced.

These tales represent the celebrity side of witchcraft. For the ordinary woman, accused of overlooking her neighbour's livestock, cursing her fellow villagers, or causing a woman's husband to become impotent in response to some imagined slight, there might be a quick and probably brutal response from her own people. For every accused witch who was questioned in accordance with the *Malleus Maleficarum* of 1486, which gave full instructions regarding the method of such questioning (and torture) of suspected witches, there must have been dozens of helpless females upon whom suspicion fell. The woman suspected of being a witch might then be thrown into the nearest pond with her skirts tied about her knees, and her thumbs tied together. This was the common way of 'testing' a witch at grass-roots level. The assumption was that if she floated to the top of the water, as she may well have done as her bound skirts and petticoats would have trapped air, then the water was said to have rejected her and she was certainly a witch. She would then be hauled out and either hanged or burned, with the locals feeling fully justified that they had rid themselves of some evil influence. This would be the case however many times they may have bought potions from her

themselves in the past.[34] If the poor woman sank like a stone and drowned, she was then declared innocent, as the water had 'accepted' her. That she was dead was then considered a great pity, and the people could look elsewhere for the source of their problems. Many women must have had to suffer the terror of a death such as this, which never came to be officially recorded, and would mean very little except that a shabby hovel would eventually disintegrate.

The local priest may well have stood back on such occasions, and let the locals do their worst, on the assumption that they may have been correct and the woman was in some way a focus for evil. If so, it was best that she was prevented from spreading her pernicious influence over the parishioners. This is another sad example of the small value placed on the life of any woman unfortunate enough to be obliged to live without the protection of a man.

It is relevant here to describe a famous sixteenth-century case, that of the disappearing husband, Martin Guerre. Though it took place in France, it raises some very interesting legal points in relation to medieval and later medieval marriage customs, as well as demonstrating the attitudes prevalent at that time.[35] Martin Guerre and his wife Bertrande married in 1538. Both were from prosperous peasant stock. Unfortunately, the marriage remained unconsummated for eight years. This was a very humiliating situation for the couple and they had to put up with a good deal of local gossip and bawdy jokes. The first legal point is that Bertrande could, by canon law, have had her marriage dissolved after the third year of non-consummation. In fact, she was pressed by her family to do so, though she resisted any attempts to force her to separate from her husband. Why was that? Could it be that she was at least in a familiar situation with Martin and astute enough to realise that her family would press her to remarry as soon as she was free; she may well have

feared being put back on the 'marriage market' by her relatives. After the eighth year, the local wise woman gave them some advice and made them a 'special' cake to eat. They also had four Masses said by the local priest on their behalf, and whether it was the cake, the advice, or the holy priest that did the trick, things between them improved and Bertrande conceived. In due time, a son was born. However, Martin was not happy being a farmer and shortly after that he left his wife and their new baby. (It may in fact have been his reluctance to settle down that had caused their problem in the first place.) It was rumoured locally that he had gone to Spain to serve in the army of Philip II, but the family heard nothing of him. While first married to him, Bertrande could have been awarded an annulment due to his impotence, but once she'd had a child, and he had abandoned her, she had another humiliation to face. As an abandoned wife she was thrown back on her family, found herself living again with her mother, and could not get her marriage dissolved. The relatively lax laws of the twelfth century had been altered, and by Bertrande's time it was no longer possible to assume that her missing husband had died. In 1557 the Parliament of Toulouse cited those changes during the case of another abandoned wife: '... during the absence of the husband the wife may not remarry, unless she has absolute proof of his death. Not even if he has been absent for twenty years or more. The death of the husband must be proved by witnesses, who can give the court sure depositions.' So Bertrande was stuck, neither wife nor widow, and with no support, other than that of her increasingly unwilling family. She was said to have lived 'virtuously and honestly' during her time alone, raising her son. She must still have been lonely. In 1556 a man arrived in the village claiming to be the missing husband. There was a superficial resemblance, and some people agreed it was Martin, while others were less sure. Bertrande certainly had reservations at that time, but her sisters-in-law both claimed

that he was their long-lost brother and she was pressured into accepting him as such.

Bertrande had lost status because of her abandonment. She had become a burden to her family, and her chances of having further children were nil. Her position in the village depended on her being a wife and mother, and this may well have been a factor in her agreeing to accept this man as her husband. Not all the family were happy about it, as the supposed husband then became heir to the holdings, but on the whole they lived together peaceably, and developed a fondness for each other. They had a further two children together, with one daughter surviving. Family arguments eventually arose as the husband then wished to sell some of the family land, and he even asked her family for an account of their administration of the property while he had been absent – rather pushing his luck you might think. Resentment and gossip began and a witness statement was produced by another man passing through the village, who claimed that he had fought with Martin Guerre in Spain, and that Martin had lost a leg! The new husband had to be an imposter.

Before the new learning had begun to catch on in Europe, Bertrande would have been put into a convent at this point, to await trial. In this case, however, she was placed in a house of 'respectable people' away from her family, to avoid further pressures. When the trial got under way, it was considerably enlivened by the appearance of a one-legged man, who claimed that he was the long-lost Martin Guerre. Bertrande was then accused of not only being a liar but also an adulteress. The returned husband blamed her for everything and legally he was in the right. She had lost her honour by accepting the other man, and not only living with him as his wife but also producing two children by him. The fake Martin Guerre was accused of 'stealing a heritage' in that he had not only enjoyed the inheritance of the real husband, but the wife as well. In producing children with her he had misrepresented them into the family and his surviving daughter was another possible heir, even though she was technically illegitimate. The first husband's abandonment of his wife and their child for eleven years was not considered relevant.

The Toulouse court was at that time handing down the death penalty for adultery, in cases where 'social obligations' had been violated. In 1553 a judge's clerk had been hanged for sleeping with the wife of his master, and in 1556 a sharecropper was also hanged for sleeping with the wife of his landowner. The 'fake' Martin Guerre, then known to be one Arnauld du Tilh, was also sentenced to death. He had imposed himself in the place of the genuine husband, to the disgrace of the whole family. However, his daughter with Bertrande was not declared illegitimate after all, due to the good faith rule. This rule stated that if at least one of the parties of a marriage entered into it 'in good faith' that is, believing it to be good and valid, then any children of that union were to be regarded as innocent of illegitimacy. The little girl then took her real father's name and became his general heir.

Bertrande may well have known the truth all along. It was said in her own time that 'there can be no mistaking a man's touch on a woman' though perhaps she simply preferred the new husband to the old, uncaring one. The missing Martin also went free of punishment, as his desertion of his family for so long was attributed to 'the heat of youth, boiling up in him'. The imposter, Arnauld du Tilh, was to be hanged, on a gibbet erected outside what had been the marital home. Towards the end of the matter he showed great fondness towards Bertrande, and displayed some jealousy towards the returned husband. He pleaded with Martin not to be harsh with her, and referred to her as 'a woman of honour and virtue'. Bertrande had already shown some attachment to him, and the knowledge that he must die must have been a torment to her. She probably also feared what life might be in the future, living with the husband who had first abandoned her and then blamed her for everything. He would also be hardly likely to accept her daughter by Arnauld with equanimity and the prospects of her marriage must have seemed bleak indeed. Bertrande then had to suffer the horror of seeing the father of her daughter being hanged outside her windows. Her feelings at the time were not considered to be worth recording.

This shows that even by the sixteenth century, life had not really improved much at all for the married woman. They were still considered weak-willed and unreliable creatures who could be easily manipulated and must always be controlled for their own good. Bertrande's sorry story brings to the surface the undercurrents of daily living, in which a woman could be moved from place to place like a game counter, unable to decide for herself how and with whom she preferred to live.

5

STRUGGLES FOR SEPARATION

While most marriages were able to muddle along, for others there came a time when such compromise was no longer a viable option. Divorce was not, of course, a possibility, so the ways of freeing oneself from an unhappy marriage were very limited. Simply running away was always possible, but this was usually far easier for young men who found family responsibility irksome. Women were usually more tied down domestically, with children, aged relatives, and all the other baggage of maturity. There would also be the risk of having to forfeit all one's possessions, plus the dower that the wife would otherwise be entitled to, had she stayed with and outlived her husband.[1] The woman contemplating jumping ship would have to face the very real terrors of becoming a lone female, out in the world, where no unprotected woman should be. If a woman's marriage had become intolerable, there was always the slight possibility of taking desperate measures such as putting something toxic into her husband's food, but this would lead her to the crime of petty treason[2] for which the penalty was death by burning – a far worse fate than having to put up with him and hope that he would turn his unwelcome attentions elsewhere, or even die first of natural causes.

If a husband was blatantly unfaithful to his wife, she could complain to the local court where he would probably be made to pay a fine. His sexual laxity was considered far less important than hers, and the fine would be more for a prospective breach of the peace and local good order, than for the sexual irregularity itself. Taking one's husband to court, however, and causing him embarrassment among his friends, was more likely to make his behaviour towards his wife and his indifference towards his marriage vows worse than before. The marriage would remain unhappy and the wife would have gained nothing at all for her public protest.

Only in certain very clearly defined circumstances could any marriage be ended legally, not by a divorce, but sometimes by an annulment, which was effectively a way of declaring that the marriage had some impediment to its validity and, technically, had been void from its beginning. One of these was to find some flaw in the legality of the union itself, some way of proving that it should never have been entered into. One of these would be a pre-contract by one of the parties, in which they had promised to marry someone else. If this pre-arrangement were not properly dissolved before the present marriage took place, it would create an impediment. The nature of such contracts was often confusing and many people remained unsure just what formally constituted a fully legal tie. Nor was it always clear what had to be done to end the betrothal, if the parties changed their minds before the official marriage ceremony took place. Merely declaring that the marriage was 'off' was not enough. The tie was there and it could, and often did, cause problems (or an escape route) for any subsequent marriage if not properly dealt with.

Another serious impediment to legal marriage was if there existed a too-close relationship between the parties. There were strict rules to prevent inbreeding that excluded many levels of relationship that in the 21st century might be considered unimportant.

In medieval society, when people still tended to marry within a fairly close-knit social circle, one might expect that a marriage with someone from the next village would be sensible and present few problems. But others would have had the same idea over the years and their marriages could easily form a blood relationship within the prohibited degrees. There were also bastard children to be concerned about, as all those erring husbands may well have fathered children who themselves could prove too closely related. These complications were supposed to be dealt with by the village 'kin-book' kept by the local priest. This was for recording the marriages and births of the villagers. Unfortunately, not every local priest had sufficient education to keep the book correctly, or he may simply have lost interest or become mentally infirm. Many priests were merely acting as assistants to another who held more than one living, and would not be personally aware of all the local blood relationships.[3]

Marriages may have taken place that were technically invalid, due to being within the prohibited levels of kinship and it was always possible that one or other of the parties concerned might eventually try to make an issue of it, in an effort to end the union. The two basic criteria for marriage at that time were that the parties were expected to be able to 'make an informed decision' to marry, and that they then should be legally in a position to be able to contract such a marriage. Certainly in some cases, particularly in cases of noble marriages, the first condition could easily be a problem, given the ages sometimes claimed for first marriage. It was supposed to be twelve years of age for boys and fourteen for girls. There had to be some understanding that parental pressure had been brought to bear. However, if this did not go so far as to be considered 'undue force,' then it was permissible.

Johannes Gratian[4] had introduced the distinction between *conjugium initium* and *conjugium ratum,* which describes initiated and ratified marriages. Both of these states created bonds of affinity, a man could not marry his wife's sister for example, or a woman her husband's brother, even though those people had no actual blood relationship. However, only the ratified version of marriage would create an indissoluble bond between the parties. Therefore, the distinguishing feature became the *commixtio sexuum,* which was literally 'the mingling of the sexes' referring to consummation itself and including cohabitation. Much legal discussion centred on solving this problem, as the definition used in cases by Popes Alexander III and Innocent III removed the 'demonstration of consent' from being a visible exterior action, making it an expression of interior consent only. What this meant for the ordinary couple who simply wanted to get married was that it became entirely a voluntary act between the two parties. No priest was necessary and the union could take place almost at almost any time. If one party coerced the other that could invalidate the union.[5] No wonder people became confused. Any young man and his sweetheart, after spending a pleasant hour alone, might be forgiven for being unsure whether what they had done together meant that they were actually married or not. The point of any case before a ecclesiastical court, therefore, had to be the nature of the consent, to define whether any decision to marry had been definitely intended to be either there and then, *verba di presenti,* or was deferred to some later date, *verba di futuro*. If vows had been exchanged *verba di futuro* it was more in the nature of a betrothal and that would make some act denoting full consent to be necessary at a future date in order to make it binding. But even without witnesses, or the priest, the arrangement still created a legal bond, just as the vow of *verba di presenti* would have done. These rather lax rules allowed early marriage to all classes of people, even if most working people did not have the money to take advantage of them as a matter of course. The rules had been intended to be understandable to lay people, and had actually created a form of 'common law' marriage, but one that was accepted and acceptable for all purposes.

The problem was, of course, that any agreement made without witnesses was liable to be denied if one of the parties then changed their mind. From the thirteenth century, the Church began to use the system of enforcement to ensure justice in such cases. It had proved far too easy for one party to make the usual promises, in order to achieve intimacy, and then attempt to deny that they had taken place at a later date. All this had achieved was an increase in the number of bastard children, rather than easy facilitation of the sacrament of marriage for poorer people, as had been intended. For this reason, each diocese operated courts to hear cases touching on the matters pertaining to the Christian soul, such as the abandonment of such a vow could be taken to be.[6] Consequently, the Canterbury Synod of 1213–1214 forbade the private union arrangements, which had already proved too easy to abuse, and demanded that a more public form should become the rule for future marriages. Foundations had been laid for the provision of separate Church courts just after the Conquest. After the fourth Lateran Council in 1215[7] much further development was achieved, particularly in the revision of marriage rules. By the time of the publication of the *Liber Extra* in 1234,[8] regular courts with their own personnel were formed and procedures rapidly developed. Canterbury and York recruited their members from Oxford and Cambridge and these universities began to include canon law training as a part of their curriculum.

The areas covered by these courts varied in size, although that of the York Courts was huge. It ranged from Lincoln, Coventry and Lichfield in the south, meeting with the jurisdictions of Carlisle and Durham in the north. Even in Carlisle and Durham, any cases on appeal were referred to York.[9] Certain areas were outside the jurisdiction of the Archbishop of York and these exemptions were called 'peculiar distinctions'. They included some of the most powerful of the religious houses, such as Fountains, Rievaulx, Whitby, Kirkstall, Meaux, Byland and Furness, as well as collegiate foundations such as Beverley, Ripon and Southwell. By the fourteenth century, the Diocese of York included Durham and Carlisle within its jurisdiction and litigants covered by the large area of its control seemed happy to have their disputes settled by the Church courts, due to the high level of academic expertise acquired over the years. The level of knowledge, or otherwise, of the laity was crucial. Although there were opportunities for people to familiarise themselves with the laws that affected their domestic lives, they at least had legal advice on hand if they found themselves in need of it. It is seen as one of the turning points in the history of the medieval Church that such canon law could be available to the laity in this way. It allowed them a way of settling disputes over marriages that not only could decide their validity, but also the legitimacy of any offspring produced during that marriage.

When a marriage was in the process of breaking down, however, a woman still had few ways of enforcing her rights against her husband. Although the Church still expected people to treat each other with affection and respect,[10] it was, unfortunately, extremely unwilling to admit that any marriage had irretrievably broken down, even in the face of much evidence to the contrary, preferring to take the optimistic view that everything could be mended. Could, then, a litigant actually expect any favourable reception at the courts, particularly if she had few witnesses to speak on her behalf, or even none at all? As Professor Pedersen sensibly remarks: 'Plaintiffs must have been convinced that they had a fair to good chance of winning a case in York, otherwise it would not have been worth while spending their time and money.' Unfortunately, throughout time, potential litigants have been only too easy to convince that their time and money would be well spent in going to law, while those who had no money to risk would simply have to do without it.

The Consistory Court[11] was the one with the largest volume of work. Ethical standards were high, and the aim was to see justice done, rather than simply to win cases. In 1311 Archbishop Greenfield ordained substantial punishments for members who prosecuted cases they knew to be unjust. Access to legal advice was intended to be available to almost everyone, with a scale of fees for services provided, though there was some provision made for those in need to be able to approach the court and be dealt with gratis. Nevertheless, one must remember the penniless woman, living some distance from the courts, who would be unable to get there to plead her case at all if her husband was unwilling to allow her to go, or if she had nobody to take her. These legal arrangements show the best-case scenarios on paper, but for the abused woman, probably with children in tow, the sheer logistics were a barrier. There must have been many people in dire circumstances for whom the prospect of travelling a long distance without help or financial aid made the idea of attending the courts at all quite impractical, even if a free service might be applied for when the complainant got there. The assumption was always that the woman would have family and friends who could assist her, but clearly this was not always the case. This situation is common even now, so must certainly have existed on a greater scale during the medieval period, when ideas regarding the rights and position of women were so much at variance with most modern thinking.

However, for those fortunate ones who could manage to attend court, it was in session for 200 days a year, which testifies to the amount of work generated. None of these litigants would be appearing before the court at all, had their problems not been considered in some way unusual. The documents of the Consistory Court, which was held in the *Locum Consistorii* within York Minster, are now held by the Borthwick Institute of Historical Research[12] and show an otherwise quite unreachable area of medieval life: not only people's approach to the legal issues involved, but also their thinking and attitudes about the responsibilities and duties imposed on them by their marriages. The cases naturally vary. They include claims of bigamy, which was unfortunately all too easy to fall into as a technicality, if a previous occasion of whispered sweet nothings had included some form of vow, however tenuous, with a former lover. There were several cases which attempted to unravel the complexities of whether a marriage was legal or not, and of the eighty-eight matrimonial cases on the files, which are the largest single group, forty-five deal with the problem of trying to dissolve an unsatisfactory marriage. Two of the cases presented were concerned with alimony, two were for the restitution of marital rights, with a few referring to breach of promise actions and otherwise 'various' matters.[13]

By the fourteenth century, a large number of people could claim the right to have their case heard by the ecclesiastical courts. The most important of those groups were clerics themselves who, as members of the Church, could claim benefit of clergy if they were cited for any wrongdoing by a secular tribunal. As might be expected, they feature only rarely in the matrimonial case papers, but they do pop up occasionally.[14] One William Alman, who was a special commissary in a marriage enforcement case in 1389/1390, had the validity of his sentence challenged because Alman was himself suspected of being a bigamist, surely a case of the pot and kettle! Another matter, originally heard in relation to the antics of two monks belonging to the monastery of Furness, concerned their sexual relationship with two women of the town. It was heard in York as a challenge to the right of the Archdeacon of Richmond to excommunicate the monks, after the local scandal caused by them and their paramours.[15]

Perhaps as a counterbalance to the idea that all medieval women were helpless, the case of Maud Schipyn should be mentioned. She pleaded her case in November 1355, about six weeks after an alleged exchange of vows. She claimed that she had married Robert Smyth in October of that year, and had two witnesses to back her up. These were William and Margaret Theker. Margaret testified that she and her husband William had been at home in the basement of the house of Robert Smyth at Bolton Percy.[16] She claimed that Robert had pushed and pulled Maud Schipyn into his house and had there attempted to have sex with her. Maud had protested to him that it was forbidden unless they were married, at which Robert said to her 'behold my oath that if I take anyone to be my wife, I will take you, if you will yield to me.' Maud had apparently considered this good enough, despite the rather unspecific wording, and had answered to him 'behold my oath, that I will be at your disposal.' The said Robert was then accused of having thrown her onto the ground and known her carnally. This rather unsatisfactory exchange shows that Maud believed that such a vow, even without a priest, constituted some legal bond between her and Robert. Robert's words to her seem to have been intended to represent *verba di futuro* or a promise to marry her some time in the future, if indeed he took a wife at all.

No doubt he thought that the rather ambiguous phrase used would protect him, but it did not. Although there is no record of what sentence was passed in the matter, Robert must have been advised that he had no chance under the law. He chose to argue his case not on the legal implication of his words to Maud, but on the grounds that Maud's two witnesses were not actually present at the time. Again, insufficient care had been given to the distinction between *verba di futuro* and *verba di presenti*. Although Maud had made him say the words that she believed would make them married, he had not used the correct format, nor had his vow been made before the witnesses in the approved manner.[17]

Another, similar, case concerned the matter of Greystanes and Dale.[18] Margaret Greystanes had cited Thomas Dale before the Bishop of Durham in 1394. The case was transferred to York on appeal in 1395. The alleged marriage had been preceded by some talk of betrothal, and Dale had gone to his uncle's house in March 1394. There Margaret joined him. Thomas's aunt, Emmota, claimed that Thomas shared a bed with his uncle and Margaret had shared a bed with her. At some point Thomas went to the women's bed where he proceeded to make declarations to Margaret, including the words 'in future, when I plan to have a wife, I intend to take you as my wife.' Margaret had replied that she did not have possessions to compare with his and he said that he would make her the mistress of the goods he had. The conversation continued for some time along those lines, and his aunt, Emmota Cokefield, said that they did not have intercourse that night, but five weeks later, and then only once. This evidence helped Margaret to win her case in Durham. However, Thomas appealed the case to York, arguing that he was married to one Emma Corry. He had found this more suitable wife only two weeks after exchanging his vows with Margaret. The marriage with Emma Corry was done publicly and officially, with a celebration and a marriage settlement of twenty marks as a dowry. Both parties had sworn that they had no claims to any other partner. The banns had been read for three Sundays in the parish church at Staindrop and on 10 April 1394 the marriage was made before a priest outside the church door. However, the witnesses were aware that there could be legal problems, due to Thomas's earlier declaration to Margaret. Again, unfortunately, the outcome of the case is not preserved in the existing York archives, so we do not know whether Margaret's prior claim to be married to Thomas was recognised or not. However, her case was weak, in comparison to that of the second wife, Emma Corry. It was only after the Durham court had found in favour of Margaret that Thomas had appealed to York, and Emma made her appearance. Thomas must have seen the advantage of the better match. The case may well have ended in deadlock, or been settled out of court. A *causa matrimonialis et divortii,* as these types of cases were called, was to determine the validity or otherwise of a previous attachment. It would, of course, mean that if the plaintiff were successful, one marital tie would have to end, to allow the other to continue.

Other cases point to the laity being fairly well informed regarding the laws of consanguinity.[19] They could certainly be used in an attempt to end a marriage, as in the case of Boton and Acclum in 1337.[20] The defendant, John Boton, had for some time been having an affair with Mariota Lesci, who was the second cousin of Johanna Acclum. Witnesses confirmed that there had been a relationship for more than a year, during which John Boton had regular intercourse with Mariota, before John contracted a formal marriage with Johanna. They had actually been given a penance to perform, by the priest, for their lewd behaviour. The witnesses also confirmed that there was a blood relationship between Mariota and Johanna and this was widely known. It is another odd case, in which the sentence of the court does not survive. Obviously, the long standing affair between John and Mariota was sufficient to produce an impediment to any marriage between him and Johanna, and it makes one wonder why he attempted it, unless there was a compelling financial incentive.

A rather more impressive attempt to get around the law characterises the case of Midelton and Welewyk, in 1358.[21] Alice Welewyk claimed that she had contracted a marriage *verba di futoro* nine years earlier with Robert Midelton of Bishop Burton, during which time she had conceived and borne a child. However, Robert had, with all the proper procedures, then made a marriage with Elizabeth Frothyngham, eight years prior to the case going to court. A witness confirmed that the first union, with Alice Welewyk, had taken place before the date of the official marriage, although the nature of the vow that Robert had made to Alice was *in futoro* and therefore lacked something of the official and immediate nature of the subsequent one to Elizabeth. The witness also made it clear that Robert had confirmed to Alice that he needed to make sure she could have a child before exchanging any more formal vows with her. Alice had eventually agreed to these terms and had called servants to witness that he then made his vow to her, to that effect. Their relationship then actually lasted just under a year, as during that year Robert had begun negotiations with the family of Elizabeth Frothyngham. She was from a more wealthy family, which resulted in protracted negotiations, but these were eventually concluded to the satisfaction of all. The marriage then took place three weeks later in the private chapel belonging to the bride's family. The wedding was attended by in excess of a hundred guests and was a talking point in the vicinity, it was therefore far from being clandestine in any way. Alice, strangely, appears to have actually been present in the church on at least one occasion when the banns were read, as usual on three consecutive Sundays, in the parishes of Frysmersk and Burton. Even more strangely, she appeared to have made no attempt to object to the proposed marriage during the reading of the banns, which was of course their purpose. According to William Wetewang, who was a canon and master of the hospital of St Giles at Beverley, Alice's silence had been pre-arranged. Robert had appeared to be distressed and had promised her that he would compensate her and their child financially, if she refrained from making any public objection to his marriage to Elizabeth. Her silence was apparently bought for twelve silver marks. The judges who heard the case found against poor Alice, and Robert and Elizabeth went on to have five children of their own. Alice persisted in trying for justice, and actually appealed the case before the Apostolic See. Before the case could be transferred to Rome, Robert was called to York, in October of 1359, to acknowledge that his arrangement with Alice had in fact been valid. A memorandum, dated 14 October 1359, was attached to the case admitting his exchange of vows with her, and the birth of their child, before he made his marriage contract with Elizabeth. However, the court still ruled in favour of the second marriage, and the case did eventually go to Rome. Robert was obviously aware (as Robert Smyth may not have been), that the vows and subsequent intercourse had made the promise of *di futoro* into a binding marriage.[22] The confusion created, as well as the years of worry, must have seemed to him to have been worth the effort, given the far grander scale of his union with Elizabeth. Although Robert was said to have been 'distressed' at his break with Alice and their child after only a year together, he was still prepared to sacrifice his first family in order to acquire the benefit of the connection with the far more wealthy Frothyngham family.

In 1390 the York Courts heard the case of Robert Handenby and his wife Margaret.[23] Margaret was suing Robert on the grounds of cruelty, though the court, as might have been expected, wanted them to attempt reconciliation first. It was stated that 'if the aforesaid Robert shall in the future treat the same Margaret badly, and if this can be proved by two independent and legitimate witnesses, then the said Margaret may effectively secure a divorce with respect to bed and mutual servitude, between herself and the said Robert.' The court usually required a pledge from the husband of goods and/or money. If it went so far as a full legal separation (which is what they actually meant by 'divorce' at this time), then provision would need to be made for the support of the wife and any children of the marriage.[24]

Of course, there were bound to be the sort of parishioners who merrily went their own way, and simply ignored the authorities, or indeed anyone else who appeared to be standing in their way. One such couple were Hawisa of Sherington and her chosen partner Thomas de Shirford. Hawisa was from a well-off peasant family, and had been married to her family's choice of husband. She was also endowed with some property at the time of that marriage. She then deserted her legal husband to live with Thomas Shirford, with whom she had an illegitimate son and two daughters. As the couple lived in adultery, their union was illegal and the children were all considered bastards, but the family went their own way, even ignoring the reprimands of the famous Robert Grosseteste. The lay authorities chose to do some ignoring of their own by turning a blind eye to the irregularity of the association and permitting the eldest son to claim the estate, as a legitimate heir, after Hawisa's death.[25] It is rather refreshing to find a couple who lived so happily together throughout their lives, albeit illegally, and were able to raise their family without too much interference from authority. They seem, to the 21st century way of thinking, to be a shining example of how the marital partnership ought to have worked, with free choice and tolerance.

Even the most pragmatic and mercenary arranged marriage had the potential to develop some genuine affection and respect, as many undoubtedly did. But marital affection was not a state to be wished into existence, or even worked for, in the medieval mind. It was also a legal term, and married people had a legal right to expect at least a basic level of this elusive commodity from their partner. It did not necessarily equate to fondly tactile behaviour but was more concerned with treating the other person with civility and some consideration. It was intended to provide the necessities and to ensure the honouring of the marriage debt, always with the aim of producing children. Even such a basically impartial and tolerant way of living was, alas, not always possible. John Colwell and his wife asked the courts for a legal separation on the grounds that they 'lived in daily fear of their lives, and would each of them rather live in a prison than be together'. Their separation was finally allowed, though one wonders how much that was gained with their personal happiness in mind, or whether their mutually violent animosity was too disturbing for their neighbours to bear.[26]

Thomas Waralynton was taken to court and had to swear to treat his wife Matilda Tripes with marital affection in the future. This was in respect of bed and table, and he was also sworn to supply her with all those things that were necessary, such as food and clothing, according to his ability. His wife Matilda was sworn to obey him as her rightful husband.[27] One wonders whether such promises would hold for long, once the couple were back in their normal routine. Unhappily, the habit of unreasonable or immoderate behaviour quite quickly becomes fixed and very hard to break once the pattern is established. The crux of the matter, though, is that Matilda still had to swear to obey her husband, despite his attitude towards her. If he failed to keep his promises, she would no doubt have to go through the whole sorry process of taking him to court again. It was still her duty to obey him and it was likewise his duty to ensure that she did. That was the cornerstone of the state of matrimony.

One poor woman asked for a separation on the grounds that her husband had attacked her with a knife and had broken her arm. The husband was unrepentant, having seen nothing wrong with his 'chastisement' of his wife. He was still able to claim openly that he was 'perfectly reasonable and honest in his dealings with his wife' although he did admit to attacking her. He claimed that the attack was solely for the purpose of 'reducing her from her errors'. Unfortunately for her future safety, let alone her peace of mind, the court agreed with the husband, and her request for a legal separation from him was denied.[28]

The position of husband carried with it certain responsibilities as well as the right to have absolute authority over one's wife. The husband was required not only to provide the wife with the necessities of life, but to also acknowledge her right to have a sex life and a chance of motherhood. If he should prove demanding sexually, she could not refuse him without incurring censure, yet the idea of having to provide sex on demand for a man who had violently attacked and injured you is distasteful in the extreme. Yet the expectation was that the marriage should produce children – that was its function – not only to continue the family, but to contribute to the household economy, before the progeny married and started families of their own. The medieval marriage was not really expected to provide the companionship and closeness that we would now expect or hope for.

The couple would not be able to go their separate ways if the relationship became toxic, yet the one fault in the husband that would allow the wife to sue for legal separation with some hope of success was if he was unable to consummate the union. This was to deprive her of the hope, indeed the right, to produce children if she could. If, after three years, the union had not been properly consummated, either party was entitled to bring a suit for the ending of it. Because there was always the possibility of some deceit, perhaps even collusion if the couple were not satisfied with the general state of the marriage, it might be necessary for the woman to be examined by a group of 'honest women' to ensure that she was still a virgin. However, even that was insufficient. The man, being accused of impotency, found himself in a very difficult and humiliating situation. He would certainly have to be examined, to ensure that he was indeed incapable of any natural response to a woman. If this could be proved not to be the case, he would face the dishonour of being considered less than a man, and this was likely to end his current marriage and he would also have to suffer the maliciously coarse and facetious humour of his friends and neighbours. He would also have to suffer the knowledge that he was to lose the consolation of a family life, and that it was highly unlikely that any other woman would be willing to marry him. No wonder then that the men were extremely reluctant to initiate these cases.

In Canterbury, in 1292, a woman succeeded in having her marriage dissolved after her husband had been examined with regard to his potency by a group of twelve women of 'good reputation and honest life'. They did their best to arouse him sexually, but without any success at all, until he was officially declared to be 'useless'. A similar case, won by a woman in York in 1433, involved her husband being tested for potency by a local prostitute. Possibly the jury of 'good and honest women' was not available, or merely unwilling to take part. Such cases generally tended to draw a crowd of interested spectators, who took delight in the discomfiture of the man who failed. The local 'woman of the town' exposed herself to this man, referred to in the records only as 'one John' showing him her naked breasts. As he appeared unenthusiastic she went further, embracing and kissing him in attempts to arouse him. When even her eager and experienced embraces failed, she warmed her hands at the fire in order to stroke him, 'holding the penis and testicles of the said John' while admonishing him to then and there 'prove and render himself a man'. However, despite all these efforts she and her witnesses, (six female companions), reported that throughout the examination John's penis had remained a mere three inches long. She and the witnesses then left, but found time on the way out to curse poor John for his failure. One wonders how much of his failure was due to the situation in which he found himself. He was not alone with the woman, who may indeed have been more skilled at provoking male response than his own virgin wife, but having to be fondled in front of six other females, all eyeing him cynically, perhaps even nudging and giggling, would surely have been the absolute nadir of shame for any man.[29]

In the case of Lambhird and Sanderson, brought before the York Courts in 1370, John Sanderson of Wele was cited by his wife Tedia Lambhird, who asked for her marriage to be dissolved on the grounds of his impotence.[30] They had cohabited for four years, after which Tedia had left John. The couple had taken advice from the Dean of Holderness, who ordered them to resume their original cohabitation, as if further familiarity was likely to produce some miraculous change in their unhappy circumstances.[31] They did obey the Dean for some time, but eventually separated again. John had to face two different tribunals. The first was intended to find out if his impotence could be cured, the second was the formal physical examination at York. The first tribunal met in a barn in the grounds of John Sanderson's father's house. The witness, Thomas of Wele, reported that he had seen Tedia and John attempting intercourse 'in a barn at Wele, which belonged to John Sanderson who was the father of John the defendant'. He gave the date and time of this attempt. He stated that they performed with 'due diligence for the work' but that John was 'lying low and in no way rising or becoming erect.' He also, more surprisingly, said that John's brother was present, and that he actually stroked 'the said member of John' without success. When the case was heard in York, the investigation gave fuller details of the examination by a group of women who had been appointed especially to try to arouse John. The description given by the three women concerned stated '…the member of the said John is like an empty intestine of dead skin, and the middle of its front is totally black. The witness stroked the member in her hands and put it into semen, and having been thus stroked and deposited it neither expanded nor grew.' When asked if John had a scrotum with testicles she said 'there is in that place the skin of a scrotum, but the testicles do not hang in the scrotum but are connected with the skin in their extremities, as is the case among young infants.'[32]

Professor Frederik Pederson has given his opinion that this man suffered from hypospadias, which is a fairly common condition, where the urethra opens in an unusual place at some point along the penis. The penis will not then function normally in other ways. The marriage was annulled.

Another case shows Katherine Paynel taking to court her husband of four years, Nicholas Cantilupe.[33] This couple was of a rather higher social status and either knew how to manipulate the law, or had advisors who did. One of Katherine's witnesses said that Katherine had often tried to 'find Nicholas' genitals with her hands, when he was asleep but could neither touch nor find anything there and the place where his genitals ought to be was flat, like the hand of a man.'[34] Nicholas seemed, quite naturally, to be afraid of having an examination, both of being stripped naked and of having the 'committee of honest women' handling him and commenting freely upon him. He attempted to delay the matter at every point and was actually threatened with excommunication for his non-appearance at three consecutive meetings of the court. At another time he'd had Katherine abducted and placed in one of his castles in Nottinghamshire. He forced her to swear that she would not proceed against him, cursing her and saying, 'you know well that I am sufficiently potent to copulate with you, having genitals that are good enough for married life.' He added, 'I demand that you will swear that I am able to have intercourse with you, having sufficient natural instruments.' He also forbade her to leave without his permission. In the private chapel she was forced to swear to his declaration, but she eventually managed to escape with the help of her servants. When the court decided that the marriage should be annulled, Nicholas still did not give in. He took the matter to the Apostolic See. However, he died just over two years later, while the case was still being prosecuted in Avignon. As Katherine was still technically his wife at his death, she inherited lands and money from his estate. Nicholas would probably have been about twenty-nine or thirty years old when he died. Again, Professor Pedersen has done some investigation into the possible cause of the man's problem, and has stated his belief that it was congenital adrenal hyperplasia, (or male pseudo-hermaphroditism). This results from a mutation of genes and can result in ambiguous genitalia, or apparently external female genitalia. It is found in approximately one in six thousand male babies, shows insufficiently developed sexual organs, and an inability to procreate. Among other symptoms there can also be a shortened life expectancy. For Nicholas it had created a sense of deep humiliation and he had reacted with anger at the idea of being examined in public.

The examination for potency would seem to have been one of the few ways in which women could legally 'get their own back' on men, with the law usually working in their favour for once. It is not surprising that they then cursed or jeered at any man who had to undergo the process and indeed failed to 'render himself a man'. It does show a rather unedifying glimpse of personal male to female relationships. The man was keen only to be seen to be able to perform his function, while the woman demanded that he did so, citing her right to have children as her excuse for dragging her husband through a degrading process. If she succeeded, she could then free herself from him in the most abject circumstances, leaving him humiliated and unlikely to remarry. There is little sign in these cases of what we might call any natural affection. These people had often cohabited for several years, without appearing to have formed even the most basic emotional bond, the possession of which would surely preclude exposing one's partner to such mortification and public derision because the process could only deprive the partner of any personal self-esteem. It seems a sad indictment of the duties and expectations of marriage in those times that there was such a lack of any personal connection or sympathy between the couple, even after several years of what would appear to be otherwise amicable cohabitation. Again, the closeness and support that is expected from modern marriage seems entirely absent in these cases. However, in an effort to be fair, it must be remembered that these are the nadir of personal relationships, and as such may be equated to the great antagonism often shown in our own divorce courts when a relationship has broken down. It is always a pity when a union, which started off with the usual high hopes, is brought down to the level of combat. However, it often happens and these cases show that it always did.

There is, in fact, one type of case heard by the courts that may shed a different light on the matter. These are the cases known as *sub poena nubendi* (under the penalty of marrying). This is a penalty that could be imposed by the court, if it was found that a couple were habitually having sexual intercourse[35] and it was intended to prevent such fornication from becoming a public scandal. However, it often worked out another way. Sometimes plaintiffs, usually women, would use it as a means of obtaining a marriage that might otherwise not be forthcoming. The court would usually impose an oath on the couple concerned in the terms of 'I swear that I will here take you as my lawful spouse if I know you carnally from this time forward.' In its most basic sense, it would seem to be a good way to elevate an affair into a regular and legal relationship. The extant cases were brought by women who probably hoped that the court, after evidence had been produced that the affair was continuing, would declare that the union had to be made legal. However, it was open to abuses and could work in quite another way to its original intention.[36]

One of these cases, that of Rowth and Stry,[37] shows how the man realised that he was being trapped into a marriage. Hugh Stry argued that he had not sworn before the Dean of Beverley's official that he would marry Cecilia Rowth if they continued to have sexual intercourse together. He claimed that he had agreed that he would be 'lashed around the church and marketplace in Beverley on six separate days, as a penance for having sex with her, if he could obtain no better grace'. The York court, after the case had been referred from Beverley, was not impressed by his claim that he would prefer to be publicly lashed on six occasions, rather than marry the woman he had been sleeping with. It may well have merely been his attempt to delay the matter, and particularly having to cohabit with her before the case was transferred to York, which would have effectively ended the validity of his objections to the forced match. He did eventually win his case, by being able to prove that he was somewhere else entirely on a date that Cecilia Rowth claimed he had again had sex with her.

The case of Partrik and Mariot[38] was obviously an attempt to trap the man into marriage. Alice Partrik from Thirsk appeared before the York court in 1394. She requested that it enforce her marriage to John Mariot from Sowerby, claiming that it had already been contracted by abjuration *sub poena nubendi* that had been enforceable as it was followed by further sex between the couple. It appears that some close relationship between them had already lasted for a considerable time, for she claimed to be the mother of several of John's children. However, John was actually living alone, not with Alice, and however long the matter had gone on, he seemed determined to finally put an end to the relationship. Probably fully aware that John wished to be rid of her, Alice was equally determined to trap him into a marriage. She told William Stabyll and Richard Lambe, a parish clerk, that she intended to have sex with John on a particular evening. She asked that they be available as her witnesses. They agreed to this, and a little while after Alice went to John's house they appeared, only to find to their surprise that John had rejected Alice's advances. At the subsequent hearing, the two witnesses were quite vague about the date of that unsatisfactory meeting, and Alice lost her case against John.

Such cases often caused serious confusion for the court, and this is shown in the matter of Forester and Staynford in 1337.[39] In 1329 John Staynford had been compelled to marry Alice Forester, with whom he had been having an affair. Unfortunately, the Archdeacon of York, Ralph Cournebourgh, who had passed that sentence on John, had not taken into account the fact that John was already married. He had appeared before the same court eight years earlier, as the defendant in a divorce case in which his *de facto* wife had pleaded to have their prior marriage enforced, and this later court demanded the 'marriage' to Alice be annulled. This had already been 'compelled' as a result of a previous conviction for fornication with her. The court had granted the annulment at the time, confirming John to be the legal husband of his first wife. However, Alice appears to still have had a powerful hold on John's affections, and their relationship had continued. This had resulted in a second conviction for fornication with her, and a second demand that they should subsequently marry. John seemed to feel that he was unable to claim the previous marriage as his defence against the charges of adultery, yet that would surely have naturally negated the court's second demand that he should marry Alice. Perhaps he preferred Alice anyway, but had no grounds for separation from his first, legal, wife; he might also have preferred to be considered a recidivist with regard to his adultery with her, rather than have to give her up. At least this case showed that some natural affection was present and could be long-standing, even though it was directed towards what the court would consider was the wrong woman.

There is also a case in the York archives that showed a young man steadfastly refusing his already arranged, and properly performed, childhood marriage, on the grounds that he found that he had 'no natural affection' towards the young woman chosen for him.[40] William Aungier, in 1357, applied to the York court to have his marriage to Johanna Malcake annulled. He was fourteen years old and his wife was then sixteen years old. His close family had all died in the plague and he had passed into the guardianship of an uncle, one Thomas Bekyngham. At the end of a year, the uncle sold William's wardship to Thomas Malcake, who was the steward of a local noblewoman. Malcake had a niece, Johanna, two years older than William, and Bekyngham and Malcake persuaded the boy, when he was only eight years old, to exchange marriage vows with Johanna in the chapel of the manor of Fenwick. They were put into the nuptial bed together the following night. This marriage, despite having fulfilled the necessary legal criteria, would have needed to be ratified once the parties became of age. Only the consent of both of the parties, when they were old enough to make their own decision, could make the early marriage vows binding, as no consummation had taken place due to their extreme youth. William had then lived with Thomas Malcake for a further six years while Johanna had lived elsewhere. During this time the pair saw little of each other, with only a couple of short meetings, which were arranged to find out if they could get along with each other. Some little time before the marriage was due to be ratified, on William's fourteenth birthday, there were rumours that Johanna was no longer a virgin. It was said that she had had sex with 'several men' whose names were not recorded. This made her uncle send William away to Fenwick, where she was then living, and he stayed with her in the house for a week. Obviously the uncle was hoping that William would have sex with Johanna, which would confirm their marriage. However, William absolutely refused to consummate the childhood marriage, even though towards the end of that week he and Johanna had spent one night in her bed together *solus cum sola, nudus cum nuda*.[41] This term usually implied that the parties concerned had in fact had sex, but it appears that it was not so in this case. William was very displeased at being put under such pressure to accept Johanna and he discussed the situation with his friends. One of them, who was a witness on his behalf, confirmed that William had declared 'it displeases me that I knew her once, for she does not prize an affection that is upheld. Therefore, for sure, I never intend to consent to her that she be my wife, nor to cohabit with her.' At the end of the week he moved away, to live alone, before starting his claim at the court in York. William is the only litigant in the surviving fourteenth-century cases in the archives in York, who declared that he wanted to have a marriage based on 'an affection that is upheld'. This makes his case unusual in that he wanted not only a marriage, but one based on an emotional involvement and hopefully leading to a long-standing fidelity between him and his wife. William Aungier was using the legal term 'marital affection' *(affectio maritalis or affectio conjugalis)* in an entirely different way to the strictly legal application and in a far more literal sense. He felt that he required a different level of personal commitment from any future wife, wanting her to be both physically and emotionally at one with him. This was considered unusual at the time, and he could almost be said to have been ahead of his time in refusing to accept less.

The ambiguous Latin term used, *affectio maritalis,* was concerned with a purely formal contract, intent on merely indicating an acceptance of each other as legal spouses, and mainly as a method of transferring ownership of lands or goods, rather than a designation of any more personal feeling. It did not need to denote any deep emotional involvement. Even canon lawyers at the time were hard put to define exactly what *affectio maritalis* was supposed to mean. The requirement of marriage partners to grant their spouse sexual intercourse on demand was already in force, with or without any display of real marital feeling as we might understand it. It was purely a part of the contract. Conjugal rights could and would be demanded whether the couple had any affection for each other or not, therefore it was not a requirement for a seemingly successful marriage. In the end, the law made no attempt to define the term in any way that would make it possible for a court to decide whether or not it actually existed. It tended to remain an implication that spouses agreed to this as part of the basic contract with each other.[42] Except in the case of poor idealistic William Aungier, the term did not consider any emotional content of people's lives together.

Some people already suffered from marriages that were highly unsatisfactory in other ways. Cruelty cases, for example, were notoriously difficult to deal with as one side or the other would be expected to lie, or have witnesses to testify on their behalf, yet that did not always make their evidence convincing.

The situation in a request for a divorce (which, it must be remembered, was more correctly merely a judicial separation, rather than full divorce as we know it) was named *mensa et thoro* which meant 'from bed and board'. In effect, this was a division of the two people whose continued cohabitation might be expected, at some point, to result in serious injury to one of the parties concerned. The case of Nesfield and Nesfield, which came before the court in 1395, was one of these. Margery Nesfield claimed that her husband Thomas had attacked her with a stick, and beaten her with it. More importantly, she claimed, he had stabbed her in the arm with his dagger and had broken her 'spelbon' (a bone in her arm) so she wished to be separated from him legally due to his cruelty towards her. It was further claimed that his anger towards her was so great that he would surely have killed her, if he had not been pulled away from her by her witnesses Johanna White and Thomas' own servant, John Semer.[43] Margery left her husband as soon as it was possible for her to do so, but it took her a fortnight to be recovered enough even to walk. However, the case proved not to be the usual simple wife-beating matter. Thomas was able to produce three witnesses who testified to the several occasions when Margery had threatened to kill him. It was claimed that at least once Margery had provoked him to make an attack upon her, so it would appear to their neighbours that he had beaten her for no reason. John Semer went on to explain and the court recorded that 'the witness says that on a certain day around the feast of St John the Baptist, four years ago, he was present in the house and heard Margery threaten to kill Thomas her husband. She said that she could kill him in his bed if she wanted to. Moved to anger, Thomas wanted to strike her a blow, but she escaped outside the door, bellowing and crying, and publicly saying that her husband Thomas wanted to kill her.'

Two instances of the court held against Margery and upheld the marriage, denying her the separation she asked for. They did require that Thomas gave surety that he would not maltreat her in the future. Margery attempted to appeal against the court's decision to the Holy See, but the officials refused to refer the appeal.[44] The problems may have been twofold in the decision against her request for a divorce *mensa at thoro*. One was that any reconciliation between the parties after any incident of cruelty was held to condone or forgive the incident and therefore denied the divorce of the parties with relation to that act of cruelty. So, until there was further cruelty, the claim could not be made. The second problem with this case was that the cruelty appeared to have been mutual, with either violence or threats of violence from both sides, making it impossible for the court to decide who the instigator actually was.

One case with a different sort of plea, which may well have resulted in a separation *mensa et thoro* (although full documentation is lost), was that of Devoine and Scot, in 1348.[45] The cruelty and violence in this case was extreme. Richard Scot had been called to the court some years earlier to answer charges of adultery with five other women. The adultery had resulted in a number of illegitimate children, and all of these children were being cared for by his long-suffering wife Margaret. He had, at that and other times, shown what sort of man he was, when he claimed that he had every right to beat his women. According to several witnesses, a little while before the case was heard, Richard had attacked Margaret and beat her with a stick so badly that her eye fell out of its socket. A doctor was called who recommended that she should be taken to the local hospital, but Richard threw him out of the house. Margaret eventually reached the hospital under her own steam, and then refused to leave it, being in fear of her life. She brought her case from the hospital, with the support of a cleric, John Halghton, who appeared as a witness on her behalf. In this case there was no attempt at reconciliation after the specific act of cruelty referred to, and the cruelty itself was of sufficient severity to endanger her life. Although the full papers are lost, it seems safe to assume that in this case the court found in Margaret's favour.[46]

One further case from the York Cause Papers may show a variation of matters that were put before the court, as this is initially a case of non-consummation, culminating in abduction. In the matter of Marrays and Rowcliffe,[47] Alice Rowcliffe claimed that her marriage to John Marrays had taken place when she was under-age. A witness on her behalf agreed that her uncle had said that she would receive no dowry if she did not agree to the marriage. Also her brother had threatened her that if she still refused, he would throw her into the well. Alice had lived with John's family before being married to him, and she had been heard to express a wish to marry him on several occasions. During the hearing both partners were represented by proctors. John claimed to have married Alice in the presence of her parents and family, to which she had consented. He also claimed that she was then of legal age. Many witnesses appeared and John claimed that the marriage had taken place in the steward's chamber of the monastery of St Mary at York, at around Christmas of 1364. After this, the couple spent the night together and behaved as a married pair. Whether or not Alice had been pressured into the marriage received special attention from the court, but she was reported to have 'consented freely and with a happy face'. After that, Alice stayed in the household of Annabile Wastelyn, John's sister (where he had lived for the two weeks prior to the wedding), until the following July of 1365. During that time she was treated as John's wife and received several gifts from him. Also during her stay with John's relatives, witnesses claimed that they attempted on several occasions to have sexual relations, but with little success. Johanna Rolleston, one of John's cousins, said that they had had intercourse at least two or three times that Easter, saying that she had 'heard noises between them as if they were having intercourse'. She said that Alice had two or three times moaned quietly, as if she had been hurt by the activities of the said John. Annabile claimed that Alice had wanted to have intercourse with John and repeated a conversation they had had. Alice was reported as saying 'I will not lie in bed with you any more until my marriage is solemnised, because I am sufficiently old to be your wife, and not your lover.' John had then stopped her and said that he had entered into a contract with her parents to marry her at a specific date, that is, that the ceremony had actually been conducted *verba di futoro* and not *verba di presentii* as John's witnesses had testified.

One witness said, that on being questioned whether or not she liked her new master, she had said 'I am fully sufficient to be his wife, and not his whore!' Matters seemingly came to a head when a local nobleman, Lord Brian Roucliffe, who had become interested in the case, 'abducted' Alice, probably to give her a breathing space away from John's family and her own, who were all importuning her. Again, unfortunately, the full papers are not available, and all we know is that the court convened again in September 1365. One hopes that the intervention of the local lord helped Alice to have a fair hearing, despite the many witnesses on behalf of John's family, whose evidence seems shaky at best. It does seem clear, by John's own admission, that the ceremony they had all attended was only a formal betrothal rather than a full marriage. Alice was resentful of John and his family pressuring her to have sex with him, even though the proper marriage ceremony was only intended to be 'at a future date'. The situation had made her feel used. It also shows the very unpleasant position a young girl could find herself in, if both families were keen on the match, and wished it to be consummated without delay, in order to establish that all-important legal tie. Despite the law in force at the time, it is rather disturbing to realise that at the time these incidents took place, Alice was only twelve years old.

It is sometimes difficult to remember that while these cases are interesting in an abstract way, they were indeed real cases, not fiction, and it was someone's human misery involved. This held true whether the case was salacious, as in the impotence ones, causing extreme embarrassment for the men, or a case like Alice's. In her case, a very young girl had been pressured, by threats, into accepting a marriage and then had to suffer what we would consider to be sexual abuse. It is no wonder that the local landowner had taken it upon himself to intervene, bearing in mind Alice's youth and the pressures upon her. One can only be relieved that he did, and that someone cared enough to try to shield Alice from the situation in which she found herself. Even her own family were inclined to allow her to be forced into a marriage which she did not seem to want. They are as culpable as John's family in trying to force the girl into a situation for which she was not ready. On the other hand, one has to respect Alice for the steadfast way in which she insisted that she preferred a proper marriage, legally performed, rather than the ambiguous position that had been thrust upon her.

It would be far preferable, of course, to be able to see how all these matters turned out, but we have to reconcile ourselves to the idea that medieval people were rather more pragmatic about marriage than we tend to be. They generally seemed to expect less emotional involvement, or even sexual satisfaction, and tried to live their lives sensibly for the most part. But human nature will out, people become involved where they should not, which causes complications of all kinds. Unfortunately, money has been an ever-present incentive to force people into wedlock, or have them force others into it, if the benefits seem to be great enough. The Cause Papers dealing with such marital disputes offer a fascinating insight into the real lives of these people, which are sometimes just as far from the ideal as our own.

6

THE FALLEN WOMEN

The fourteenth century was a time of huge changes, largely due to the effects of the Great Plague, or Pestilence, which struck England in mid-century at the end of its long sweep of devastation across Europe. It had started in China in the early 1330s accompanied by drought, famine, floods and other disasters, which culminated in the plague itself. This illness was first reported to have spread into Europe in 1347, first in Constantinople and Sicily. Moving very quickly, at about a mile a day, like a comet with a tail of horror and suffering spreading behind it, it reached England, via Bristol, in December of 1348 and within a year had spread all the way into Scotland.[1] The most obvious result when the horrifying disease finally eased, was that there were far fewer people in England at its end than there had been when the pestilence first arrived. Estimates vary, with some areas, and not always the urban centres, being far more severely affected than others. Overall, there was a probable population loss of approximately thirty to forty per cent during that terrible time, with a further fifteen to twenty per cent population shrinkage over the rest of the fourteenth century.[2] The social and economic impact was inevitably enormous. Medievalist Thorold Rogers:

The economic results alone could hardly mean less than a great overturning of the usual, with people who had previously even considered themselves to be of little value suddenly finding themselves immensely more valued. Men could suddenly command proper wages and free movement of labour to wherever they were most needed. Parliament immediately produced legislation in an attempt to halt such changes, but to a certain extent the clock could not be turned back, despite all attempts to make it do so. The tide would prove, eventually, to be unstoppable, even though in the short term the discontents would lead to the Peasants' Revolt of 1381.[3]

Women would also find that there were changes that meant that they too had acquired some value. Indeed, every living creature able to produce a day's work had found its value increased, for the work still had to be done. The female population had to provide the hands to ensure that necessary work could be completed but that was a short-term solution – there was an even greater service for them to render their country, which was for all women of childbearing age to attempt to replenish the almost halved population. A real resurgence in numbers would take far longer to achieve than might have been expected, and it was not until the 1630s that the total population of England again reached five million.[4]

There were, of course, other changes. Surviving the plague that had taken the lives of so many, must have been rather like surviving a particularly fierce war. The first reaction was probably simply stupefaction, a bewildered looking around to see who and what was left. Then there would be grief. After that, in time, might come euphoria, the feeling that one had been preserved for something better than a life of misery and drudgery. This would mean not only a desire for more opportunities in life but also a desire for more pleasure, for real pleasure itself had previously been the preserve of only the fortunate few.

Gradually, and it must have only been very gradually, the country got back on its feet. The majority of survivors may have been relatively young, with fewer elders from whom to ask advice. This also meant, of course, that there would be fewer older people around to express disapproval. A woman at that time would be considered in her prime at around seventeen, fully mature at around twenty-five, but she would be definitely over the hill by her mid-thirties.

There was the desire for change, and gradual change was then inevitable, though legal discrimination against women still continued. However, it was often not working quite as strongly on a personal level, and this allowed women sometimes to prevail against their husbands. If any woman managed to survive the dangers of childbirth she could hope to live to a ripe old age, with increased respect, and hopefully increased wisdom. In this women tended to do rather better than the men, as very old men became rather pitiable creatures when they were unable to fulfil the primary masculine functions, and they lost power in consequence. A woman, even when her childbearing was over, could become a centre for advice and assistance to her younger female neighbours.

With new hopes came other changes, new boundaries. Sumptuary laws became necessary to prevent people from attempting to wear clothing deemed suitable only for those at a higher social level. Sumptuary laws have been promulgated at regular intervals since Roman times, when even the Roman dictator Lucius Cornelius Sulla[6] found it necessary to attempt to stop the citizens from wasting their money on vain display after a time of national emergency. After fear and destruction has passed, it seems to be the norm for extravagance to emerge. However, the very regularity of these laws show just how difficult, if not downright impossible, they were to enforce for long. Naturally, anyone in a position of prosperity wishes to flaunt that prosperity in dress and ornamentation, and efficient enforcement of such a rule becomes unfeasible. What was considered appropriate for every social degree varied with time and circumstances, but the clothing regulations that were imposed by the sumptuary laws of 1363 were roughly as follows[7].

Lords with lands worth £1,000 annually, with their families, were not subject to any restrictions. Knights with lands worth 400 marks annually (or £266 13s 4d) along with their families, were allowed to dress as they preferred, except that they may not wear weasel fur, ermine, or clothing of precious stones, other than jewels to be worn in women's hair.

Knights with lands worth 200 marks annually (£133 6s 8d) and their families could wear fabric worth no more than 6 marks for the whole cloth, no cloth of gold, no cloak mantle or gown lined with pure miniver, no sleeves of ermine, or any material embroidered with precious stones. Women were not allowed to wear ermine or weasel fur or any jewels except those to be worn in their hair.

Esquires with land worth £200 per year, and also merchants with goods to the value of £1,000 and their families, were allowed to wear fabric worth no more than 5 marks (£3 6s 8d) for the whole cloth. They were allowed to wear cloth of silk and silver, or anything decorated with silver, and their womenfolk could wear miniver, but not ermine or weasel fur, or any jewels except those worn in their hair.

Esquires and gentlemen with £100 per year and merchants with goods to the value of £500 and their families were allowed to wear fabric worth no more than four-and-a-half marks (£3) for the whole cloth. No cloth of silk, gold or silver, no embroidery, no precious stones or furs. Women and their families were to wear fabric worth no more than forty shillings for the whole cloth. No jewels, gold, silver or silk, embroidery or enamelware, and no fur except for lamb, rabbit, cat or fox. Such women were also not allowed to wear silk veils.

Servants and their families were allowed fabric worth no more than two marks for the whole cloth, no gold, silver, silk, embroidery, or enamel. Women's veils should be worth no more than twelve pence.

Carters, ploughmen, drivers of ploughs, oxherds, cowherds, swineherds, dairymaids and everyone else working on the land, who did not own forty shillings worth of goods, were pretty much at the bottom of the pile of respectable people. They were to be allowed no cloths except blanket or russet worth twelve pence per ell[8] and these had to be fastened with belts of linen rope. However, as they were considered negligible, nobody really bothered what they wore, as they couldn't afford anything much anyway. Many would consider themselves fortunate to have a change of work clothing at all, and be able to change from wet and muddy clothing into something dry.

Nightwear could range from the sumptuous, with bedgowns sometimes being fur-lined, to being obliged to lie down in one's undergarments, or at least change into a clean shift if there were others to choose from. Everyone wore some kind of nightcap or linen bonnet, as the heat escaping from the body via the head was considered to be detrimental to health.[9] Naturally, the poorest people and those considered outcasts in some form or other would be fortunate if they could sleep warm and dry, which was often not the case.

Clothing, ornate or otherwise, has a function other than mere warmth and even more important than display of wealth or rank. For those who still had youth, health and leisure, indeed anyone over and above the very poorest subsistence level, the real function of clothing was to attract the opposite sex. It was at this period that dress actually began to fit, and even to exaggerate, the body – becoming more than merely a covering for modesty or a way to keep warm. Women certainly began to wear dresses drawn more closely to the body, and with a rather lower neckline. These were much disliked by the clergy as being immodest and an unnecessary allurement for men. There were even early drawings of devils wearing tight dresses, which showed the bosom, or riding on the trailing train of fashionably vain females attracting attention. Men were equally guilty, and enjoyed even more extreme fashions, easily beating the women at their own game. They quickly abandoned the sensible doublet and hose, or the long gowns, in favour of showing off their legs in very short doublets and tights. The codpiece[10] became a centre of attention, often padded and decorated. This was similar to a woman pushing up or padding out her bodice, which was considered equally disgraceful by the clergy. This exaggeration was also reflected in the footwear of the more fashionable man. Their shoes became longer and longer in the toes until, in some cases, they eventually became so ridiculously long that they needed to be fastened to the wearer's knees with laces or small chains, to prevent him tripping over them.

Naturally, these excesses were considered to be a sign of general moral degradation and dire warnings were regularly given, to the effect that the devil would take over the wearers' souls and carry them off if they did not mend their ways. The temptations of these extremes of dress and the waste of money they represented were signs that the country was going to the dogs, but that has been the opinion of every age, when the young and the old have disagreed about the suitability or otherwise of clothing.

Not everyone had a stake in the fashions of the times, and not everyone could afford to follow the trends anyway, but for certain sections of the community a good appearance was essential. One of these groups consisted of the women who needed to attract the attention of men in order to earn a living, the prostitutes. They occupied all levels of society and had many levels within their general grouping. They ranged from the rich man's mistress who might consider herself to be, or might actually be, a lady, to the poor, worn-out creature who had slipped down the rungs of the ladder of success instead of climbing them. The profession also included part-time members, who probably did not consider themselves to be whores at all, and who only worked as such when things became difficult, in order to earn a little extra.

The Church and the municipal authorities had a serious financial stake in the sex business. Many brothels were in property owned by the Church, to which they paid their rent. The Church turned a blind eye to the goings-on within their premises when such rents became due. Municipal authorities also owned property used as brothels, and both sections of the community also patronised those houses, as clients. The toleration of the Church towards the members of the oldest profession was summed up by St Thomas Aquinas himself, who remarked, 'if prostitution were to be suppressed, the careless lusts would overthrow society.' This was the usual method of double thinking regarding the sex trade. On the one hand it was sinful and any participation in it should be discouraged, but on the other, more pragmatic, level it was a very necessary evil and provided an essential safety valve for all men who did not have their own women,[12] men who might, if unable to control their natural urges, become a threat to respectable women and girls, so without the use of these 'common women' there would certainly be one less method of social control.[13] The love of money was the real driving force, almost as uncontrollable as the lusts of those men who were, allegedly, roaming the streets looking for women to rape. It was certainly money that concerned the brothel and bawdy house keepers, and also money, or lack of it, which drove so many women into the trade in the hope of at least making a living when they had nothing else to sell but themselves.

The almost respectable type of prostitute would ideally be a member of a brothel or bordello. She would be expected to wear some item of clothing in order to mark her out, to differentiate from respectable, decent women. This could be a yellow veil, but sometimes other items might be required, such as the wearing of a simple yellow stripe on her clothing. In some other areas red was required. These restrictions were in direct contradiction of the mores in some countries abroad. In Venice, courtesans were very finely dressed, were famous for their beauty and were much sought after. They were often painted wearing fine clothes, lots of jewellery, and with their hair showing. This was not allowed for the most respectable women in England; all married women covered their hair, with a veil, or a headdress of some kind. It was considered highly unseemly for a decent woman to be seen in public with her hair loose, as that was a style suitable only for a young girl or, conversely, a loose woman. A bride could wear her hair loose on her wedding day, which was intended to show her virginity, if she still possessed it; this was a social convention, like the modern-day bride wearing white, even though she may very well not be virginal. A queen being crowned could also wear her hair loose, to signify her spiritual marriage with her subjects, but the loose woman who was seen with loose hair was using her crowning glory to attract the attention of male clients. For a married woman, having her hair covered in public was a convention followed more or less until the 1950s, after which it was only considered necessary in church, and finally not at all. It was a very long-lasting belief that a woman's hair was a sexual attraction in its own right, and once she was 'spoken for' it was covered to show that she was no longer available on the marriage market.

The part-time sex worker might rely on the fact that she appeared to be an ordinary member of the public, as it gave her more freedom, even if she did not then have the protection of an official establishment. She may have nurtured the hope of finding a permanent 'keeper', or even a husband, from among her part-time lovers and this was not an impossible hope, though probably less regular an occurrence than such girls may have hoped. For most men, the use of a whore for sexual release was without any emotional involvement and that was a large part of its attraction.[14]

Brothels were not really intended to allow married men within their doors, or clerics either, but both these groups did not find any real difficulty in getting in, using brothels as they wished, even though some of them may have exercised a little more discretion than was usual. The clergy were, of course, supposed to be celibate, but few people actually believed that they all were, as there were many clerics who found the vow of celibacy particularly difficult to observe. The prohibition of married men being admitted to brothels was intended to prevent the spread of infection back home to respectable women, but whether this actually worked is debatable. Jews were also banned from using brothels, a religious prejudice rather than a hygienic one.

Brothels or bordellos were expected to hang a red light outside their premises, to show when they were open to receive clients. This is the origin of the red light district. Brothel keepers, always with an eye on the cash flow, would provide not only a room for the women in their employ, but also often their food, clothing and ornaments, to enhance their charms. The women would naturally be expected to pay for these commodities out of their earnings, and the unscrupulous bawdy house keeper would ensure that these were kept at such a rate that they often took all of the earnings of the women concerned. Not only did that mean leaving no cash for extras but also no possibility of making any savings, and therefore being able to leave. The women were also prohibited from having any special lover of their own, as this would distract them from their other clients, and make them far more likely to entertain such ideas as running away. The women were supposed to be thrown out of the brothel if they became infected, though this was more concerned with the good name of the house, than with any desire to stem the possible spread of social diseases. Any woman rejected in that way would end up on the streets, where she was not only still spreading diseases, but on a personal level was working in a far more dangerous environment. At that level, a beating, rape, or even murder was possible, once she had lost the doubtful 'protection' of an established house, however sordid it may have been. The bordellos, brothels, and stews[15] were likely to have had some sort of bodyguards working there, not only to keep an eye on the women, who were considered unreliable and low creatures at best, while prostitutes might be said to be women at their very worst; the main object of the bodyguard was to act as 'chucker-out' for men who became belligerent, either through drink, or in a belief that they had not received their money's worth.

Whatever services the working girls offered, the Church was determined to have its say, in this as in everything else. Even presumably decent women, that is, those not involved in the sex trade at all, were subject to being harangued about their natural urges and the services they might be inclined to perform for their husbands. A Church Penitential questioned women as follows:

Have you done what certain women are accustomed to do? That is, make some device in the shape of the male member, and of a size to match your sinful desires? If so, you shall do penance for five years on legitimate saints days.

It seems an extreme penance simply for the use of such a 'device' – should the women thus interrogated have had any idea what their confessor was talking about. There was always the problem that the thought might be the parent of the deed... The Church's obsession with the sex lives of the laity was all-embracing. They not only told people what to do and not do, but also how to do or not do it. Some Church writers went so far as to describe the various sexual positions, making lists and then ranking them in order according to which was the most, or least, morally damaging. As clergy, they would probably have been better occupied with higher thoughts, or perhaps having a cold dip in the nearest river, rather than getting so bogged down with intimate details about which they were supposed to be ignorant.

St Albertus Magnus[16] ranked five sexual positions, all but one considered extremely questionable.

1. The missionary position, which was the only one that had any clerical approval at all, and even then was preferably used only for procreation. The church always had a bit of a problem with the idea of the 'marriage debt' of sexual responsibility to one's partner, preferring to ignore the idea that anyone might want such a relationship other than as a duty.
2. Side by side. The medieval mind, or more precisely the clerical medieval mind, found it bizarre.
3. Sitting.
4. Standing.
5. Oral or anal sex.

All the latter part of the list was objectionable, with oral and anal sex being considered detestable. This was because they affected the potential procreation of children. The woman on top in any way reversed the normal male and female roles of domination, but anal sex was the one the church had the most difficulty with. Peter Damien[17] in his *Book of Gomorrah*, which was an ecclesiastical discipline written in 1049, defined sodomy as 'an act against nature'. His distaste was so extreme that in copies of his book reference to it was often left out completely, as if it did not exist, as he probably wished. Not only sodomy got him hot under the collar, he also strongly objected to masturbation, mutual masturbation, copulation between the thighs, and copulation from the rear. Some sexual positions may well have been attempts at contraception, hence the disapproval, but in other cases the intensity of hostility shown perhaps gives more information about the restricted and unnatural lives of the Church Fathers. They wanted to cut the ordinary person off from all the instincts of life, attempting to take away even the innocent pleasures of a respectable married couple.

St Thomas Aquinas actually expanded 'sodomy', which was in his eyes the ultimate sin and degradation, to cover all sexual variations except face-to-face vaginal intercourse, also naming lesbianism as a sin.

The upper classes did have some release from the stultifying obsession with what one should not do, should not enjoy, should not even think about, with their 'courts of love'. This exercise, familiar to the court life of Eleanor of Aquitaine[18] was ideally suited to the warm, sensuous climate of her homeland and was concerned with the pretended affection of nobles. This was often the affection of a young man directed towards an older lady. It showed itself in flirting, public adoration, respectful attentions, songs, poetry and declarations of love. No physical contact was intended, and as the woman was usually already married, none was expected. This extravagant love play did presumably offer some release from the constraints of an arranged marriage, giving an emotional outlet for a lady of equal or superior rank to that of the young man, just as the local village girls would provide him with a physical one. For the lady, it gave the assurance that, despite marriage or increasing age, she was still desirable, and so long as it was kept within proper boundaries there was a certain amount of pleasure to be had, with no harm done. Look, but don't touch, in fact.

For the ordinary person, with no education or time for such play-acting, it would appear that the only release to be found was in having an affair with a neighbour's wife, which might well land one in court. The alternative was to visit a brothel, which might very well have even more distressing and long-lasting effects, even if any moral or emotional responsibility was entirely absent.

For those who could afford minor luxuries, bathhouses had opened in London by the late medieval period. These had to battle, up to a point, against the general medieval prejudice against entirely immersing oneself in water. Unless known to be clean and pure, water was likely to infect through the pores of the skin.[19] The Flemish women whose entrepreneurial skills had established the first bathhouse in Southwick, had got around this prejudice by providing for their male clients rather more than the opportunity for cleansing. The bathhouses flourished due to the attractions of the young ladies who attended the bathers and were willing to share the water with the men. In some delightful drawings of the time there are bathers sitting with ladies, enjoying food in the warm water, a very civilised way of being washed. It was apparently all perfectly respectable so long as the ladies concerned kept their headdresses on.

Unfortunately, where there are women prepared to offer sex for cash, there are always human parasites living off them; not merely the pimps and bodyguards, but the madams who run the brothels and the thieves who prey not only on the prostitutes, but also on their clients. Prostitutes have always been suspected of being in league with thieves, if not actually thieves themselves. The men with them might be expected to have their minds fixed on other things than keeping a close eye on their belongings, which they would find were missing when the excitement was over. Too much of that sort of thing gave a brothel an even worse reputation than it started with and was bad for business, so the madam might take a dim view of the house being too often involved in more than mere petty thieving.

That did not stop roughs from following clients who appeared to have sums of money with them, or even decent clothes, and accosting them in the darkened streets, for which the brothel could not directly be blamed. The unwary client of such pleasure houses could never guarantee that he would not one day find himself lying in the gutter in a filthy alleyway, missing not only his purse of money, but probably his doublet and shoes too. This could be hard to explain to his family. The event might be expected to spoil whatever pleasure he had had. Some women, on the fringes of the criminal fraternity, acted as lookouts for thieves, or perhaps as temptresses themselves, trying to entice some gullible man to what he hoped might be a romantic tryst, then either robbing him or leaving male companions to rob him.

Then there were the refinements of seduction. These might include giving one's sexual favours freely to some married man, perhaps a decent middle-aged businessman, with the intention of blackmailing him once he was enmeshed. The threat of informing his wife, or more importantly, his business associates, might be enough to get him to pay, and continue paying, for the silence that maintained his aura of respectability. Any man of reasonable position, acquired after years of hard work, would abhor the idea of being exposed as an adulterer, let alone a dupe, which could cause him real humiliation and embarrassment. Such a demand might provide a woman with a small income for some time, particularly if she could claim that he had seduced an honest woman, and therefore ruined her.

Wherever prostitutes were, there were likely to be disturbances. The women often quarrelled fiercely among themselves, with their male protectors, and sometimes with their clients. It was good reason for the authorities to prefer to keep them within one area of the town, preventing them from taking their discord elsewhere. Every town had its own red light district where the men knew where to find what they wanted, even if the general ambience became rougher and more dangerous because of it. There were, of course, punishments for anything other than the most minor infringements of the city code and prostitutes could easily find themselves at the wrong end of a cart, being whipped through the streets. For the most hardened of them, such a penalty became an occupational hazard, with the woman capable of screaming insults back at the amused crowd who were enjoying insulting her. Any public punishment was guaranteed to draw a crowd, it was entertainment for the masses, and free too.

A couple caught out in adultery, who had produced a child together, risked having to face the penalty of being stripped half naked, tied together, and whipped as they were paraded through the parish.[20] Being paraded through the parish was also common for the convicted prostitute, with the added problem of being banned from that particular parish, which forced her to move along to the next one to set up business afresh. York's famous Cherrylips was 'moved on' so often from one parish to another that she eventually found herself back where she had started, no doubt to the delight of her regular clients. The borough records of York for 12 May 1483 state that the 'whole parish of St Martin in Micklegate came before the Lord Mayor and complained of Margery Gray, otherwise known as Cherrylips, that she was a woman ill disposed of her body, to whom ill-disposed men resort, to the annoyance of her neighbours.' She was before the mayor again on 28 July, when York was busy with the preparations for a visit from the new king, Richard III. He was due in the city in August, for the famous crown wearing. On that occasion, after it had been claimed against her that 'she had a bad disposition and governance of her body and was a scold to her neighbours,' she was expelled from the city so that she did not offend the sensibilities of all the dignitaries due to attend the Church of the Holy Trinity on Micklegate, during their time in York with the new king.

A prostitute could be constantly pestered by the clergy to alter her lifestyle, though it is doubtful whether their suggestions would appeal to many. Only if she were sick, or old and unable to attract clients, might she be likely to consider becoming a Magdalen. The Church counted every such conversion as a triumph, but they were far more likely to be due to simple necessity, the same kind of necessities which had driven the woman into the life in the first place, and from which age and infirmity would eventually exclude her. The women did not have it all to themselves. In York, the records show that there was at least one male transvestite prostitute who was able to make a decent living in the town, and there must have been more than one.

For a man, the punishment could be even worse than that prescribed for women, as sodomy, that most unspeakable sin, could be punished by death. This could be by burning at the stake, hanging, or in the case of a priest caught in the act with another man, being suspended in a cage until starved to death.[21] This would not apply, of course, to the well-known homosexuals of medieval times, with both Richard I and Edward II having intimate relationships with other men. However, the full penalty of the law could still be exacted from their favoured companions. Richard the Lionheart was several times officially reproved by the Church for his affection for men, and he made promises to reform, though without obvious success, both kings married, as many homosexuals were obliged to do, living a life of pretence to protect themselves from the law.

The tumbril was a favourite device used to humiliate offenders, causing a good deal of local amusement. It involved plenty of mouldy vegetable throwing, though it was preferable to the serious injuries inflicted by the regular authorities. Several instances are recorded of women being carried through the streets after being found guilty of selling the sexual services of their daughters. The tumbril was also used for the punishment of other sexual offences, such as a man and women found 'in naked bed' together. In one of the cases recorded they were brother and sister.[22] This brought them well within the prohibited degrees banning a sexual relationship, as delineated by the Church, even though incest was not actually a specific offence which could be dealt with by the laws formulated by Parliament.[23] No doubt being jolted around the parish in a tumbril, while being jeered at by excited locals who liked to use any such occasion as an excuse for a little mild rioting, was unpleasant. But it was far less unpleasant than any formal punishment might have been, even if it meant that the offenders might have to leave town afterwards, if they were to get any peace.

This rather humorous if noisy image, however accurately the cabbages may have been thrown, is only the tip of the iceberg when considered against the wider picture of the number of sexual offences that were actually dealt with by the medieval church courts. Essex at that period had an adult population of around 30,000 but at least one-third of those people were arraigned for sexual offences of one type or another. It would appear that the court in York dealt with even more cases, which suggests that there was a great deal of sneaking around going on.[24] Most of the people involved found themselves in court because they had been reported by a disgruntled neighbour, or by the jealous husband or wife of one of the parties concerned. Perhaps it became obvious in a natural manner, when some woman became pregnant when she had no legal partner to account for her condition. Even merely being under suspicion of having committed a sexual offence could land one in court, having to prove oneself innocent, if that is ever entirely possible, rumour being rife in small communities. Any person summoned by the churchwardens to appear before the court would need to take witnesses with them. These would have to be prepared to testify that the accused was a decent and respectable person, unlikely to be involved in such shenanigans, and this would involve considerable expense if the court happened to be several miles away. If the accused was not believed, despite all protestations of innocence, or unable to produce witnesses willing to swear on his or her behalf, they would be required to perform a penance as punishment. Unfortunately, this would not merely consist of series of prayers, said privately. It would be a public matter, involving standing at the church door every Sunday for a specified period, wearing a white sheet, carrying a white wand, and being obliged to confess the fault to all fellow parishioners. During the service in the church, the offender would have to stand before the whole congregation while the priest read a homily. This could go on for several weeks, but even that was probably preferable to having to stand barefooted in the marketplace, wearing a paper hat, with the word 'fornicator' or 'adulterer' written on it.[25] If a married woman were involved, she would have to stand with her hair hanging loose as a sign of her laxity. If the lover was from another parish, then the disgrace had to be witnessed by both, so it would have to be done twice. If the offenders could not be bothered to argue the charges, or had good reason to believe that they would lose anyway, they had the option of doing nothing towards their own defence and letting the law take its course. This then provided the punishment of minor excommunication, which meant being suspended from all church services, excluded from the taking of the sacraments of communion and marriage, and generally becoming a religious outcast, at the risk of one's soul, for the duration of the ban.[26] Most people sentenced in this way would make an effort to improve their behaviour for a time, for their soul's sake if nothing else. If they were hardened and indifferent to the state of their immortal soul, they might be more careful not to be found out.

Most alehouses, even in quite small villages, would have a resident harlot, plying her trade to the customers for a few pence at a time. They often combined the provision of sex with the serving of drinks. These enthusiastic, or not, amateurs would be on a level with women who entertained local men within their own homes. Being a part of the village community may have made it easy to develop a few 'regulars' though it may have attracted the attention of the parish priest and the even more unwelcome attentions of the wives of those customers. They were likely to take a very dim view of the siren living alongside them and could make her life extremely unpleasant or even dangerous. They could easily make an example of her, with the help of relatives and friends, and their punishments might make it a poor return for her selling of her services so cheaply. The risk of reprisal ran alongside the risk of contracting a disease, which made the prospect of being the sole prostitute in a small area seem rather dire.[27] It cannot have been laziness that made women pursue such an occupation fraught with hazards, especially when it involved not only the odium of the local women but also the risk of punishment from the authorities. Nor can they all have been nymphomaniacs, prepared to take anyone to satisfy their own sexual needs. It is far more likely to have been sheer destitution that drove them, forcing them into an antisocial form of employment and creating a very uncomfortable co-existence with their neighbours. In a time of few opportunities for women, particularly if they were poor and uneducated, it must have seemed as if there was little choice in order to live and perhaps feed children.

Any woman could easily fall into this trap, if her circumstances changed. Abandonment, widowhood, or being 'ruined' by an early seduction could all help to make the vulnerable woman or girl into a lonely figure, without the obligatory male presence that alone provided some protection. Charity could be highly erratic and alms insufficient to ensure reasonable survival, while any idea of properly organised financial help was merely a pipe-dream. Any woman who could not work on the fields or in the usual feminine occupations would be obliged to fend for herself as best she could, and accept the drawbacks of her trade. The health issue was a particularly awkward one in medieval times, as many illnesses were firmly believed to be some form of punishment from God for past behaviour. Sexual diseases as a result of sexual irregularity seemed a logical enough result.[28] There was also the problem of general cleanliness, or lack of it, to be contended with, which would be only slightly mitigated if sex took place in a bathhouse. Hot water and a good scrubbing might make the clientele more presentable, but could do nothing to prevent the eventual spread of venereal diseases.

For the unfortunates working on the streets, or even working from home, there was no such refinement as a good wash first, or indeed afterwards. If disease was contracted, and eventually ended in the death of an acknowledged prostitute, she would be denied the benefit of burial with the more reputable citizens, and their wives, in her hometown. Prostitutes were often buried outside the walls, in a graveyard especially for outcasts such as whores, itinerants, and criminals. This stemmed from the ancient Roman idea that prostitutes, actors, actresses, and other entertainers such as circus people and gladiators constituted the dregs of society and were to be excluded from the society of decent people in death, just as they were in life.[29] In Roman times the prostitutes even had their own goddess, Venus Erucina, to worship and to whom they paid over a share of their earnings in good times. For them, and their spiritual descendants in medieval England, interment in death with ones friends and colleagues was probably preferable – better than being buried with the very people who had been so disapproving during life, and who had forced the females of the trade to both live and die apart from their fellow citizens.

Some towns were far stricter than others with regard to tolerating such people. Coventry, for instance, during the reign of Edward IV, required all single women up to the age of forty to take chambers in the home of 'honest folk' or go into service until they were married and presumably of no further worry to the authorities. The Mayor of Coventry also decreed that any person 'entreating for the favouring of any misliving woman' was to be fined twenty shillings.[30]

York's most famous red-light area, Grope Lane, now discreetly renamed Grape Lane, was quite close to the centre of town. Many towns and cities later renamed their areas of brothels and bathhouses, changing Grope, or the even worse Gropecunt Lane, to Grape Lane. Many places also used the term 'Magpie' for areas frequented by prostitutes and their clients, so there are several

Magpie Yard and Magpie Lane addresses, testifying to the original purpose of the area. Some local authorities may have had difficulty in forcing the prostitutes out of the areas they had occupied for generations as the towns expanded and the usual attempts to tidy up the town centre were made.

This was a problem affecting even the most prominent people, as is shown by the area of Southwark in London, which was notorious. The Liberty of the Clink, forming part of Southwark that was actually in Surrey, was exempt from the jurisdiction of the County Sheriff as it came under the direction of the Bishop of Winchester. He had his London residence, Winchester House, there – surrounded by pleasant parkland. But it would not always be the most salubrious place for his Lordship to spend the hot summer weather, away from the noise and stink of the city. Because the area was outside the jurisdiction of the City of London, as well as that of the County of Surrey, activities banned by both those authorities were allowed in the Liberty of the Clink.[31] In 1161, the bishop was granted the power to license prostitutes and brothels within the Liberty and women subsequently employed there became known as 'Winchester Geese'. If a man caught a disease from one of them, it was said that he had been 'bitten by a Winchester Goose', which is where the term 'goose bumps', for swellings, comes from. When the 'geese' died they were of course buried in unconsecrated ground. However, in this case, the Cross Bones in Southwark was used over a long period of time for the burials of these poor outcasts and is now preserved by the local residents, with a small memorial to commemorate their lives. In that at least they turned out to be slightly more fortunate than many of their colleagues, who are buried in unmarked graves throughout the country and not remembered at all. The Bishop of Winchester's licensing of the trade in that area was the beginning of a scandalous if highly lucrative business, which would eventually come to define the area, much to its detriment. By 1422, when Henry VI took the throne, the 'stews' in Southwark were at the peak of their earning power. The stew-holders had become prosperous enough to be able to buy property elsewhere and property ownership was considered to be a mark of respectability, despite the fact that the properties they owned, often inns and taverns, also functioned as illegal brothels. In the fifteenth century any property owner was eligible to serve on a jury, which gave further opportunities for corruption.[32]

One case, that of Elizabeth Butler, shows how the system could be made to work. Elizabeth was visiting a friend in the area when she met Thomas Boyd. He appeared to be respectable and offered her some work as a maidservant in what he said was a Bankside inn. She accepted the offer, but on arrival quickly realised that it was a brothel. She later claimed 'he would have compelled me to do such things and services as the others of his servants did there.' She refused to comply, after which he claimed that she owed him rent and she was taken to the Bishop of Winchester's court. While there, he demanded a sum from her so large that he knew she would be unable to pay it. She was found guilty and spent three weeks in the Clink, where Boyd made it clear to her that he would cancel the debt if she would agree to whore for him. She continued to refuse and managed to get a petition sent to the Bishop of Durham, pleading that her case be heard in the higher Court of Chancery. Unfortunately, the rest of the documents are lost, so we are unable to find out whether Elizabeth was freed.

One Bankside stew-holder who was tried for an offence of procurement very similar to that of Thomas Boyd got his comeuppance. Fabyan's *Great Chronicle*[33] reports that 'upon the second day of July was set upon the pillory a bawd of the stews named Thomas Toogood ... The which before the Mayor he was proved guilty that he enticed two women dwelling at Queenhithe to become his servants and to have men in common within his house.'

In April 1439 a bawd named Margaret Hathewyk was charged with procuring a young girl named Isobel Lane for a group of men from Lombardy. When the Lombards had used Isobel, Hathewyk then delivered her to a Bankside brothel 'for immoral purposes with a certain gentleman on four occasions, against her will'. Hathewyk ended up in the Clink, to which she was apparently no stranger, as her name appears in its records repeatedly over a period of twenty years.

Some of the women who worked as whores in the area had originally lived in the city, but went to Cock Lane[34] near Newgate, or crossed the bridge into Southwark daily to work, but soon they were barred from even lodging within the city. An ordinance of 1383 stated that any whores caught within London itself were to have their heads shaved and then be taken through the streets in a cart, while minstrels played around them to attract public attention to their shame. This is the origin of the 'rough music' that even as late as the nineteenth century was used to shame sexual offenders and adulterers in English villages. Sometimes the offenders would be bounced along on a plank to add to local amusement or, failing their actual presence, a model would be made to resemble them. The women suffering such humiliations in medieval times were required to wear a trademark hood, and after a noisy and uncomfortable ride in the cart, would be taken to a prison to be pilloried and publicly whipped. By 1393 the rules had been strengthened by further demands that they 'keep themselves to the place assigned thereto, that is to say, the stews on the other side of the Thames, and in Cock Lane.'

Although Henry V had attempted to ban London's Aldermen and other senior citizens from letting out their properties to tenants who had been 'charged or indicted of an evil and vicious life', by 1436 Parliament was to hear an urgent petition from Southwark's citizens. They were complaining that illegal brothels were still operating all along the length of Borough High Street.

The petition claimed that 'many women have been ravished and brought to evil living and neighbours and strangers are oft-times robbed and murdered.' Parliament could do no more than reiterate that the stewhouses be restricted to the licensed areas, but with little lasting success.[35] The laws of supply and demand would preclude any permanent change, the profits were far too tempting and women were always available to feed the requirements of the clients. This provided not only an easy but very lucrative living for the bawds, both male and female, who pandered to the local men who used the bordellos and kept the trade going. It had been a self-perpetuating circus almost since the beginning of time, so any attempts of local authorities to impose real control, or the attempts of churchmen to bleat about sin, were chaff in the wind. The resurgence of the trade after every attempt at restriction showed that pimps, bawds and brothel-house keepers eagerly got business under way again as soon as possible.

The cases of procurement, distasteful though they are, can only show one side of the argument. There must have been a fair percentage of women who were suited to the life and did not regret their choice of occupation, though the sadness of the lives of those who were forced or seduced into it against their will is not to be ignored or minimised. They were incarcerated in a form of slavery almost impossible to escape.

One fifteenth-century ordinance banning whores from the town indicates the level of moral outrage against them. It is a particularly harsh example on the theme of the supposedly uncontrolled lusts of women, which to the modern mind seems ridiculous – it was the men who were pursuing and paying prostitutes. Women were also often guilty by association, with certain types of people being tarnished, it was not necessary to prove that any accused harlot had actually solicited or received payment from a man[36] for her to become as reprehensible as any other woman of loose morals. Indeed, the fear of female sexuality is far from confined only to women in the sex trade, as the ordinance makes clear:

> For to eschew the stinking and horrible sin of lechery, the which daily grows and is practiced more than it has been in days past, by the means of strumpets, misguided and idle women, daily vagrant and walking about the streets and lanes of the city of London and suburbs of the same. Also repairing to taverns and other private places of the said city, provoking many other persons into the said sin of lechery. Whereby many people, as well men as women, being of themselves well disposed, daily fall to the said mischievous and horrible sin, to the great displeasure of almighty God and disturbance and breaking the peace of our sovereign lord the king and of the politic guiding of the aforesaid city...[37]

As any woman who has had sexual relations with more than one man (outside of legal marriage) was adjudged a whore, this dragged in women who were not professional prostitutes, as in the case of one Margaret Hopper. She was convicted of being a whore for committing adultery with two men, over a seven-year period. It was the fact that she had had sex with more than one partner that was the key. It was common to describe any woman who had lovers as a 'common whore' whether or not any financial inducement was involved.[38]

The Southwark suburb could come under the heading of 'official brothel', which is why the authorities were so keen to have loose women kept in it, even when they wished to be elsewhere. Sandwich in Kent had a similar system, as had Southampton in Hampshire. Both Sandwich and Southampton had a regular clientele of sailors, who might turn their unwanted attentions towards the decent wives and daughters of its citizens if their needs were not catered for. A part of Hull also rented property to brothel keepers with the same idea, though the records for Southwark are more detailed.

It is interesting to note, however, that despite the women being vilified, no great attempts were made to persuade them to entirely give up their evil way of life. There were very few Magdalen houses in England, in comparison to on the Continent, and the women had no alternative means of support offered to them if they wanted to, or were able to, leave their employers. Life in the sex trade was already difficult enough, with the threat not only of disease but age creeping on. In most cases it was highly unlikely that the woman would be able to save enough from her earnings to start up her own bawdy house, given that her handlers would take almost all her money from her during her working life. The Magdalen houses abroad were intended to provide an alternative for the woman who wished to make the change, they were somewhere she could stay and earn her living in a respectable way by simple menial work and restore her self-respect. The houses were run by churches, which at least practised what they preached. However, in England there was little organised salvation for those women. Coming out of the trade, as in going into it, they were pretty much on their own and expected to fend for themselves. It must have been particularly galling to know that, although the churchmen professed to deplore one's lifestyle, and felt entitled to treat one as a leper and excoriate in the most extreme terms, so many of the properties in which these women were abused were owned by the Church. In some cases the clergy even formed part of the clientele, yet they did nothing realistic to help the women who might be held under duress there, seduced to the life, or taken into those places against their will.

The regulations forbade the stew-holders to beat the prostitutes, which suggests that they regularly did, and the bishop's officials were instructed to search at regular intervals to find any women who might be held there by force. However, the ease with which even these safeguards were evaded gives no confidence that any serious attempts were actually made. Even if some women did manage to free themselves from the bondage of the life, they could quickly and easily be replaced by others. The laxity of the officials themselves is made clear by the case of Alice Skelling, who was involved in a debt case between 1504 and 1515. She openly complained that the jurors themselves, who were in judgement on her, were 'only bawds and watermen who regard neither God nor their consciences but only their own appetites and the pleasure of the great officers of the court'.[39]

Any regulations were, in any case, intended far more to protect public order rather than the women involved in the sex trade. Male customers were not supposed to be harassed in the street, or pulled into brothels by their clothing. The banishment of any woman suspected of having 'the burning disease', which could refer to almost anything from syphilis to leprosy, was intended to protect him from the most obvious contagion, yet the protection even of the customers came a poor second to the need to keep the peace. There was a provision that required a prostitute to spend a whole night with her client – but this was not to ensure that he got his money's worth from her, rather to prevent men wandering through the streets at night, looking for women and causing trouble. The whole idea was to make the women available to men, yet keep them under firm control, hopefully preventing them from 'contaminating' decent women. Decent women were defined as those already under the legal control of some man, husbands or fathers. Any women in a different situation came under the regulations of the civil authorities, becoming known as 'common women' who had forfeited the right to choose their own lovers, yet were still available to all. They were expected to accept these restrictions and not bother anyone. The civil authorities generally emphasised the point by referring to all prostitutes as 'single women' although it did not imply that all prostitutes were unmarried or that all unmarried women were prostitutes.⁴⁰ It merely defined the prostitute as being a woman who was not under the legal authority of a man, and was intended to ensure that she was made to behave in a way society considered appropriate to her station.

Medieval opinion – and preaching – contained a strongly misogynistic element, with all the negative views of women centred around their sexuality. All the criticisms of females, whether they were decent women or whores, came down to the threat they were believed to present. This was not only towards men but also towards society in general, a fear of the turmoil women could create within the social order and against civic peace, which was so easily overturned. A list of the 'twelve abuses of the age':

> A wise man without works, an old man without religion, an adolescent without obedience, a rich man without alms, a woman without modesty, a lord without virtue, a contentious Christian, a proud pauper, a wicked king, a negligent bishop, the masses without discipline and a people without laws.

Despite all the potential horrors of anarchy, the one woman mentioned in the list is presumed to be some kind of sexual rebel, which is the only criticism in the list aimed at women in general – but the only one that was considered necessary. A man could be many things, good, bad, or fairly indifferent, but a woman was delineated by her lusts alone, as if every one of them was a predator that men should fear, as her blandishments were guaranteed to lead him astray. What sane and sensible men, and there must have been some, thought of this after watching hard-working mothers and harassed wives going about their daily routines, or seeing innocent female children, charitable widows and holy nuns living their lives peaceably, is difficult to know. Were they really expected to believe that all these women and girls were continually stupid with lust?

Right: VIRGIN AND CHILD. The contrasting and mutually incompatible expectations of women, the innocent virgin, yet also the mother. (Author)

Below: 'OUR LADY'S ROW' Goodramgate, York. The earliest surviving houses in the city. They stand on part of the original churchyard of Holy Trinity, which lies behind. The rental income from these properties helped to maintain the church. (Courtesy of Brandon Strafford)

STONEGATE. York. Six feet below this street lies the Via Praetoria, which connected the Basilica of the Roman Fortress with the bridge over the River Ouse. In medieval times this was the centre for goldsmiths, printers and stained glass merchants. (Courtesy of Brandon Strafford)

SNICKETS and GINNELS abound in the city, connecting roads and streets. Many are extremely ancient pathways. This one leads from the Shambles to the main market. (Courtesy of Brandon Strafford)

LENDAL BRIDGE TOWER. This building is 700 years old and formed part of York's water defences. A chain could be pulled between it and the Barker Tower opposite, to prevent access. Loaded boats were charged 4d to enter the city. (Courtesy of Brandon Strafford)

BARKER TOWER. Not only helped to control the water defences, but was in the centre of the tanning and leather industry. Also sometimes referred to as the 'Dead House' as the unfortunates drowned in the river could be stored there temporarily. (Courtesy of Brandon Strafford)

MONK BAR. A 'bar' is a gateway, like a self-contained fortress. This would have had an outer Barbican, as did all the gates of York. It also has a working portcullis and 'murder holes' from which stones or liquids could be dropped onto attackers. (Courtesy of Brandon Strafford)

MULBERRY HALL, STONEGATE. This beautiful building was originally three shops, with living quarters above on the jettied first and second floors. It was extended during the sixteenth century. (Courtesy of Brandon Strafford)

BARLEY HALL, YORK. This was built as a Hospice for Nostell Priory and was extended during the fifteenth century. Now owned by the York Archaeological Trust. (Courtesy of Brandon Strafford)

BARLEY HALL, INTERIOR. This is an example of a comfortable medieval townhouse, which would be an unattainable level of luxury for many of the city's inhabitants. (Courtesy of Brandon Strafford)

ST. CRUX CHURCH HALL, WHIP MA WHOP MA GATE. The church hall is all that remains of the church of St. Crux, mentioned in the Domesday Book but unfortunately demolished in 1887. Whip Ma Whop Ma Gate is the shortest street in York, and the Saxon name means 'neither one thing nor the other'. It was later the site of the town pillory where offenders were punished. (Courtesy of Brandon Strafford)

POSTERN TOWER, FISHERGATE. This delightful relic once formed part of the early medieval wall defences, where the city wall met the River Foss. (Courtesy of Brandon Strafford)

MINSTER CLOSE. This is a large walled area, known as the 'Liberty of St. Peter'. It provided enviably comfortable housing for senior officials of the Minster from as early as 1086. (Courtesy of Brandon Strafford)

ST. MARY'S HOSPITIUM. This is an original guest house of the Benedictine Abbey, offering accommodation for travellers such as merchants, who would not be permitted to stay within the Abbey itself. The building dates from around 1300 and is now part of the Yorkshire Museum. (Courtesy of Brandon Strafford)

ST LEONARD'S HOSPITAL, UNDERCROFT. This was the largest hospital in the North of England, containing some Roman stonework. The previous hospital on the site was damaged by fire in 1137. It was designed to care for the sick poor of the city, having accommodation for several hundreds, and it also provided meals for the prisoners in York Castle. (Courtesy of Brandon Strafford)

NAUGHTY NUNS. Redrawn from a medieval original in the MS Douce 264, showing disobedient nuns being taken home to their convent in a wheelbarrow, pushed by a naked man. (Author)

SPRINGTIME SEDUCTION. 'If we were found, we would be dishonoured.' 'But inside you must come, for our love!' Redrawn from Giacomo Jaquerio's fresco at Castella della Manta in Saluzzo. (1418-1430). (Author)

TIMBERED building of the period, a lovely survivor of the black and white buildings typical of the middle-class medieval properties in any prosperous city. This one is in York. (Courtesy of Brandon Strafford)

ST. THOMAS HERBERT'S HOUSE. Pavement, York. A very fine example of a large and imposing timber-framed domestic residence. This one also boasts fine wall paintings. It adjoins the medieval Lady Peckett's Yard, named after the wife of a former Lord Mayor of the city. In the thirteenth century the yard had been named Bacusgail, or Bakehouse Lane. (Courtesy of Brandon Strafford)

ANCIENT FARMHOUSE at Charleston in the West Riding. This shows the domestic and working environment, built in the local stone, that endured for centuries, with very few changes. (Courtesy of Brandon Strafford)

CHARLESTON, West Riding. An open area, now used as the village green, that is popularly believed to be a tourney ground or tilt field. There is a raised area to one side which corresponds to a grandstand for seating. (Courtesy of Brandon Strafford)

GEORGE SAVILE GRAMMAR SCHOOL. Wakefield. (W. Yorks). This dates from a slightly later period, when education began to be more easily available outside the home, for the sons of the middle classes. (Courtesy of Brandon Strafford)

BUTTERCROSS. Pontefract, (W.Yorks). A lovely market day survivor. Every large town and city would have had its own Buttermarket. (Courtesy of Brandon Strafford)

THE ROMAN BATH. St Sampson's Square, York. Not just a pub! This building actually has the remains of the original roman bath house underneath. The precursor of the medieval bath houses. The public house stands next to Finkle Street (a finkle is an angle, or a street leading out from the corner of a square.) It was originally called 'Mucky Peg Lane', not in reference to a dirty woman, but regarding a passageway used for the driving of pigs to market. (Courtesy of Brandon Strafford)

THE SHAMBLES. The original butcher's row in York. A lane of prosperous shops and living accommodation, backing on to the main market square. (Courtesy of Brandon Strafford)

GRAPE LANE. Originally Grope Lane, or earlier still known as Grapcunt Lane. One of the busiest of the city's red-light areas, the Viking version of its name dates back to 867, but was later 'gentrified' to avoid embarrassment. (Courtesy of Brandon Strafford)

A female falconer depicted in the Fécamp Psalter, c. 1180. (Courtesy of the Koninklijke Bibliotheek)

A scene from the Luttrell Psalter showing a dining room scene at Sir Geoffrey Luttrell's house. His wife, Agnes Sutton, is seated to his left, and another lady is on his right. (Courtesy of the British Library)

'Herr Wernher von Teufen, or Man and woman with a hawk'. This miniature from the German Manesse Codex shows a high-class couple; this offers another rare depiction of a highborn woman practising falconry. (Heidelberg University)

A female hunter depicted as a centauress. (Courtesy of the British Library)

Harrowing as depicted in the Luttrell Psalter. A man can also be seen warding off crows with a slingshot. Women were expected to take their part in such agricultural activities. (Courtesy of the British Library)

A detail from the Luttrell Psalter showing a woman encountering a grotesque. Some women must have felt like this upon meeting their husband-to-be, if the marriage was forced on them by their fathers. (Courtesy of the British Library)

Ladies encountering knights. It was crucial in the medieval era for a highborn woman to engineer a good match for herself. (Courtesy of the British Library)

A lady gives her heart to a man – quite literally. (Courtesy of the British Library)

Prostitutes were often depicted as mermaids, as in this illustration from the Luttrell Psalter. (Courtesy of the British Library)

Above: The siege of the castle of love from the Luttrell Psalter, showing women defending their maidenhood from suitors. (Courtesy of the British Library)

Below left: Women could and did defend themselves; in the Luttrell Psalter a woman can be seen beating a man. In his pocket is a stick with which he could legally beat *her*. (Courtesy of the British Library)

Below right: The stereotype of the harried husband was alive and well in the medieval era; in this manuscript from the early 1300s a rather unhappy man supports his posing wife on his shoulders. (Courtesy of the British Library)

It was hardly likely and was an insult not only to the women so maligned, but to the men who loved their mothers, respected their wives, and adored their daughters.

Of all the offences committed by women, adultery was believed to be by far the most common. Even when presented as a masculine sin, the suggestion was always present that the women were still 'available' for it. This was emphasised in a sermon in which the extreme fashions favoured by young men were blamed, not on the foolishness of youth, but on female passers-by who were likely to be inflamed by the sight of them.

> Many have their clothes so short that they barely cover their shameful parts, and certainly show women their members so as to provoke lust. Similarly too, some women artificially decorate themselves by painting their faces to please the eyes of men. Indeed, those who do so have the likeness of whores.[41]

After beginning a criticism of the prevailing male fashions, the writer then turned it around to become yet another stab at women – a dangerous and confusing species who, even under a cloak of respectability, were positively seething with lechery and likely to drag some unsuspecting youth off the streets to have their wicked way with him. It is a wonder that any male could walk the streets unmolested, in view of the raging desires of women, hidden under a benign exterior. This particular attribution of lust to women is an effort to displace onto them the responsibility for the sins of the men who could not, or would not, control themselves.[42]

A story then commonly circulated was that of a priest, who had a vision of his dead mother in Hell, where she was surrounded and tormented by vermin as evidence of the adulterous behaviour of her sinful life. A fifteenth-century version claims that her head was tormented because of 'the whorish ornamenting of my hair' and her lips and tongue 'because of my vain speech and adulterous kisses'.[43]

Even if a woman did not use the extremes of fashion to tempt men with her clothing she was still likely to be considered guilty of allowing the Devil to use her. Her soul was to be held responsible for any excesses, desires or temptations of others in respect to her body. Bromyard tells of two women who prayed earnestly for disfigurement because their natural beauty was a temptation to others and of a young girl who had herself locked up for life because she instilled in a man the temptation to sin.[44]

The *Destructorium vitiorum* holds women fully responsible for all the lusts of men, even if these are provided inadvertently.

And if some say that women decorating themselves exquisitely to improve their beauty does not have evil intent, I respond that nor does the sword have an evil intention when someone is killed with it. Still he who turns the sword to unjust killing has evil intention and thus the Devil uses women thus adorned. Like a sword has evil intentions, who gives the occasion of harm, gives the harm.[45]

Many preachers recognised other causes of the lusts of men besides the beauty of women, but still argued that women bore enough responsibility for it even to justify their self-mutilation. This echoed the blame apportioned to prostitutes, rather than the clients who used them, for all the social disruption caused, directly or indirectly, by their trade.[46] Social disruption was only to be expected. The brothels must have become a real nuisance to their neighbours in areas where they abounded, but people would already have been aware of the reputation of the area and knew what to expect there; unless, of course, they formed part of that unfortunate nucleus of residents who were there all along, and were dismayed to find that their area was 'going down' along with their property investment in it. Some places were certainly more offensive than others, and the stewhouse of one Angelo Taylor in King's Lynn was accused of 'causing many quarrels, beatings and hues and cries at night'. Also in King's Lynn was Petronilla Bednot's stewhouse. There 'about midnight on several nights, when the neighbours were in their beds, malefactors and disturbers of the peace came with sticks to their windows and beat upon them maliciously, saying to the neighbours 'you who are in there, come out and be beaten.' A Henry Cook and Nicholas Wick quarrelled when the former interrupted the latter with three whores, but the dispute ended badly for Henry, who died from a stab wound.[47]

Some locals became so furious that they took the law into their own hands. In 1305 the Prior of Holy Trinity in Aldgate was accused of trespassing on the house of a neighbour. He said that the place housed whores and the beadle had made no attempt to evict them, so he and others had removed all the doors and windows in an effort to force the prostitutes to leave. The Prior won his case and the court ordered the women should indeed be evicted, as they were still in residence. They were apparently still carrying on business even without doors and windows, quite oblivious to the draughts.[48]

One Katherine Worsley got her own back on the young men of the parish who had used her services and then accused her of whoredom. She 'reported to divers women of the said parish that their young men, who were in contemplation of marriage with them, had not what men should have to please them, and this she knew for a truth. By reason whereof the said men were refused by the said women, to their great hurt.' Robert Harding, who related the tale, said that he was afraid Worsley would 'make report of him to the rich widow he wooed, by reason whereof the said widow should have in like manner have refused him'.[49]

Those people who rented property to prostitutes could also be accused of being thieves or vagrants and of prompting illicit activities such as gambling. In 1281 the Clerk of the City of London lumped together a group of men arrested 'for divers trespasses as homicides, robberies, beatings, assaults and being vagrants at night after curfew within the city. With swords, bucklers and for instituting games near the jetty and for the keeping of brothels'.[50]

Nevertheless, if a brothel keeper or even a lucky prostitute managed to prosper they were then looked on by their colleagues as being, and certainly considered themselves to be, as respectable as any of their neighbours. Alice Stapleton in her will of 1494 left money to the local church to pay for a canopy over the altar. She also left gowns to her female friends and a fortunate boy of her acquaintance was to receive six shillings and eight pence for his school fees. Perhaps the bequest to the church was for her soul's sake, and perhaps her friends of later life did not know of her origins, or they did and simply did not care. In that case she would have acquired, finally, the cloak of full respectability and acceptance.

One case, from December of 1395, shows some variation from the usual reports of the carryings-on of local females of ill repute. John Rykener, who was caught in an 'unmentionable act' with John Britby, was arrested in a stable in Sopers Lane just off Cheapside. He was seen to be wearing women's clothing and he was calling himself Eleanor and claiming to be an embroideress. When he appeared before the mayor he was still dressed as a woman and cheerfully admitted to having committed several similar offences, saying that he had been paid for sex by 'three Oxford scholars, six foreign men, three chaplains, two Franciscans and a Carmelite friar'. Though he admitted that he charged men for sex he said he also gave his sexual services free to women, including a few nuns. Strictly speaking, he should have been condemned to be burned at the stake for sodomy but he seems to have had a great deal of charm and an insouciant attitude to life. The authorities appeared to be reluctant to have to impose the extreme penalty on him, and didn't seem to know what to do with him. Finally, they decided to charge him with 'misrepresenting himself as a woman, confusing his male clients, and failing to provide them with the womanly services they had paid for'. It is highly unlikely that any of John's male clients were unable to tell the difference between him and a woman, and they had probably got from him exactly what they had paid for, but the lesser charges saved his life. Unfortunately, again the documents are incomplete, so there is no surviving record of what penalty they did impose on John.[51]

7

THE TRIALS OF WIDOWHOOD

For the fortunate woman, at the end of a satisfactory marriage, perhaps left in comfortable circumstances and with family and friends around her, widowhood need not be feared, it was merely another of life's transitions. But for too many others it exemplified the contradictions of prevailing attitudes towards women in general. This ambivalence, built up partly of respect but also of misogyny, was there at the latter part of any woman's life, a continuance of the paradox she had always lived with.

The Church was very fond of widows who were respectable, charitably minded and who had no desire to remarry. These women were the backbone of any local church from whom it might expect support, alms and a substantial bequest at death. The Church did not like the 'flighty widow', perhaps still young and in control of some money of her own for the first time in her life. She would probably still be attractive enough to be on the lookout for another man and in no mood to turn her mind towards her soul's salvation.

Widowhood was taken into account as early as the marriage contract, when 'at the church door' in the sight of all, a man promised his wife her dower.[1] This could be a specific piece of land or property, or could be the standard rate of one-third of the husband's own holding. If left a widow, she would be in full charge of her dower for her lifetime. It would then be hers whether or not she remarried, unless she had been legally divorced from her husband and her marriage therefore declared invalid. Of course, there could be other bequests from the husband, in addition to the dower. These ranged from personal gifts, to household goods, and even the wife's own clothing.[2] Such clarification of detail may seem to be rather over the top, but as mentioned earlier, unless the goods were specifically mentioned as belonging to her by her husband, they were very likely to fall into the hands of some rapacious heir. They would then become merely a part of her late husband's general estate, in which case they would be lost to her.

Life was often shorter then, and more than one marriage was commonplace. Not due to divorce, as in present times, for as we have already seen divorce or annulling a marriage was a very difficult process and by no means possible for everyone. In fact, unless there was a very serious legal reason why the marriage should not continue, the wedded pair was pretty much stuck with each other for life, come hell or high water. But then, 'life' did not mean then what it does now. Diseases and childbirth were perilous, accidents which would now be considered fairly minor could easily lead to death, and for many – indeed most – people, a full-length marriage might be expected to last no more than twenty or so years. Compare that with the life expectancy of the early twenty-first century, when vowing oneself to another person 'for life' could mean sixty years or more – quite a different prospect, which is why pragmatism has had to step in and allow that many people cannot be expected to stay the course, despite all the fond hopes at its beginning. People change a great deal over half a century, or even more, of living together and nature never intended it to be such a long commitment.[3] During the medieval period, nature did step in frequently, in ending a life one way or another while the person was still comparatively young. This could very easily mean that a woman might have more than one husband, and also might very well be married to a man who had had more than one wife. This could mean that her husband's heir was not necessarily her own child. In some cases, bringing up a deceased woman's child or children, even giving them as much love and care as her own, did not guarantee a stepmother the affection of her husband's sons when it came to the division of property. This was particularly the case if she had produced children of her own who also had a claim, thereby dividing the inheritance. This led to many very serious clashes, when a widow would need all the help she could get to allow her to retain the things given to her during her husband's lifetime.

Any medieval landholder approaching death could also grant his property to one, or more, feoffees on trust to deal with it as he directed.[4] By using this device he could hope to avoid the medieval equivalent of inheritance tax or death duties, also circumventing the prohibition on devising freehold land by will. (Freehold was not as we know it. In theory all land was held by the king. It was only passed down to heirs with his agreement, hence payment of heavy taxes on inheritance.) The landholder could instruct his feoffees to hold the land for his own use during his lifetime, and after his death it could then be conveyed to the widow, or eldest son, or whomever he chose. This had the advantage, as with modern-day trusts, that when he died there would be no feudal reliefs due to his lord, as only the deaths of the feoffees (who were then the nominal authorities for the time being), would occasion such payment. This exercise in tax avoidance was to become so efficient and successful that eventually Henry VIII would attempt to abolish its use, after realising that mass tax avoidance on this scale made him the chief loser.[5] Even a 'reversion', which was a right to the future possession of land, usually after the death of someone who held a life interest, could be inherited. One licence to inherit in the

1494/1495 Court Roll of the Manor of Wakefield uses the phrase 'to hold to him and to the heirs of his body legitimately begotten'.[6] After the death of the head of the family and the payment of the heriot, or mortuary fee (which was usually the best beast or some other item of value), the succession to the unfree holding had to be dealt with. In theory, all land belonged to the lord, so he could re-allocate it as he wished. Usually, the original family took over the holding of the deceased, after due payment of a fine and the swearing of loyalty to the lord.[7] Once the transaction was entered onto the Court Rolls the peasant family were back in possession of the land they had worked on in the first place. The entry on the roll was their 'deed' and would support their right to it in the case of any dispute.

On some manors a widow could hold the property for her own lifetime and this was known as a freebench. She would be entitled to keep it so long as she remained unmarried, and it was considered a mark of villein tenure when the whole of the tenement went to the widow. She would have received only the usual third in a 'free' holding, or if the property had been leased for a fixed price.

Some men made a 'fictitious' surrender of their holding during their lifetime, then received it back again after payment of a fine, with the provision that a son or daughter should eventually succeed.[8] Another ploy was to obtain leave for the wife to have half the holding for her own lifetime, to ensure that she would be properly provided for.

Each manor tended to work slightly differently, even when owned by a religious house. For instance, the manors of the Abbess of Shaftesbury were subject to many complicated arrangements from around 1343, designed to ease the passing of the land from one tenant to another.[9]

However, the widow who had been left her husband's holding might not be in quite as enviable a position as might at first appear. Having the ability to run the holding correctly was paramount, and this generally necessitated having able-bodied sons old enough to do the work. It was unthinkable for any lord to allow his property to deteriorate and lose production through neglect, and in addition there was the obligation of the work that had to be done on the lord's own land, which formed part of the tenancy agreement. For this reason alone the presence of at least one healthy and strong man was essential. If the widow, being alone, was forced to surrender the holding back to the lord due to her inability to cultivate the land properly, she would be left with nothing and find herself thrown upon the charity of her family. Usually, she would try to make some arrangement with a relative, or some other man, whereby she handed the land over to him in exchange for provision for herself. This could not, of course, be merely a private arrangement. It would have to be sanctioned by the lord of the manor and enrolled at the manor court, to make it a binding agreement. Nothing could be left to chance in the event that the lord's property could lose its value. One example of this in action was a case at Hales in 1281 when Agnes Bird surrendered the property to Thomas, her elder son: 'All the land held in the vill or in other places, on condition that he will, so long as she lives, fully and honourably provide for her as follows...' There then followed a long list, closely detailed, of all the items that Thomas was to provide for Agnes in exchange for the land. These included wheat, oats and peas that were to be delivered at regular intervals. There were also five cartloads of sea-coal, the provision of a suitable house for her to live in (30 feet in length and 14 feet in width between the walls with three doors and two windows), plus five shillings in cash at Pentecost. All was to be carried out 'fully from year to year so long as the said Agnes was to live'. Thomas also agreed to pay the fee of half a mark to the Pittancer of the Convent, should Agnes ever need to appeal to the abbot. In the case of failure Agnes was to resume possession of the land to do with as she pleased, despite any agreement. To ensure that the agreement was fully understood, it was read out word for word in full court before being written down in the rental book, and signed by Nicholas the Abbot and Brother Geoffrey the Cellarer.[10]

Other entries showed that such formal agreements were common, with sometimes a father making over a holding to a son, a brother to a brother, or occasionally an old man who presumably had no sons to work the land making an agreement with his lord, in the same way as a woman alone would be obliged to do. In one case a woman surrendered her tenement to the Abbot of Warden who gave her 'in regard of charity a messuage and two pairs of shoes at Christmas'.[11] The Durham Halmote Rolls did much the same as was done in the case of Agnes and Thomas Bird, when a case was recorded in which a son, William, took over his father's holding.[12] He then promised officially to 'sustain him *honorifice pro posso suo*'. On another Durham manor it was agreed that the parent be lodged and also given three rods of land, that is, one in each of the manor's strip fields, for his own use.[13]

This meant that a widow in reasonable circumstances could expect to be provided for in a way that ensured her future, rather than having to depend merely on some verbal promise that could be easily forgotten or denied. If the widow had been given a life interest in the lands left by her late husband it usually contained the proviso that this would be forfeited if she remarried without the permission of the lord of the manor or if she was found to be guilty of unchastity. In the case of hasty remarriage, which was not approved by the lord, the inference is clear. If the man she chose proved to be a bad husbandman it could seriously affect the holding, therefore both the lord and the woman's family would consider they had a say in whoever her next husband was to be, if indeed she was to remarry at all.

On many manors, a second husband would have rights over the holding only during the lifetime of the woman, and any children of such a second marriage would have to take their place in line, after the children of the first marriage. However, if the woman had been allowed to surrender her rights and seisin[14] to the new husband, and that had been granted and legally agreed, it would mean that any children of her first marriage would be barred from the holding in perpetuity; it gave the property entirely to the issue of the second, the first having no inheritance rights over it at all. This meant that a second husband was usually only allowed to enter onto his wife's holding on a temporary basis, during the minority of any children of the first marriage. On the death of the wife he would then be expected to give up the holding, surrendering it to the next legal heir.

The second reason for a woman forfeiting her holding was if she was found to be unchaste. While, to modern eyes, this would be a private matter, the medieval system did not consider it so. If the widow was still of marriageable age then her behaviour mattered. If she cheapened herself by immorality then her value as a marriage partner to another man was subsequently lessened. Therefore, a feudal lord had the right to be aware of her conduct and if necessary could remove the holding from her control.

One West Country custom, reported to have been in use on several manors, claimed that an unchaste widow who had lost her rights on the manor could recover them if she rode into the court on a black ram. She must repeat the words: 'Here I am, riding a black ram, like a whore as I am. Therefore I pray you, Mr Steward, let me have my land again.'[15] This may never have actually taken place, as the riding into court on the back of a recalcitrant ram would have been quite a feat. The story may be apocryphal, but had any woman attempted it, she may possibly have caused enough amusement by her daring to have been awarded her disputed land. Unfortunately, there is no real evidence either way.

What we do know is that on the death of the widow, with her life interest, the holding would go *in toto* to one of the children. It did not necessarily have to go to the eldest, but it would not be divided, as such divisions would eventually lead to parcels of land that were too small to be viable. In some areas, most particularly in Kent, the succession of the youngest son was widespread and tended to be known as 'borough English'. An article in the archives of the Suffolk Institute for Archaeology says that this strange custom was the law on eighty-four manors in Suffolk, twenty-eight manors in Surrey, and on 135 manors in Sussex.[16]

Chaucer's *Canterbury Tales* deals with a great variation between the comfortably provided for, and those suffering abject poverty. In *The Nun's Priest's Tale* he describes a poor widow, stooped with age and living in a narrow cottage beside a wood, in a dale, therefore very damp. Her life was hard and we read of her 'little rent' and having to somehow keep herself and her two daughters. They had three pigs, three cows and only one sheep. In describing her home he says 'full sooty was her bower, as was her hall, in which she ate many a slender meal.' No doubt she did, as did many others in a similar situation. It is not difficult to imagine her living quarters, damp, dark, with a central fire providing more smoke than heat and her few animals still living at one end of the building, in the old manner. At least they would have helped to maintain the heat in the small cottage, even if they also added to the smell.

A different sort of widow was also described by Chaucer in *The Wife of Bath*. She could certainly have been called 'merry'. Rather naughty too, as she claims that as she pleased her husband every night in bed, he would have had to be a miser to have denied some other man the pleasure of 'lighting a candle at his lantern'. She went so far as to admit that on the very day that her fourth husband was buried, she seduced a twenty-year-old lad. It was typical of Chaucer's wit and common sense to use a loud, bawdy woman to argue the case that women had been badly portrayed, because all the stories written about them were written by men![17] It was true, but what it also showed was that for many women 'attitude' was essential. The way a woman faced life with all its difficulties had a great bearing on whether or not she was able to enjoy it, and get the best out of it. Although financial and social considerations always played their part, it was still the woman herself who finally decided whether or not she would allow life to get her down, or whether she was fully determined to tackle whatever was thrown her way, if she intended to live her life, not merely exist in it, whether her husband doted on her or made her miserable. As at all times, and in all walks of life, a sense of humour and a good solid dose of pragmatism stood her in good stead, changing life's perspective for the better.

The medieval sense of humour was, in fact, very earthy, bawdy, and perhaps to us often cruel and unsympathetic. It centred on old men being cuckolded by younger wives, people falling over and hurting themselves, or young men tricking pretty girls into sleeping with them after making false promises of marriage. Such promises were often pledged with a ring made of rushes, designed to fall apart as soon as the man had had his wicked way with the girl. Other amusements varied from cruel blood sports to the simple pleasure of throwing cabbages or whatever was available at whoever was unfortunate enough to spend market day locked in the pillory. This is not to say that charity and sympathy did not exist, they did, as many of the court cases show. There was often a genuine desire to do good even though life was acknowledged to be hard and often painful, so the person who could not develop a thick skin and a firm sense of perseverance was likely to fall by the wayside.

Even a troubled king could be cheered by a sense of the ridiculous, as with Edward II. One day the king was reported to have been riding along with his household, and one of his staff, a man named Morris, fell off his horse. Remounted, Morris fell off again, until he was thoroughly muddied. Edward II laughed and laughed at the man's hopelessness and, after laughing until he cried, he awarded the man the equivalent of a year's salary as a gift for providing so much amusement.[18] Likewise, many a wife, or widow, would need a robust sense of the ridiculous to be able to survive the vagaries of medieval marriage, and still be hale and hearty at the end of it.

One of the few benefits during those times was that if an army was summoned, the women were not included, except when they followed their men. Of course, if a woman had sons that would be a worry when they were taking part, and any woman could fall victim to collateral damage if a rioting army were to occupy her home area. If she were highborn, a general muster could mean that she was likely to become widowed even sooner, as lords were targets for either death or ransom. If an estate was obliged to find sufficient ransom money to bring home its lord, it could be bankrupted or be subject to long-term financial disaster. Once widowed, however, the noble lady would keep not only her dower rights but also her title, even if she were to remarry with a man of lesser rank.[19]

On a humbler level, the same applied in the sense that any widow with more than her leg in her stocking could be deemed an attractive prospect for another man. A woman married to, for example, a tradesman, could sometimes become one herself. One Margaret Russell of Coventry is an example of a wealthy female trader. One of her ventures to Spain consisted of goods worth £800.[20] A woman like that was fortunate indeed, at a time when most women had little or no authority.

Even the second richest person in fourteenth-century England, Queen Isabella, with her wealth and unassailable social status, found it could do her little personal good when her husband had the power to make her personal life deeply unhappy. Her husband's preference for his male favourites, who were permitted greater power even than her own, eventually led to insurrection, but that was hardly an outcome most women could expect.[21]

One of the few areas in which a woman was at some kind of advantage, if she survived the perils of childbirth, was that she was likely to live longer than her husband. This, too, could be very much a two-edged sword, for if young and presentable, or merely comfortably provided for, she would be expected to take another husband and start the process all over again. These forced remarriages must have seemed particularly cruel if the woman had only recently been freed from an unhappy relationship and then had to face the risk of another. For the woman who had loved her husband, and been kindly treated by him, it could also be a trial, for she could hardly expect to be so fortunate a second time.

Even the highest born of women could be subjected not only to an arranged marriage, but actually a forced one, achieved by abduction. This very nearly happened to the redoubtable Eleanor of Aquitaine after her divorce from her first husband Louis VII of France. With the king she had managed to produce only two daughters, and France was subject to Salic Law, which meant females could not reign. It was necessary for Louis to remarry and Eleanor's vast lands were returned to her. This made her the most eligible woman in the world, and on her journey home, well guarded though she was, an attempt at abduction was made. Count Theobald de Blois, despite being only the second son of Theobald of Champagne, thought it was well worth his while to attempt to capture her and make her his wife, possession being nine-tenths of the law, in defiance of the Church ruling that the lady needed to be in agreement. However, in this case the lady had heard rumours of the hopeful groom's intentions and left the area just in time. She had only travelled a short distance when scouts informed the party that another attempt was about to be made, by Geoffrey of Anjou, which was also avoided. It may seem almost unbelievable to us that such an important person should face two such attempts on a journey home, at a time when no conflict threatened. That these two young men decided that it was well worth the risk to marry the lady, by force of arms, may well have testified to her charms. She was certainly reputed to have been a beauty in her youth, but her physical appearance had far less to do with it than her vast lands. These stretched from Aquitaine, Poitou and Gascony, and from Indre to the Basses-Pyrenees and were greater than those at that time controlled by the king. They were a powerful lure for any man wishing to make his mark. She eventually married the man who became King Henry II of England and her life was a roller coaster of events, showing that not even the highest rank could protect a woman from the vagaries of fortune.[22]

For the ordinary woman, widowhood, which might have at first appeared to be a release, could also turn out to be perilous. One found that her stepson refused to allow her the dower that was hers by right of law. This case, from the York Court, was between Katherine Hiliard, widow of John Hiliard and her stepson Peter.[23] After the death of her husband, Katherine found her stepson unwilling to give her control of the dower, and to back up his position he claimed that the marriage between her and his father had been invalid as being within the forbidden degrees. If the marriage was invalid, then he need pay her nothing. Katherine claimed that John had had the control of her dower lands passed to him at their marriage and that she needed them back. They consisted of a third of twenty-four messuages, a mill, sixteen bulls, twenty-one bovates of land, five acres of meadows, pasture for 300 sheep, plus annual rents of eight shillings. The dower covered the villages of Arnall, Dripole, Riston, Preston, Sutton Hedon and Careton. Small wonder that Peter was reluctant to let it all go. The marriage had taken place at dawn in late October or early

November of 1363 in the chapel at Riston. The witnesses agreed
that the sun was up when it was celebrated, so that it could not
be considered clandestine. No impediment to the marriage had
been claimed at that time. Peter's brother Thomas, however,
claimed that the marriage was clandestine (i.e. not with sufficient
public view allowed), and the church windows had been covered
to prevent the candlelight being seen. Peter also claimed that
after this, the couple had been denounced to the Archbishop by
their parish priest. The Archbishop then demanded they live as
brother and sister. Katherine and John cohabited for another five
years and Katherine's stepsister said of them that they had 'lived
like true and legal spouses with marital affection, until the death
of John. They were believed and publicly reputed to be true and
legal spouses in the village of Riston and neighbouring areas.'[24]
Peter brought in other witnesses who claimed that Katherine and
John had not slept together after the Archbishop's sentence on
them, but that they had also tried to obtain a dispensation from
the Pope, which was unsuccessful, shortly after which John had
died. No sentence survives in the records for this case, but the
couple's attempt to obtain a Papal dispensation surely shows that
they were aware that something was wrong with the legality of
their union. However, if the marriage was invalid from the start,
then Katherine's personal property, that is her dower lands, had
never belonged to John in the first place, and certainly did not
belong to Peter. If she had passed her right of seisin over to John,
there would have been a record of it in the courts, and no such
record was ever produced.

In the case of Hopton and Brome from 1348,[25] Constance,
the daughter of William Brome, was a widow with two children
(though one of them died in 1348). She was attempting to
get out of an alleged marriage to another William, the son of
Adam Hopton, who was her guardian. She claimed that not only
was there an affinity between her and her guardian's son but that

she had already married another man, of her own choice, named William Boswell, the year before. Either Constance had a good knowledge of the law, or had access to advisors who did, for her case was presented clearly and with all the facts witnessed. Two of her witnesses were clerics and there was also a notary public prepared to speak on her behalf. Her claim was that there was an affinity between her and William Hopton, the man her guardian was trying to marry her to. William Hopton was also the cousin of her first husband, who had been one John Rotherfield. This man had unfortunately been murdered (no details of this homicide were given), and she had then married William Boswell of her own free will. The son of her guardian was not only related to her first husband, but was actually underage when her husband had died. She claimed that she had had 'marital affection' with her first husband, which was attested to by several witnesses. These were apparently people of education and great respectability, though it later transpired that one of them had actually conspired with Adam Hopton to force through the marriage with his young son. Another of the witnesses, knowing of Hopton's intention, had warned him to 'have nothing to do with it, as no good would come of it'. At the time of her first marriage, Constance was the ward of Adam Hopton, and her husband John was his nephew. It was very clearly a matter of her guardian wishing to keep his ward's property within the family and as soon as she was widowed he had tried to arrange the match with his son. The attempt had been scuppered by her marriage instead to the man of her own choice.

It was testified that when the match with Hopton's young son was put to her, she had remained 'quiet and unresponsive'. After this disappointing reaction her guardian had threatened 'to break her neck'. Faced with physical threats she had to acquiesce, although most reluctantly, and it was further reported that when the Hopton marriage did take place, both

Constance and her nine-year-old bridegroom had to be dragged to the altar, 'crying and resisting'. The tangle took some time to sort out, dealing with claims that her first marriage had been invalid, but eventually she was successful. It was recorded that her chosen husband, William Boswell, had a marriage that had been 'entered into legally' so she was able to break free from the guardian's hold over her and over her property.[26] One of the most shocking aspects of the case, to modern eyes, apart from the age of the nine-year-old bridegroom who seemed highly unsuitable for a woman who, though still young, had already borne two children, was the admission that both parties had been dragged to the altar. Their vigorous resistance to the marriage contravenes the Church's requirement of free consent of both parties. However, this proviso must have frequently been ignored when financial considerations made it convenient to do so; there is a wealth of evidence that so-called consent was often nothing of the sort, with threats of physical violence being the least of it. Not every reluctant bride was able to free herself and forced marriage was merely one of the perils of young widowhood.

The transference of any woman's property to her husband, which was the immediate result of marriage, made such abuses all too common and this situation was one that would continue for in excess of 500 years after Constance had so nearly been trapped by it. It was not discontinued until the Married Women's Property Acts of 1870 and 1882. Throughout those centuries, married women throughout the country were reliant on their husbands to handle their affairs wisely, even though many did not. The result was that a man could, and often did, go through his own inheritance like a drunken sailor on shore leave, then marry a woman who had property of her own and do the same with hers. Any debts run up by him would cause his creditors to seize her property as well as his own, to gain payment, leaving her penniless too. [27] Denied legal safeguards, the medieval woman was obliged to accept her inheritance being passed on to her by the husband who had control over everything; though many husbands were careful to settle this with specifics.

Thomas Warham, a carpenter of Croydon,[28] made a very detailed will, specifying all the household goods that his wife Elyn was to have after his death, with the proviso that if she remarried she would lose the bequest. These items included curtains, wall hangings, 'ledes, vessels, hustilments and all bruying necessities'. She was also to receive six of the best cattle, hogs, geese and poultry. Her husband also added 'I bequeath to my wife, the said Elyn, all the array and apparell to her own proper body belongyng, and all other goods and money in her own propre keping, being at the time of my decease.' Elyn was to show herself content with the bequest for if she was not, the household stuff was to be bequeathed elsewhere. A slight sign of friction there?

One Robert Bifeld,[29] an ironmonger of London, behaved in much the same way, saying 'to Johanne, my wife ... my goods and catalles moveable and unmoveable, all the array and apparell to her owne person bilongyng ... Plus 1,800 marks.' Again, if the widow chose to dispute the bequest she would lose it, and receive no more than her legal dower third.

This kind of bequest also held good if the proposed marriage had not yet actually taken place. William Stepham[30] had made his will in Bruges on 12 September 1472 before a public notary and witnesses. He died shortly afterwards. He was betrothed to Margaret Wodehows, and his will reads as if the property referred to was already in her possession, as well as the wedding trousseau he had collected for her. Also 'he willed that the lady Margaret Wodehows his declared betrothed should kepe and retain as her own possession all goods moveable and unmoveable that she held before the promise of marriage between her and William was made.' No share or division of these goods was to be made with the heirs or successors of William. Furthermore, after his debts had been settled he 'gave and left to the lady Margaret his betrothed, all the jewels, garments, precious objects and womanly adornments (*jocalia, vestes, clinodia et ... ornamenta mulierum*) then in Calais or Bruges, that he had intended to give to her at their marriage.' He then required his executors to treat her in a manner that would give her no cause for disagreement, so that in future she could say that his behaviour towards her had been the behaviour of a good, just and honourable man. It would certainly seem to have been so and the handsome bequest would go a long way to making her a desirable party to some further marriage, or at least ensure that she was safe and comfortable.

Richard Tillys[31] in his will makes his wife Margery his sole executrix so he must have trusted her good sense. He had perhaps consulted with her regarding the bequests, which included a 'silver gilt saltsaler, with a body of coral and a girdle called a dimycent, which belongs to her mother and also a primer belonging to my mother'.

Some men had held onto the clothing and other belongings of their deceased spouses and were to mention such items in their own later wills. Roger Lawkenor[32] died in August 1478 and his will includes: 'item, my second wife's russet satin gown to be made into vestments for the church at Tratton ... item, that my second wife's bones be laid in my tomb with me.' He declared that the marble stone that he had bought for his first wife's grave should be laid upon her at Arundel, as he had decided not to be buried with her, preferring to lie for eternity with his second.

Thomas Brampton[33] made his will in September of 1485. He made the Duchess of Norfolk his executrix. Brampton left his cousin Rowlesley one of his own 'best gownes' and to Rowlesley's wife 'one of my wife's best gowns, the best she will chose with a dimycent such as it will please my lady's grace to give to her'.

Also, 'I will that mistress Jane have one of my wife's gowns.' His marriage appears to have been without issue and he had not remarried. He left all his lands and tenements to his brother Robert and his household items to be divided between Robert, his other brother William, and his sister Elizabeth. Although Brompton had no relict for whom to make a bequest, he had carefully saved the clothing of his late wife. The cynical might consider that this was due to the inherent value of the garments, but several men had done this, passing on to other women the belongings of a wife long gone. It would seem churlish to imply that no affection was involved or to deny that the late wife's possessions evoked no sentiment.

This can be balanced by the fathers who were so afraid of family land or possessions passing to a stranger that they were even prepared to disinherit a daughter who looked like becoming the main heir, for fear that her eventual husband would take all.[34] Ideally, land and real property would go to sons, while daughters tended to receive smaller items and sums of money thereby ensuring that the holding passed down through the male line whenever possible. The English peasant shared the European view that the generation controlling the family lands was more a stewardship than an owner, that they were holding them in trust for future generations. This accounts for the great desire to pass on *in toto* and keep the family name connected with the property.

The Church, while encouraging people to make wills, it being for the good of their souls to leave their affairs in order at the end of life (and also leaving the customary bequest to the church), was in accord with the landowner. They too benefited from a smooth and easy succession to the next in line. Theoretically, of course, the landowner could take back the land at any time, but this could be counter-productive and consistent husbandry was far preferable.

The two basic types of inheritance that appear from the studies may appear to make the process rather more straightforward than it may actually have been in practice. We are familiar with the old adage, 'where there's a will, there are relatives', and the common customs were intended to make things clear and cut down the almost inevitable squabbling that tends to mar the passing of a relative.

Impartible inheritance, which was the intention to keep all the land intact and the inheritance of only one person, could be the usual primogeniture (inheritance by the eldest son), or ultimogeniture (inheritance by the youngest son). Partible inheritance, known in Kent as 'gravelkind' required a division of the property into separate and obviously smaller units. By the fourteenth century primogeniture had generally taken over. At Bookham in East Surrey in 1339 two leading villeins, Gilbert Luwyne and Thomas atte Hache, asked the lord if the rule of the youngest son inheriting could be changed in favour of the eldest son. The old custom, though being the one used by their ancestors, was 'to the grave damage and detriment of the whole homage of tenants'. The lord, who was also the abbot, agreed to the change and within a year other villages also wished to make the change to primogeniture. They were allowed to do so, on payment of a charge of forty shillings. It was speculated that they wished to follow the example of the noble families, who had long practised primogeniture.[35]

Unigeniture, whether the land was to be inherited by the eldest or the youngest son, had the advantage of keeping the property intact and preserving it as a far more viable unit. This was certainly to the ultimate benefit of the landowner and, if the family economic unit was prosperous, this benefited all its members – not just the land-inheriting males. Daughters would also receive greater bequests though theirs were usually in the form of animals, household items, cash or a small portion of land taken from the whole. The fact that for the daughters their inheritance would usually be in the form of moveable goods reflects the expectation of their marriage, helping to found a family elsewhere, rather than continuing their own parental line, as was expected of the chief male inheritor.

However, this ostensibly sensible theory tended to fall by the wayside if the father merely instructed his heir to 'look after' the non-inheriting siblings, rather than specifying particular bequests for them. Far too often reliance was placed on the good nature of the heir, and although the widow's portion was fixed in law, the dowry of unmarried sisters would need also to be specified. They might very well end up with nothing if their brother, perhaps encouraged by a greedy wife, was empowered to decide for himself how much they should be allowed.

One example of this in action comes from the Syward family,[36] who went to court to try to settle the argument of how much the non-inheriting sisters could legally expect to receive from their deceased father's property. They may well have been disappointed by the final judgement, which was that they should each receive a lodging and a stated amount of corn, which was fixed at half a ring of wheat and half a ring of peas.

Naturally, even with partible or divided inheritance, the siblings could receive viable holdings if the original patrimony was large and there were few people for it to be divided between. This could work quite adequately in areas where other economic activities were available, as in woodland or in the fens, where hunting and fishing could provide food and less land might be needed to actually support the family.

Succession of any kind could be long delayed if the widow had a claim on the land for her own lifetime. In common law, the widow was allowed the usual third of the property for life, through her dower. However, customary law tended to treat the widow rather more generously. On a number of manors in the West Midlands the widow could be granted part – or sometimes the whole – of the manor for her lifetime. The most common arrangement was that she would receive half.

The right of the widow was as the continuator of her late husband's tenure, so she was not obliged to pay any entry fine.[37] There were however variations in the settlements of the dower. In one area the widows were given interest in the family land only until the heir reached his majority, but even this could vary. Some areas left the widow in control until the heir was twenty-one years old, after which time she could claim her lodging or 'houseroom' from him to secure her a home. Some areas allowed the heir to claim his full inheritance as young as fourteen years old.

Chalgrave Manor in Bedfordshire had in its records a case where Richard, the son of Thomas Ballard, claimed that he was the eldest son and should therefore inherit. The jury were told that he had once had an elder brother, who had died, but the deceased brother had left heirs of his own. If the elder brother had actually held the land during his lifetime then his heirs would have taken priority over Richard, but as the brother died before he had inherited the rule did not apply. Richard's other problem was that his mother was still alive and the manor had a rule whereby 'no customary tenant can enter into the land after the death of his father while his mother still lives, unless the mother does agree. The mother may hold the land for all of her life if she so wishes.'[38]

One man had given his wife a choice of future living arrangements, with the proviso that if she was still not satisfied she could take her third of the estate, in accordance with common law, after which she could provide her own home.

If no widow, or surviving son, was available the succession also involved customary rules. If only daughters remained, the land could be divided up between them, unless one of them – perhaps an elder daughter – had already received her inheritance when she married. Another of the Chertsey Abbey records gives details of a case where the younger daughter was declared 'impotent' and her claim dismissed in favour of the elder daughter receiving all, which was not a happy prospect for family harmony.

One rather complicated matter in the Chertsey Abbey records involved a dispute between half-sibling and in-law inheritance. Peter Bernard died leaving a messuage and half a virgate of land to his son by his second wife. This boy, William, died while still a minor so his half-sister from the father's first marriage claimed the inheritance. The court argued that she was not William's sister, but merely the daughter of Peter's first wife, saying 'none of the half-blood may inherit by right.' The land was eventually awarded to the man who married Peter's widow, the understanding being that at least there was someone who could adequately maintain it.[39]

A bastard could be looked on leniently by some manors, if the person concerned was the sole heir. Otherwise, he might be given land for his lifetime only, but the Church and the lord of the manor were often generous in accepting legitimacy. If a marriage had ended on the grounds of consanguinity or affinity, the children were still considered to be legitimate. Even a child produced from an obviously adulterous relationship could be deemed to be so too, as in the words of one jurist, 'whoso bulleth my cow, the calf is still mine.'[40]

Widows with land could also rent it out, to save having to struggle to cultivate it themselves. This would be on the understanding that it would revert back to the family once the heir grew to maturity. Occasionally, mature sons would be settled on their rented land until the parents were ready to retire. After the plague years, land was in any case more readily available and if the family could afford to rent vacant tenements, then even the younger children could expect to have land, rather than having to do without as previously. People who had little money or none at all could hope to work and save something to acquire a little land of their own, or at least arrange a 'retirement' contract with an elderly neighbour who had no heir. This led to an increase in land transfers to people outside of the usual family unit, while land holdings themselves tended to increase in size, from an earlier average of around twelve acres to double that size.

Differences also became apparent in the way that land and property could be passed to a widow. The widow's rights were, of course, assured at her marriage. The careful husband could surrender the holding into the lord's hands, then take it back in the names of both himself and his wife. Then when he died, the widow could continue to hold it by right, without requiring special permission to keep it and also without having to pay any further entrance fines. Similar arrangements could be made in respect of a son or even a daughter, enabling the family to pass on land even during the lifetime of the father. Poorer families would have sons who could do nothing but wait. They might be able to establish themselves by means of wage labour, or be lucky enough to find a widow with land who needed some man to help her work it. Unfortunately, that too often brought them into conflict with the sons of the widow when they matured, or even found them fighting off competitors for the widow's attentions in the first place. There were plenty of second or third sons from better-off peasant families who had the same idea and would also be on the lookout for marriageable women with some inheritance that made them a good prospect for penniless and land-hungry males.

Poor families had to juggle the resources they had in attempts to provide in some way for all of their children. In this they did not always feel bound to honour the local inheritance rules, which led to many permutations influenced by talents or even simply favouritism, with younger ones being again dependent on the heir, sometimes receiving nothing at all. However, it seems to have been the immediate family that mattered, and a testator who died without children of his own did not tend to leave land to cousins or nephews, but preferred to leave instructions that it be sold, and the proceeds put to the benefit of his soul. If the land was rented, then it would revert automatically to the landowner in any case if there were no obvious heir to it. There would, however, often be some attempt to find a person in direct line of relationship to take on the property, before it was offered to strangers.

After the Black Death people quickly appeared to take up land left vacant by the decease of the holders. Many of these people claimed kinship with the previous landholders, though one wonders just how many of these so-called kin were in fact related in any way, or were merely landless men taking the opportunity of a lifetime to become established in a market suddenly desperate for farmers. The landowner, faced with land likely to remain uncultivated, probably did not enquire too closely.[41]

When a widow was left the right of 'houseroom' this could vary enormously. It was, strictly speaking, the right to have a room in which to live out the rest of her life, within the family unit. This accommodation was to be provided in addition to the dowry she had brought with her at her marriage. This dowry would have been returned to her on widowhood, unless she had chosen to legally pass it on to her children. The widow might be granted the right to remain within the main house for a number of years, and later move into a dower cottage when the heir needed extra space for his own growing family. Alternatively, she might have been given a house and parcel of land separate from the family holding in the first place, or in a more humble family it might merely consist of a place at the hearth and a bed to sleep on. Sometimes the will of the husband would instruct a specific amount of money, goods, or foodstuffs to be apportioned to the widow at regular intervals.

A young woman left a widow with small children and land to cultivate must have found the responsibility taxing. If she arranged for some other man to take over the cultivation of the land until her eldest son was old enough, she had to pray that the arrangement entered into with him worked out well. Sometimes it did not. Eve de Colley was obliged to sue John Payne because he had failed to plough and sow the land for her, as he had agreed. There must also have been many cases where the sub-tenant was reluctant to leave the property when the heir was old enough to take over. Recourse to law in these cases could prove very expensive, particularly if the agreement had been a rather informal one, in which case the result could be unreliable. Looking from the other side of the argument, it must have been galling to have to leave land upon which one had worked for several years, and probably improved, handing it over to a raw youth. The temptation to bleed the property of its profits in such cases may have been great. In all of these arrangements human frailty and greed must have come into play, and even if the matter was then taken to some form of legal arbitration the resulting decision may often have been unsatisfactory.

In some cases men felt obliged to bequeath their property to their son, even if the personal relationship between them was faulty. Thomas Clay of Potton directed that his tenement and lands in Potton should pass to his son Richard after the death of his widow. He did make the proviso 'on condition that his behaviour improves in the future to the satisfaction of his mother and the executor'. The executor was Richard's uncle, John the Chaplain. In other words, he was giving the widow the right to disinherit their son if he did not conduct himself correctly.

Not all all widows were living in penury and misery, though it must be emphasised that many did, eking out an existence in dire conditions and having no hope of any improvement to their lot. One such case of abject poverty was that of Matilda Sherlock of Pinchbeck. She was a widow and a beggar, with two sons, John and William, who is recorded as being six years old, and a small daughter. They lived in a house in Spalding lent to them by

John Herney. One night on retiring to bed Matilda placed a candle in a wall niche and forgot to extinguish it. It fell, setting the house on fire and the whole family was killed. The case is mentioned by Elaine Clark in her article 'Some aspects of Social Security in Medieval England'. This kind of tragedy must have been one of many similar ones when the modern safety nets did not exist and charity to widows and orphans was a matter of personal conscience.

For the more fortunate, widowhood could be a time of release and personal freedom. The widow no longer faced the inconvenience and personal risk of repeated pregnancy, and the duty of obedience to the husband had also ended, along with his legal control. If left with a reasonable income, and if unlikely to be pressed into another marriage, it could become a time when a woman could flourish and enjoy her freedom for the first time since childhood. The manorial courts show prosperous widows still in possession of full tenements as well as merely living in cottages, and show them also buying land and pursuing trades.[44] One Johanna, the widow of William de Bothes, arranged for her son to take over eighteen acres of land and the buildings of his father while still a minor, but the property was to remain in her custody, along with his inheritance. She was then able to purchase a further two acres of new land for herself. One Matilda, the widow of Elyas, could afford to sue another couple for seven shillings and fourpence worth of flour she had sold to them, showing that not all women were easily put upon.[45]

Not all widows would wish to try to carry on alone, finding the responsibility irksome or were simply desirous of adult male company. In the thirteenth and early fourteenth centuries widows of reasonable age tended to remarry quite quickly, though the marriage market for widows did tend to fluctuate along with the availability, or otherwise, of land. On manors where no land was vacant, men naturally looked to widows and often married a woman older than themselves. When the woman died the man would then be likely to remarry with a younger woman, who after his death would in her own turn marry a younger man, in a recurring pattern. A widow's dower lands could usually support a new husband and perhaps new children, at least for the lifetime of the widow.

During periods of land shortage, the lord would actively encourage widows to remarry whenever possible, not only to ensure the proper cultivation of his land, but also to keep the income from the marriage fines. After 1349, when the deaths from the plague had freed up a great deal of land, widows would often refuse to take over the land of their deceased husband if they could find no man to work it for them or marry them to acquire it. At that time the young men, having greater freedom of choice, both of the land and the women, preferred to take on the land directly for themselves. They also tended to marry younger women, which not only gave them the opportunity of a more enticing bed partner but also meant that their own offspring would inherit the property, rather than the half-grown son of the previous husband.[46]

Widows in urban centres naturally had different requirements and also different arrangements. In London the city law and common law together were designed to provide the widow with a reasonable living. She would have a share of the matrimonial home for life, unless she remarried, after which she would be expected to have a new home with her second husband, rather than have him move into the original home with her. Her entitlement from her first husband's estate would in that case revert to the usual third.

The rich widow could still expect to be popular with men, and only three per cent of the London wills contained the stipulation that a wife should not remarry. In fact, in 1403, a skinner left his business and his apprentices to his wife with specific instructions that if she found she could not manage to run the business properly herself, she was, within three years, to remarry so that someone competent could be in charge of it. Widows of Freemen, who chose to remain unmarried, were permitted to take up the Freedom of the City for themselves. This was a great privilege and gave the women concerned the right to carry on business, free from tolls, throughout England, as well as having the right to take on apprentices.

Of course, working widows were not confined to the capital. In Shrewsbury and in York there are records of women taking over businesses and continuing to run them successfully, with potters, butchers, cordwainers and apothecaries all leaving their widows to continue without a halt after their deaths. Several widows inherited looms, and other bequests included anvils and a horse-mill. Alice Byngley, who died in 1464, kept up the business of shear-man. Elena Cooper made pins, and Isabella de Copgrave, who died in 1400, manufactured bricks. In Wakefield, in the late fourteenth century, Emma Erle traded in cloth and Margery Moniers was left enough property to become the landlady of the whole street.[47]

In London, Margaret Salisbury, the widow of a fishmonger, was in 1440 reported as having been for some time trading successfully as a 'femme sole'. (No pun intended, it simply meant that she was working alone.) Yet when the Keeper of the Assay of Oysters at Queenhithe farmed out his office to women, he was reprimanded and reminded that the authorities held it contrary to the 'worship of the city of London that women should have such things in their governance'.[48]

Not all women were fortunate enough to have been left either land or a thriving business. The world was still a masculine place, particularly in the courts, and widows could hold no form of office. It is fair to say that women from poorer backgrounds continued to do what women have done for centuries, that is, look after grandchildren, or work at whatever menial jobs could be found, usually domestic tasks. They were midwives or nurses for the sick, at least until they were old and sick themselves, when they became reliant on the charity of family or friends.

It is apparent from the records that able-bodied women could be employed in many types of work, though many would require them to be younger and fitter than the average widow. They worked as furriers, as assistants to timber traders, masons, tilers and wrights. If they did not own the business themselves they tended to remain only semi-skilled workers and their level of pay would have been relatively low in consequence.

Widows of plasterers, painters, carpenters, coopers and thatchers are also mentioned in the records, which show that women were prepared to turn their hands to anything with astonishing versatility despite the prevailing attitudes. They could turn out to be just as successful as their male counterparts even though they would be obliged to delegate much of the physical work to others.

Joan Clopton, who died in 1419, was remembered in her parish church as being 'unstinting to strangers', evidently a very charitable woman. However, the offence of 'harbouring strangers' might seem to be at odds with her casual charity. Rural society, in particular, tended to provide a network whereby people looked out for each other, but the locals were wary of incomers. This tendency endured for centuries. (It is echoed in modern times by the influx of 'strangers' into the countryside, whose desire to be at the heart of their local community seems sometimes to apply only to local politics, rather than giving attention to the needy old lady down the street.)

In York, Agnes, the widow of John Allan, paid for stallage in order to trade as a seller of bread in the mid fifteenth century, although the actual baking of substantial quantities of bread tended to be a job for men. There were rules about 'hucksters' trading in country-baked bread, which was considered to be a threat to the urban bakery industry.[49]

Another York widow, Alice Legh, worked at a more delicate trade and was owed the considerable sum of twenty-six shillings and eight pence by her employer, Robert Loksmith, when he died. He had been a vestment maker and had employed Alice to do 'fyne heming and broderye'.[50] A Ripon woman, Elena Fulford, also supported herself by doing embroidery, which was referred to by her own will.[51]

Margaret Hall of York who was first a servant to a goldsmith, then later became servant to a chandler, whom she eventually married, shows how necessary it was for women's lives to be fluid. A range of skills and experiences might have to be built up, from the most basic domestic skills, to assisting a husband, or later her sons, in a family business.

The women were specifically exempted from the Statute of 1363 that confined male workers to one single craft or trade, and there was steady growth in work opportunities for women due to expansion of the economy. The high point of female economic activity appears to have been during the mid-fifteenth century. Later economic depression shrank the labour market so far as women were concerned, and they were then excluded from a large range of occupations in which they had previously been employed, in an effort to protect male employment. This tended to force women, whether wives or widows, back into marginal and poorly paid work, and subsequently back into positions of dependency.[52] Once the economic status of the women was eroded, the female worker found herself pushed back into the restricted roles of wife, mistress, mother or whore from which she had long struggled to free herself. Again, instead of becoming a fairly independent worker, she was concerned mainly with finding a husband from whom she would take her identity. This unfortunately coincided with a period of falling marriage ages – and a strong prenuptial trend of pregnancies and illegitimate births, which were indicators that the role of women had again been consigned to the merely physical. This renewed emphasis on the need for any woman to be 'with' a man as a part of his household, in order to live decently, or be able to take part in business activities, was problematic. It made the woman who was alone become a problem and surplus to requirements. It must have been especially poignant for those who would have loved to be able to remarry, but found themselves without the opportunity to do so. Whether a woman was poor, or more comfortably placed within her level of society, all women tended to lose a certain amount of status when such attitudes were prevalent. Widows were once again expected to be respectable matrons, beloved of the Church for their supposed piety and willingness to engage in almsgiving. If they were of a more active disposition, eager to continue to live life in the real world and conduct business vigorously, they might in some way appear to become disreputable, as any woman who was not safely under the control of some man was largely assumed to be.

However, some women still craved male company and on them the restrictions must have pressed very hard and been difficult to live with. Some widows were known to have taken lovers and these relationships could have unfortunate, if variable, results. Isobel Edmond, a tenant at Cleeve Priory, took a lover and he paid the entrance fine on her land for her, and the banns were read for their marriage. She was one of the more fortunate ones who could regulate the relationship and regain the status of being a wife. Not so lucky was Lucy Pofoot, the widow of Thomas of Houghton. She was at a tavern one evening, and after returning home a 'ribald stranger' who must have seen her there asked her for 'entertainment'. She may have agreed to entertain him, but was found the next morning with five knife wounds in her heart. Another widow, Sarra, aged forty-six years, entertained three men at her house and was subsequently killed and robbed.[53] These women were not necessarily pushed into part-time prostitution merely because they were widows, but to suggest that a woman is not lonely, just because she is surrounded by family and friends, is to ignore the impulses of human nature. Many women, whether young or in their middle years, still require more than overseeing a house or minding grandchildren. Many still crave male company, not merely for sex, but to reassure them that they are still women and desirable. Nobody wishes to be forced into old age prematurely but for these, and many like them, the attempt to fulfil a basic human need led to their shaming and death.In itself a tragedy was the expectation that so many women, still far from old, should be content merely with a life of celibacy, or religious and family duties, once they were widowed.

8

SPIRITUAL MARRIAGE

It may be said with some truth that as the Middle Ages progressed the Church began to exercise a stranglehold over basic human desires and emotions. It was in the interest of the clergy to render all natural impulses into sins, and then profit from them, as indeed the local lord still did with his own systems of fines and fees for anything other than the most exemplary conduct. It is also true to say that, in an age when people were brought up surrounded by opportunities for the expression of piety, many were and remained genuinely pious. The colour and ritual provided by the Church often fulfilled a deep need, through the drama and excitement of the liturgical year, particularly for ordinary people whose lives could be dull. It also created a sense of belonging, of forming a small part of something greater than oneself, when that greater religious family was neither small nor insignificant. The membership of this enormous and powerful group, however indirectly, gave a sense of security and meaning to lives that were otherwise mundane, sublunary and filled with fears that the ordained could help to assuage.

For many even this was not enough. Following the routine of the holy year whilst still remaining in secular life did not always fully appeal and did not guarantee that place in Heaven that some people needed to give their lives purpose. The desire to take vows of religion was still a fundamental part of everyday life and one that had only honourable connotations. In a later time, the idea of confining oneself in a closed community, of giving up all that usually makes life pleasurable, may seem strange. However, within the context of medieval spirituality it was perfectly possible to devote one's life to God, without in any way appearing radical. This closer connection with God could even, if necessary, be achieved while still within the bonds of matrimony. While the idea of marital celibacy might seem in some ways to be a contradiction in terms, it is not at all unusual, even now, for the sexual side of a relationship to fail. Once the first flush of romantic love is over and the necessity for producing children has been completed, the sex drive may lessen. Sometimes it leads to one or other of the partners looking elsewhere for solace, but often enough the failure of the sexual side is mutual, and this is the ideal situation in which the medieval idea of marital celibacy could thrive.

Unfortunately, the public honour which the state of obvious piety, particularly monastic piety, conferred upon the family of the professed, could lead to another form of abuse. A family member who might otherwise not have thought to choose religion in that form for themselves, could be pressured into taking a vow, either to facilitate the vow of another, or because of the family's desire to have a professed religious among its members. It could also become something of a 'dumping ground' for family members (often female) who were in some way unsuited to marriage and could relatively easily be provided for by a one-off payment to a nunnery. Unfortunately for the religious houses, this shuffling off of the untrainable, the unsuitable and the unmarriageable could cause problems. The initial dowry would be quickly spent, but the permanent visitor was still in residence and likely to remain so, either as a professed religious or even as a guest, taking lodgings under the abbey roof. These people could be a great source of friction and disturbance within the house. They did not always live, or wish to live, according to the rules of the house that applied to others. They could disturb the more devoted inmates, creating their own forms of abuse with noise, pets, visitors, even lovers and the bringing of the secular world too close to the values of those seeking peace.

Medieval lay piety could often be a highly emotional state, centring of course on the life and death of Jesus Christ, and the joys and sorrows of the Blessed Virgin Mary, with some side excursions to favourite saints. This emotional response towards such figures can be compared with the rather similar response of a person falling in love, though without the sexual aspect. Unless we allow that the 'agonies' of saints can appear to represent some sort of physical orgasm, as in Bernini's sculpture *The Ecstasy of St Teresa* in the Church of Santa Maria della Vittoria in Rome, or his breathtaking sculpture *The Ecstasy of Beata Ludovica Albertoni* in the San Francisco a Ripa, also in Rome. Though these famed artworks are from a later time, they represent a continuation of a form of religious devotion that is essentially medieval in its intensity. Perhaps the medieval mind, and indeed the later one, found it easier to accept the idea of female sexual excitement if the female concerned was saintly and the object of her desire was Christ himself. Such depth of feeling was far better directed towards God, while the fundamental business of sex within marriage was supposed to be merely procreation rather than enjoyment. Otherwise anybody was considered far better staying celibate.

Conversely, the Romans viewed celibacy as an aberration. It was a denial of the State's right to expect its citizens to provide progeny for its support, either as soldiers involved in its expansion, a political elite to govern it, or dutiful females to regularly produce further children for as long as was decently possible for them.

Only the six Vestal Virgins were exempt from this requirement, and their virginity – at least while they remained inmates of the Temple of Vesta – was deeply associated with Rome's good luck.[1]

Ancient Judaism was also strongly opposed to celibacy, considering that a women's role was to be a mother, and the woman who failed to produce children often believed that she was in some way cursed. Christians were alone in considering that celibacy was a requirement of religious office, though in the earliest times even they had not believed it to be an essential part of a holy life. It was to become not only that (though often difficult to adhere to for many) but the idea gradually formed that once the laity were not active in producing children, then they should not really indulge in sexual activity either. They were far better off if they took some form of vow of celibacy, even if it only involved regular abstinence at certain times.

However, while the terms 'celibacy' or 'abstinence' are often used interchangeably, they are not at all the same. Abstinence is the requirement to abstain from some, or all, aspects of sexual activity for a limited period of time. This is usually at holy seasons, during menstruation or pregnancy, and so on. Actual celibacy must be defined as a definite religious vow, presumably (or ideally) taken voluntarily, to the effect that the subject will henceforth not engage in any sexual activity at all. This is a far more restricting vow, and also life-changing. Gabrielle Brown in *The New Celibacy* referred to the two main differences as 'abstinence is a response to what is going on with regard to the outside, but celibacy is the response to what is taking place on the inside.'[2]

The ability to live comfortably within a totally non-sexual environment is not given to everyone. Many people find it impossible to live an asexual life, even though a large number of modern people live alone, which was rarer in medieval times. The natural urge leads, and has always led, to what would once have been called sin, when the natural sex drive takes over and any vows given, however voluntarily, can be broken. The Church recognised the possibility of this, going so far as to 'discourage particular friendships' among religious communities in efforts to minimise, or preferably prevent, acts of homosexuality. Close friendships, even without any physical element, are not conducive to the performance of suitable devotions to the deity, who should be the only object of affection. Nor are they likely to produce fair and equal behaviour towards the brethren or sisterhood as a whole. Indeed, such close friendships may be considered even more disruptive to good order in the long term than a brief sexual relationship might have been, as merely physical release between partners who do not share any emotional bond tends to be more short-lived.

For the unfortunate person, placed in a religious house while not possessing any vocation, merely to allow a guardian or relative access to their lands or other property, this was not only a tragedy on a personal level. It could be considered to be a crime, having imprisoned a person without hope of release, when innocent of any wrongdoing and without any desire for such a stringent way of life. This was the fate of many women throughout the medieval period and beyond, when a guardian found it preferable to make that one-off payment of a dowry and then retain the rest of the inheritance, thereby disposing of the woman permanently. Had she been found a suitable husband then the property would become his, and the guardian would lose control.[3] This was commonly the case during the reign of Edward IV when any young woman who found herself a ward of the king was likely to be sent to a local nunnery. The dowry payment given ensured she was confined there for life, allowing the king to make use of the rest of her property. It was a very lucrative money-spinner for the guardian but a tragedy for the girls concerned.

One of the best examples of this (if from a rather later time) is the famous case of Lady Marianna de Leyva, a member of the family of the Princes of Ascoli. They were Grandees of Spain during the period when Italy was in Spanish hands. It serves to show the attitudes and problems of the system in England during a time before the country became Protestant and the religious houses closed. Lady Marianne was put into a convent just before her fourteenth birthday in 1589. Two years after she had been placed there by her widower father and before she was quite sixteen years old, she became Sister Virginia Maria, and is today well known as the Nun of Monza.[4] She grew to womanhood within the walls, while her father remarried and produced a son. It is difficult for us to imagine how this young woman must have felt, being blessed at birth with health, wealth, good looks and impeccable breeding, yet to be immured in a convent to face a life she had not chosen. The rhythm of the city outside went on without her, while she was subject to stultifying routine in the company of other women who were not necessarily her chosen friends and may have had little in common with her. She certainly appears to have desired to have children of her own, and she certainly felt the pangs of romance, though these things were officially denied her. She made the acquaintance of the son of a neighbour, whose property adjoined the convent. The young man concerned, Juan Paolo Osio, was a scoundrel and a scandal to his family, who could not control him. He may have thought that seducing the attractive nun was an amusement, but once the seduction was complete the pair fell in love. Their passion for each other not only produced offspring, but also created a complicated web of lies, deceit, accusations of witchcraft, and murder. Gian Paolo was sentenced to confiscation of all his property, the destruction of his family home, and while a fugitive he was finally killed by a man he believed to be a friend. Sister Virginia Maria was sentenced to be walled up alive in a tiny cell, a fate she endured for fourteen years, living on only starvation rations, suffering cold, illness, and total lack of the most basic hygiene, without the slightest help. But amazing as it sounds, she did survive. How many times must a professed religious have been tempted beyond endurance by the prospect of a life like other people, and how much more difficult must the life have been when the celibate was unwilling? One can only pity those like Sister Virginia de Leyva, despite their perceived faults. The crimes to which her lifestyle led her also led to her death-in-life sentence, but had she been living a normal woman's life they would never have happened. Some, at least, of the blame for what she did must be laid at the door of the father who decided on such a future for the girl.[5]

The case of the Nun of Monza is one of extremes, and no attempt is being made to suggest that murder and mayhem is a natural product of the celibate life, but there are many reports of scandals where outlets for natural desires are denied. There was an old poem of a prioress whose sexual failings caused her disgrace: 'She bore a child in cherry time, all the convent knew of it.' There are charming drawings showing members of religious orders in the stocks alongside their lady friends, or naughty nuns being carried home on wheelbarrows. It has always been a standing joke that the presumably celibate priest is really no better than he should be, or that in a convent full of nuns at least some will be eyeing the priest who comes to administer the sacraments. Such jokes are in line with the general disbelief that people are able to live successfully in such a situation. In our modern world, where every 'normal' person is expected to be enjoying a regular and varied sex life, the idea of celibacy seems pointless, even peculiar, but the medieval mind was different. Their attitude could usually find a place for not only voluntary abstinence at regular times, but also find nothing astonishing in the idea of full celibacy all of the time. This was despite knowledge of the various 'unsuitables' who stained convent life with affairs, extravagances or other attempts to continue a worldly life within the walls. Piety did exist, and some people did prefer the enclosed life away from the world and all its temptations, which seemed to them only dross. Whatever the way of life, there was still belief in the existence of the soul, which could easily be stained, damaged or subject to severe punishment for errors committed, or duties deliberately evaded. In this situation, preparation for a better future in God's Heaven was seen as a sensible precaution, not a fantasy.

There was even a belief that virginity, so easily lost, could be redeemed by an exemplary life. In this, the 'born-again' virgin was not a joke. Virginity could not only be a positive lifestyle choice, but could almost be recoverable. Not physically of course, but by confession, repentance, absolution and the determination to begin anew. This could be done by a married pair who could take a vow of celibacy together; it could be done by an anchoress who might personally decide to retreat from the world, yet remain within it, being ceremoniously locked into a tiny cell and being declared 'dead to the world'. Yet once the local bishop had pronounced that sentence upon her, she was still able to hear, see and be seen from her window. Some of them became great favourites and were consulted on many issues both political and domestic.

By 1200, belief in Purgatory was widespread with the dead occupying a separate place somewhere between the physical world and Heaven itself, which they would be obliged to occupy until their souls had been cleansed of sin. This could be achieved by the prayers of their loved ones, or by having shown true repentance at life's end.[6] The thirty days immediately after death were considered particularly important for assisting the soul through Purgatory with prayers and masses. Prayers said over the new grave both helped the departed and gave some focus to the grieving living, as they did their best to prevent the deceased loved one from becoming a revenant, or one of the walking dead, of which there was considerable fear.[7] While the Church did not actually encourage belief in these unfortunates, who appeared to be trapped between one existence and another, they certainly used them as fearful examples of what could happen after death if a soul were possessed by demons. Many popular accounts claimed that the souls of those people who had experienced a bad death would be able to return to harm the living. They could be used to emphasise the need for a 'good' death, which was one in which the Church had played its part. It was necessary to be confessed, absolved, and have the Last Rites performed, as these rituals sent the soul off with a strong recommendation to God. For the sensible person, this was all the more reason to make proper provision for future acceptance into Paradise in plenty of time, not leaving it until the last moment. The real danger was that some accident or sudden illness might catch one out, leaving the soul unable to be put into a state of grace before having to face its maker.

For careful people, a last-minute garbled absolution was insufficient, representing a huge risk of being found wanting and becoming condemned, either to Hell itself, or at least to a long and very uncomfortable sojourn in Purgatory. For the indigent, or those who had nobody likely to pray for the repose of their soul, the twin festivals of All Hallows (1 November) and All Souls (2 November) were intended as a general attempt to assist. These festivals were for souls who otherwise had no help to send them on their journey towards reward (or punishment), and formed part of a general cleansing done by the community on behalf of deceased members who had nobody to care for them individually.[8] These community devotions formed part of one's duty of charity, and were made in the fervent hope that similar prayers might be available to help pave the way into Heaven if the supplicant were ever left in a similar predicament at their own death.

Elderly widows were always considered important to their local church. They might be expected to be pious, to put their souls in good order in good time, attend to charities and church donations and if they had been left a good inheritance were a good source of revenue. There was a good reason for the Church to encourage a widow to take a vow of celibacy, which would mean that they would not remarry. That almost certainly meant more donations, which a second husband might veto.

The vows of celibacy were a serious matter, and involved the vowess receiving a cloak and a ring from the Bishop, while her vow was officially recorded. Lady Margaret Beaufort[9] was reputed to have taken such a vow while married, with her husband's permission. After this was done they lived apart, though he is said to have visited her at intervals. After his death in 1504 her vows were renewed. She may have been an unusual case, but was far from unique. Though such vows were more usually held back until the husband had died, if his permission was given it was perfectly possible for the married pair to end their physical relationship in this way. If the marriage was one of convenience, as the Beaufort and Stanley one may well have been, it probably suited both parties perfectly well to vow to have no physical contact. It would also apply to a couple who were well advanced in years and took their religious teaching seriously, in which case, as there could be no further hope of children, it would be unnecessarily sinful and indulgent to continue a sexual relationship. For the health of their souls they could then not only abstain, but also make an official declaration of their intent.

St Augustine [10] said 'in our day, no one of perfect piety seeks to have children, except spiritually.' This might seem to herald the death knell of the human race, until one remembers that the piety of most of the ordinary people, while genuine enough, was not perfect!

While there were people such as the Beaufort-Stanleys whose financial situation allowed them to live separately, this arrangement was certainly not practical for most. Others may have wished to be able to do so, for the further improvement of their souls, but could not afford two homes. The idea of 'living chastely' could even mean merely being faithful to the one marriage partner rather than being completely celibate, as we might understand the term.[11] This mixture of the meanings of the various descriptions of marital sexuality causes some confusion. The religious were intended to be celibate, but many who held high positions in the Church hierarchy simply ignored the stricture, keeping mistresses and providing for their bastard children as any layman of wealth would do. Despite these failings, the call to the life of the Church was still considered the ideal, with the married state running a rather poor second. It was useful for preventing the laity from copulating indiscriminately, but not really to be recommended otherwise. Marital duty still required the provision of children and the marriage debt was intended to provide the outlet of a sexual life, though in the case of someone like Margaret Beaufort even that desire might fail and the vow become preferable.[12]

The implication was that the married state was good enough for ordinary people who had to do their duty and reproduce. However, those of a more spiritual inclination could, and probably should, do without it.

Then there is the married couple who were not too old to produce children, and not inclined to enter a religious house of any kind. They were able to still renounce all sexual activity but not actually separate in order to do so. This concept, intended not merely for the elderly or the infirm, was actually recommended by the early Church. It implied a state of purity not usually possible within the marriage bond, and it almost equalled becoming a religious, even though it could never be quite as good. Living in the world meant that the participants were still subject to the many earthly and fleshly temptations, from which the true religious were more protected, nonetheless it was certainly better than normal married life.[13] The Church greatly approved of it and it was given a certain amount of respect by the laity. It could improve the status of those women who had decided upon it even if the pair did continue to live in the 'real' world.

While the rich couple could easily have separate accommodation,[14] the poorer couple who wished to try this lifestyle would have the added difficulty of having to continue to share a small home and possibly even share a bed. The whole point was that this celibacy, even if agreed by both parties, in no way involved actual legal separation. The vow for this was, in theory, performed before the bishop, as with the others, and the church authorities were happy to perform the little ceremony that ensured that the marriage entered a new phase, without being dissolved. While the married state was in itself considered 'worthy' it was far more so if it could be removed from the fleshly mould of procreation.

The Cathar road to becoming a 'perfect' required a married couple to separate, if they could not guarantee being able to live under the same roof in a state of 'ascetic chastity'.[15] The Church considered the Cathars to be heretics, despite their saintly lives, as they did not adhere to Church doctrine and thought the Pope was not at all special. They believed that the physical world was evil and ruled by the devil, so only the pursuit of heavenly goodness was safe. Orthodox belief didn't quite go so far as to admit that the devil ruled the earth, but it certainly acknowledged that earthly temptation was rife, and to be strongly resisted.

Peter Lombard's *Sentences*, written between 1155 and 1158 (a standard theological textbook), stated that the sex act was never entirely without sin and that even within a faithful and loving marriage it was highly unlikely that any such relationship could be without blame. This is the case wherever sex is 'indulged' in if the actual desire to procreate is absent. It also applied if the man would have 'desired intercourse with his wife, even if she were not actually his wife'. In other words, if he lusted after her. It makes plain that any sexual attraction was considered sinful. So even the respectable married couple cannot enjoy each other in private, without being censured. The inference is that the ever-present 'marriage debt' could be rather a grim undertaking, as providing one's spouse with sex on demand was only non-sinful if the pair were not attracted to each other![16] So the Church, while accepting the need to propagate the species, considered it a sin to enjoy it, and only considered it innocent if performed with someone unattractive who would not be the object of desire if one was not married to them. Some theorists even went so far as to consider that fornication with an attractive woman was more sinful than with an ugly one, simply because the pleasure was greater.[17] However, Alan of Lille (1128–1203) takes the opposing view that having sex with an ugly woman must be more sinful, as the natural compulsion must be less, making the act one of determination to commit the sin despite the woman's lack of attraction.[18] The canonist Huguccio (Bishop of Ferrara, died 1210) said that provided everyone avoided having an orgasm then the act might be considered sinless, but surely that contradicted the rule that sex was for procreation? In any case it was unlikely to be a solution that appealed to most people. If the only way one could avoid sin were to abide by a rather complicated set of rules, without any enjoyment of the act, while also trying to find some way to conceive children without an orgasm – where on earth do you start?[19]

The sainted Bernard of Clairvaux, in a sermon in 1144, protested against the possibility of 'chaste cohabitation' with anyone of the opposite sex, saying 'the Church forbids men and women who have taken a vow of chastity to live together.'

But that is a very different thing, involving a definite vow taken voluntarily. He went on to say 'to be always with a woman, and not know her carnally, is this not more than to raise the dead?'[20] This either says a lot for St Bernard's generous understanding of human nature, or displays a total lack of faith in people being able to control themselves while in the presence of the opposite sex. Most of the blame for all this lustful feeling was, as usual, placed on the women. It was widely believed that females were far more sexually oriented than men, though what fuelled that belief is difficult to see. Only Hildegard of Bingen[21] differed from that accepted male view, and put the blame firmly back upon the men.

The idea of 'celibate' marriage was a strange compromise approved of by the Church, in which man and wife both took a vow not to have any form of sexual contact with each other. Of course it was impossible to guarantee that the couple were holding to the promise. But at the same time there was the fear that female celibacy could in some mysterious way actually undermine male superiority, with men being denied their conjugal rights, thus the argument found itself back at square one. Certainly the idea of women getting above themselves in any way, including paying or not paying their marital dues, was an anathema. It exacerbated the usual fear of strong-willed women, who were not convent confined, getting their way over their men.

So far as the clergy was concerned, there was also a new need to prevent the laity from attempting to usurp clerical life, in making too close an imitation of it in their own. The constant reiteration of the need for a sinless life had rather backfired on the clergy, especially in the idea that even the most innocent sexual encounters, within lawful marriage, were still sinful. Pious lay people had begun to think that the only way forward was to copy the clerical ban on sex for their own salvation.[22] This put the clergy on the defensive and they then reared back like a frightened horse at the idea that the laity should embrace the one thing that truly set the clergy apart. The clergy had got themselves into a bind over the matter, in confusing the issue so thoroughly by their talk of constant sin whatever one did, and their claim that only celibacy could be holy. To keep themselves separate they needed a middle road for ordinary people, and this was the concept of spiritual marriage.

The original idea of the marriage debt had already raised problems with questions being asked about its application in the real world. For example, Peter the Chanter[23] asked whether if a woman suffered some kind of damage from a birth that was likely to kill her if she conceived again, must she still submit to her husband with the ever-present risk not only of conception but her own death? It was a difficult question and one that was never fully answered until the fifteenth century when denial was beginning to become acceptable in order to save a life. Aquinas agreed with this, and in fact some early Jewish writers had sensibly recommended the use of the contraceptive sponge in such cases.

One must not forget that greatest bugbear of medieval men, particularly those in clerical life, the female menstrual cycle. This provoked fear and loathing in many of them, with a terror of pollution from this natural function, which in the eyes of the clergy represented corruption itself. Indeed, corruption was held to be the fate of any offspring unfortunate enough to have been conceived at such a time. It was firmly believed that it could produce leprosy, elephantiasis, or epilepsy in children. The blood was considered to be so unclean that on contact with it crops would wither and refuse to germinate and orchards would lose their fruit. Pope Innocent III remarked 'if dogs should lick of it, then they will become mad.'[24]

If a woman had claimed that her husband was incapable of consummating the marriage, she would have to provide her proof, as the York Cause Papers have shown. But if the husband simply denied it and yet refused to submit to the physical examination, she and the court would have to take his word for it. Jacqueline Murray suggests that such examinations for impotency probably began in thirteenth century England.[25]

Gratian's claim of the absolute lordship of the husband over the wife extended to all areas, and even a charity vow made by her was subject to revocation if he so chose.[26] In fact, her ability to make such a vow in the first instance was thought to set a dangerous precedent and the husband's right of revocation was seen to be necessary. This rendered women quite incapable of undertaking any legal matter, as their given word was so easily rendered void. This 'natural order,' so important in the medieval mind and upheld beyond all common sense, was due to the belief that man was made in God's own image, and women were not. Therefore, the woman, being of a lower order, must remain subservient to her natural master. It was even said that God would prefer a woman to obey her husband by not performing acts of personal religious devotion, if told not to. In this case her duty to her husband took precedence even over her duty to God. Gratian also firmly upheld the right of a man to 'correct' his wife.

The only vow that a woman could take that could not be revoked by her husband was that of marital celibacy. In such a case the agreement for the vow had had to be made by them both, with the approval of the Church and it was not possible to take any stance on marital celibacy without the full approval of the other party. However, even in the case where the married couple did jointly take the vow to abstain completely from all sexual activity, it did not affect the husband's other rights over the wife. Such a vow could only refer to the conjugal debt and his authority over her was still valid in every other aspect of their daily life.[27] Only the vow of celibacy, made together, was inflexible. Once the bishop had confirmed their joint intention, they were expected to refrain from physical contact despite any necessity to cohabit. If they should then give in to the temptations of such close proximity, then any child or children born of their further union were deemed to be illegitimate, despite the legality of their marriage still being valid.

In the case of a single vow, that is when one of the married pair wished to retire into a religious house, the case became even more complicated. If one spouse gave permission for the other to take a vow and enter religion, yet did not intend to do the same, it left a very awkward legal problem regarding the conjugal debt. If the wife was vowed, did that mean that the abandoned husband was then free to lead his own life, as if he were a bachelor again? Not so, unfortunately. He was still married to the wife, despite her becoming a religious, so if he found solace elsewhere he was committing adultery. A case from 1329 highlights this. Beatrice, the wife of Ralph Strange, wished to become an anchoress and her husband consented. However, the bishop later heard rumours that Ralph was fornicating with others, so he felt that Beatrice could not remain an anchoress as it was forcing her husband into sin.[28] Did it mean that Ralph, then living alone, would also be obliged to renounce a sex life, because his wife had done so? Was that taken for granted and would he also be required to make a vow of celibacy, even if he had no intention of doing so? Certain authorities believed that the spouse remaining in the world should not be bound by the vow of the other. This meant that Ralph was still technically entitled to claim his conjugal rights from his wife – although she, having vowed herself to celibacy, could not do the same with regard to him. This appears to be another instance of the Church shooting itself in the foot with its entangling legal niceties. Pope Innocent IV decided that the one who remained in the world was actually entitled to recall the spouse from their spiritual retreat, to perform their marital duty; but then what about the inflexibility of the vow of celibacy? Other writers, such as Huguccio did not agree, as they put the vow to God above all earthly considerations, even to the legal spouse. Huguccio insisted that if the vowed spouse were to be recalled from the religious life by the husband to whom she owed earthly obedience, she would be obliged to return to the convent if the husband died. Pope Alexander III, on the other hand, thought that such re-entry was not necessary, although a further marriage could not be permitted. It is probably a good thing that the medieval Church did not have at that time the further complication of papal infallibility to deal with, or else all the disagreements would have been even more of an embarrassment.[29]

The insistence on the inferiority of the woman, and the necessary obedience to the man, was reinforced by the humility and passivity of the Blessed Virgin Mary. The emergence of Mary as the mother goddess figure, inevitable as it was, did little for the emancipation of women generally. The claims that she was silent, subservient and obedient echoed the qualities that men wished to see in their own women and that the Church preferred from women in general. Gratian had taught that God's will could come down to the woman through her father or husband, thus reinforcing the autonomy of the male.[30] This prevented the possibility of any individuality of thought or behaviour from women. However, Huguccio, who was generally severe in his judgements, did put the priority of the vow to God above the duties to an earthly husband, arguing that religious vows were more important than any husband's requirements. Ironically, this emphasis was rather more enabling on behalf of the woman. Any person recalled from a religious house by a protesting spouse (who had given permission initially, which technically was inviolable), was still held to being obliged to fulfil the monastic vow as soon as he or she was free to do so. This merely added to the confusion. Huguccio still denied the right of the husband to revoke any vow made by the wife, saying that the wife must do the best she could to please God, even over and above her natural master, her husband. The husband was actually forming an impediment to the wife being able to fulfil her vow, but once that impediment was removed the wife was free to return to it. This still did not address the point that the husband had presumably agreed to his wife's vow in the first place, but it did form something of a breakthrough for women. It released the widow from the pressure to re-marry and allowed for her eventual retirement from a confusing and dangerous world.[31]

Generally, the piety of females was rather suspect. Peter the Chanter was concerned about the lack of options for women who wished to devote themselves to religion, fearing that such women, in refusing marriage, might be taken to be Cathars! That much maligned sect was another source of fear and loathing within the Church establishment. Raymond of Penafort opposed Huguccio by neatly affirming that a woman most closely obeyed God when she obeyed her husband, thereby closing the door on any individuality of thought for her.[32] Although he admitted that the wife should 'sorrow in her soul' if denied the ability to fulfil her vow, the grief would attest to the purity of the intention and was to her credit. However, the wishes of the husband remained paramount. In this case it was less the outward show that counted – in performing the action she had vowed – but the inner intention. Her grief at being denied it was in the long run more important than actually having done it. This is in line with clerical advice to women, where seemingly impossible demands were placed on them. They were to ensure they performed prayers, fasts and meditations, while at the same time being bogged down by the trivia of ordinary life. It was as if they were required to be always busy, physically, mentally and emotionally, as a safeguard against them falling into sin, even the sin of thought.[33]

Even the giving of alms by the woman came under discussion – not to decide whether the family could afford to give charitable donations but whether the husband had the right to forbid his wife to do so, even though responsible alms-giving was a duty. Raymond of Penafort, while confirming the husband's right of control in financial matters, still allowed the wife the right to use any housekeeping surplus for this purpose. This was allowable even if the husband decided against it. This evasion of the man's authority is again neatly dealt with in his *Summa de Poenitentia*[34] with the excuse that although the husband was 'accustomed to prohibit the wife absolutely' he might have been doing it merely as an exercise in control. The wife could then go ahead safe in the knowledge that if her husband had seen the 'condition and misery of the poor' it would smite him to the heart in pity. Therefore the giving would 'secretly please him'. Of course there is also the proviso that if he had 'proclaimed utterly to the wife that such an act would displease and scandalise' the husband, then she ought to desist. She would then have to fall back onto 'grieving that she is not permitted to give alms', which would be to her credit. Some writers argued that any wife was entitled to 'give moderate alms, even if she knows that her husband would be displeased by it' without any pretence at cushioning her disobedience by claiming that deep down he wouldn't really mind. This is another example of the impossible task placed upon the wife, who had to walk the tightrope of pleasing both the Church and her husband. Unfortunately for her, the Church was not there to argue her case at home when she had to face the husband's anger for giving away his money when he had expressly told her not to.

Thomas of Chobham went even further in undermining the balance of the marriage. He suggested that the wife's appearance might not only be harnessed to persuade the husband to pay the conjugal debt – what happened meanwhile to the sin of lust? – but she could also use her charms to persuade him to be generous in alms-giving and good works.[35] This was one way the wife was expected to exert influence for good over her husband. Unfortunately, this advice that the wife utilise her sexuality in her dealings with him not only endangered them both by possibly committing that sin of lust, but tended to reduce her further in male eyes, reinforcing the idea that she was tempting but essentially dangerous. Wise men were advised to avoid such temptations and have nothing to do with women, except in a dominant and possibly censorious role. It was perhaps better still if the man only wrote about women, at a safe distance, from behind the security of high monastery walls.

We come then, to the opposite of women using their wiles to tempt their husband, even into acts of charity, to the idea of virgin couples. This may well seem to be yet another contradiction in terms, particularly after hearing a good deal about the duties of married people to provide that adequate sex life via the conjugal debt. Even if one of the pair wished to take some form of religious vow, it is sometimes difficult for us to see where a deliberately celibate form of marriage can fit into the equation. Why, if both parties were keen to remain celibate, did they bother to marry in the first place? Firstly, the concept of a marriage without either side requiring a consummation seems to have been largely confined to the nobility, although not exclusively so. These are the very people one would expect to be most keen to provide legitimate heirs. It would also seem that in these totally unconsummated unions, rather than ones that were originally consummated and then later became celibate, the female initiative is more pronounced.[36] However, even in unions where the wife had clearly been the instigator, the husband must have been complicit. This seems to be more unusual as family pressure to carry on the name must have been present. And yet such arrangements did exist.

The need for spiritual sustenance led many people, particularly women, to become immersed in their religion. They could be punctilious in the observance of fasts, vigils and so on. They would confess regularly and sometimes even flagellated themselves as if they were members of a religious order. This atmosphere of piety, of feeling the need for closer union with God, fuelled a great drive to reverence virginity. Those people whose virgin state was no longer a factor tended to try to replace that state of grace with innocence of a different kind, whereas someone who was literally still a virgin might come to value that state as being the most important part of themselves and something they did not wish to lose. The sanctity of virginity became so great an ideal, that even those people who had lived decent lives, given to charity, produced children and were impeccably respectable, might still believe that they had lost some irreplaceable virtue. Their lives, however good, could never be quite good enough compared to the person who was still in that state of purity and the cult of purity would include some very important women. For example, Catherine, the daughter of Bridget of Sweden, was accused by her brother of attempting to turn his wife into a Beguine, a member of a lay order who lived in semi-monastic communities but without taking any final vows. They were not committed for life, and were free to leave as they wished, but they renounced marriage and all sexuality.

The Beghards were a similar movement for men, who all held property in common, each community was subject only to its immediate head, and they were far more concerned with salvation than with the material world. Yet, where even these rather loosely formed movements can be assigned a place, it is rather more difficult for the modern mind to assimilate the idea of an actual marriage, in which neither partner wants or needs sexual contact. Except in rare cases, a later private agreement to live life on that chaste level was made. The cult of virginity in medieval life was very strong, even if the virgin state so desired was kept quiet, outside of the immediate participants. Even then, with the virgin state being so desirable in a spiritual sense, the temptation to reveal it and take credit for it must have been strong. Although openly professing to it may have caused some family embarrassment, alluding to it was not unusual. It was not uncommon to simply leave others to infer the full meaning of certain remarks. When Cunegund of Poland entered religion as a widow, she told the other sisters at the convent that she had only ever seen the hands and face of her husband, leaving them to make up their own minds what she meant. Margery Kempe was another lady who tended to extol her virtues and try to persuade others to follow her example. At one point in her life the Archbishop of York asked if she were still a virgin, despite her marriage. He then charged her with attempting to encourage Lady Greystoke to leave her husband, presumably to become a Beguine.[37]

The idea of spiritual marriage, as opposed to one suffused with the lust of ordinary sexual union, remained the ideal. It became one that the Church writers tended to praise even if, for obvious reasons, it could not be recommended for everyone. The spiritual bond was believed to be greater in any case than any physical one could ever be. King Magnus IV of Sweden was reported to have tried such an arrangement with his wife Blanche, though it became a disaster. Magnus may have had an ulterior motive, as he was allegedly homosexual, though this was quite possibly an accusation made by his enemies.[38]

Catherine of Sweden (1332?–1381), daughter of the powerful matriarch Bridget, is said to have lived in chastity with her husband. Catherine seems to have at all times of her life attempted to emulate her saintly mother's piety, but such intentions can have very mixed results. When Catherine was first married to her husband Eggard, normal marital relations were expected. Catherine was also expected to develop her spiritual life but within the context of that marriage and a family. But the marriage remained unconsummated and even Bridget appeared to have regarded the union as being void. Despite the saintliness of Bridget's life, and her good intentions, she must have seemed like the mother-in-law from Hell to poor Eggard. She obviously considered that the still virginal husband's marital claims on her daughter ran a poor second to her own maternal ones.[39] Bridget began to mould her daughter in her own image, exerting strict control over her by dictating her living place and demanding obedience from her at all times. After the reluctant virgin husband Eggard died, her grip on her daughter's life intensified, until Bridget finally had a vision of the Virgin Mary, who reminded her to use maternal kindness towards her daughter. Perhaps if she had taken more care of her daughter's marriage, and shown a little more kindness towards the totally unconsidered husband, then the family may have been happier. Saints like Bridget may be venerable, but at the same time might be quite impossible to live with. The idea of the spiritual marriage may have seemed like a good idea at the time, but it too proved impossible to live with for most people in the everyday world. It led to denial of the marriage debt, which was always one of the greatest of the clerical conundrums resulting in enormous confusion that the trained clerical minds could not unravel. It led to the female denial of male authority, which was another non-starter, and threatened to shake the foundations of married life. It also led to adultery and must have instigated bawdy and hurtful humour directed at those who tried to live with it. It caused the humiliation of such decent people as Eggard of Sweden. Only for the rare, deeply pious couple, can it possibly have worked and in that case they would probably have been better off cloistered. At least there they would have been in the company of like-minded people, rather than subjected to the constant and unnecessary pressures that added to the already fraught situation in which they lived.

To be fair, perhaps the final word on this strange lifestyle choice should go to St Eleazer de Sabran, who lived with his wife Dauphine throughout twenty-five years of total chastity. Even through early difficulties their bond not only remained, but also strengthened. When Dauphine expressed amazement at the rapid remarriage of the Duke of Calabria after the death of his wife, Eleazer replied to her:

Between husbands and wives who love the world, it often happens that the carnal love between them fails like the flesh. But between me and you there is a spiritual and pure love, and such love, just like the spirit itself, will last forever, and will never fail.[40]

The beau-ideal indeed.

9

UNSUITABLE RELATIONSHIPS

There were certainly some women who, for one reason or another, never married – quite apart from those who chose to enter religion, or had religion thrust upon them – but for the vast majority of women of all classes a marriage and, hopefully, children were the aim. This was the norm and any woman who chose differently was considered to be in some way unfulfilled. That many marriages were able to survive the years placidly enough is a given, but evidence from the York Cause Papers has helped to shed some light on the unions that were rather less successful. These have tended to be the unions of ordinary people, and the aim has been to show that the citizen and his wife had the same life problems as their more wealthy or famous counterparts. However, as the marital problems and lifestyles of the people who might be considered to be the 'rich and famous' were better recorded, it is wise to give details of a few of these too. Their personal problems were just as interesting as anyone else's, and were often accompanied by inheritance or legal problems that were rather out of the range of the lives of working people.

Pope Alexander III (Roland of Siena 1105–1181) was concerned with finding a simple formula that would be both strict and legally sound in cases of marital disputes. Though he was sitting in judgement many hundreds of miles away, which might initially suggest that he was out of touch, the ruling families of the twelfth century were in many ways more European than we are now. Due to their ownership of great estates across the Channel, they considered themselves as a matter of course to be a part of the extended Christian family.[1] Regarding the marital disputes of England's landed gentry, or indeed the landed gentry of any other European country, it must be borne in mind that the idea of clerical celibacy was in itself a new concept during the second half of the twelfth century. The change had been decided upon by the Second Lateran Council of 1139,[2] after which the promise to remain celibate became a pre-requisite of ordination, thereby abolishing a married priesthood. This decision of the Council, led by Pope Innocent II[3] was to produce wide-ranging effects and not only upon the lives of previously married clergy. The lives of all women would be affected when the generally misogynistic attitudes of many of the clergy began to make their lot particularly difficult.

One of the early cases where there are clear records is that of Richard Anstey,[4] an Essex squire who decided to claim the inheritance of a female cousin, Mabel de Francheville. He declared that she was illegitimate and that he was the heir due to being his uncle's legitimate nephew. The estates must have been substantial as Anstey was to spend large sums of money in pursuit of his struggle with his cousin, as is shown in his diary of expenses. Mabel's father, William de Sackville, had married Alice, daughter of Amfrid the Sheriff. The union was solemnised in church and many guests had witnessed it, but he had unfortunately already entered into a form of marriage with one Aubrey de Tresgoz, though despite having exchanged oaths their marriage had not been consummated. William and Alice, his second choice, had had several children, but later Alice was driven from the house. William then secured a judgement from

Geoffrey, the Archdeacon of Colchester, which annulled his already fruitful marriage to her. That this had been an unsound judgement was eventually admitted by him and on his deathbed he gave testimony that he had acquiesced in a fraud, by allowing the Archdeacon to declare his second marriage invalid. As the first promise, given to Aubrey de Tresgoz, was unconsummated it was technically invalid, although the very presence of the promise to her complicated the second marriage. There was, as usual, some discussion whether it had been a promise *de futuro* or *de presentii*.[5] The inheritance had been left to Mabel, who had enjoyed it peacefully for several years, and who had in turn married and begun to raise a family.

Once Henry II gained the throne, the courts were invigorated, and Mabel's cousin Anstey decided that it was a suitable time to put forward a claim for the estate on his own behalf. Many long delays ensued, in the king's court, in the archbishop's court, and through many hearings and even an appeal to Rome. Expenses naturally mounted, until in the end, after five years, he won his case against Mabel. One wonders how – unless his seemingly inexhaustible supply of money was a factor. By that time Peter Lombard, the great theologian, was interesting himself in 'putative' marriage, which was that any children born to a marriage, which had at the time had every appearance of being both legal and valid, should be considered fully legitimate. Unfortunately, the Pope disagreed, and he found for Richard Anstey, thereby depriving Mabel and her family of the inheritance left to her in good faith by her father, probably in the expectation that he could thereby right the wrong he had done to her mother. It seems to have been a ridiculous, even a deplorable decision, when one considers all the matters before the York courts, when the fact of non-consummation became the crux of the validity of a marriage. Despite his early promise to the first lady, Mabel's father had never actually lived with her as his wife, nor had their promise been confirmed by consummation. Mabel's father had recognised this on his deathbed, and had tried to put things right for the children he considered his legitimate family, despite his later estrangement from their mother. Reading of the matter now, it does not seem unduly cynical to suppose that the Pope may not have been in full possession of the facts of the case, although that is also hard to credit after such a long drawn-out succession of hearings. Perhaps bribery played a part in depriving Mabel and her own children of the estates of her father and their grandfather?

A few years later, Pope Alexander had an even more difficult case to deal with, regarding Agnes, Countess of Oxford.[6] Aubrey de Vere, the 1st Earl of Oxford, had married twice, but had no children. He and his brother Geoffrey de Vere then arranged for Geoffrey to marry Agnes, the three-year-old daughter of Henry Earl of Essex. By the age of six years, she was living in Geoffrey's house and treated in every way as though she was his future wife. It was later claimed that she had agreed to a betrothal, but at the age of twelve, she vehemently denied this. In about 1162 or 1163, when she reached the age of twelve, the earl himself was betrothed to her, but then her father fell into disgrace and lost his lands. Agnes' marriage value subsequently plummeted, and she was no longer desirable to de Vere, who then wished to be rid of her. However, she was not to be cast aside so easily. She won a hearing in the Bishop of London's court by 1166 although she had little reason to expect fair treatment, so she also made an appeal to Rome. The case then languished for several more years, during which the earl actually imprisoned her in a tower in an effort to make her give in, although without success. The Pope's court dealt with the matter in the leisurely way that was to become infamous, and it was not until about 1172 that a mandate reached the bishop. This was to the effect that the earl was instructed to take back

Agnes as his wife, and treat her with all respect. She was to be fully reinstated *mensa et thuro* to bed and board by him. Not only that, but he must do so within twenty days of the receipt of the Pope's mandate, or an interdict would be laid on his lands and the earl would be excommunicated. The earl complied and the marriage of Aubrey and Agnes was consummated, though with what kind of enthusiasm can only be imagined. The earl was then around sixty years old while Agnes was about twenty, and had lived in the de Vere household since she was a small child. However, despite the appallingly inauspicious beginning, the marriage did produce children, at least five of them, and the earl lived another twenty years. From this union all the later de Veres are descended.[7] This case is particularly interesting as it shows the delays that were inherent in the system and the difficulties of trying to obtain decisions from Rome. In the twelfth century, Agnes waited ten years for her reinstatement, though she had already spent all her formative years with the de Veres. She would have known no other way of life and the idea of finally being rejected by them must have been extremely distressing for her, whether or not her elderly husband had any other attractions.

All these problems could be avoided if one followed the path recommended by St Bernard of Clairvaux.[8] He firmly believed that human love was of far less value than the love of God, and married love was also infinitely less valuable than that between good, platonic, friends. Naturally in this he was referring to a situation of 'brotherhood', particularly between those in religious orders. This led to his *Sermons on the Song of Songs*, which is considered slightly homosexual in content, due to its rather erotic imagery, but Bernard probably meant it to be taken metaphorically rather than literally. This same depth of emotion can be seem in the works of St Ailred of Rievaulx. Unlike many votaries St Bernard did not exclude women from this friendship. He admitted that platonic love between a man and a woman was able to show a true depth of friendship, as deep and abiding as any kind of attraction due to a sexual love.

Hugh of St Victor,[9] while agreeing the preference for the love of God over the more flawed affections of humankind, still conceded that a woman was 'given to a man as a comrade rather than as a servant or as a mistress'. Despite these reassuring sentiments, he still felt obliged to declare that she was inferior to a man.[10] This is a contradiction that finds its way into much of the literature of the time and spills over into the judgements of the Church. Pope Alexander, in his judgement of the Anstey case, contradicts himself. He was very keen on the idea that a married couple were *una caro*, that is, one flesh. This would suggest that consummation of the marital union held the primary place in the efficacy of the bond. Yet he still preferred the first unconsummated marriage to the second fruitful one. He also rejected the claims of the offspring of the second union, who should surely have been considered a blessing from God on that marriage.

This same confusion shows itself in a case from the pontificate of Pope Innocent III (1198–1216). This matter, quoted by Brooke,[11] details the dilemma of a convert to Christianity (presumably a Muslim), who already had several wives allowed to him by the rules of his original religion. The Bishop of Tiberias dropped the problem into the lap of the Pope, as being a matter he felt himself unable to pronounce upon. It is certainly easy to imagine the time it took to come to a decision with so complex a case. Were all the convert's marriages actually legal? How could they be, if the Christian religion allowed a man to only have one wife? More importantly, where did it leave the offspring of the various wives, with regard to their legitimacy? Inheritances were at stake, and all awaited the Pope's answer. His answer, when it came, was definite. All the marriages were in fact legal, and all the resulting children of those marriages were to be considered fully legitimate. However, if the convert were actually to be baptised, and therefore became a full Christian, he would then only be able to keep one of his present wives. He would also need to understand that he would not be able to replace the ones he was obliged to reject! Here Pope Innocent quoted I Corinthians 7, where St Paul makes it clear that while mixed marriages were valid enough, they could, if necessary be terminated. This seems to be less a bending in the wind and rather more a complete overthrow of the basic tenets of Christianity. This was done to avoid frightening potential converts away from the Church.[12] The idea that medieval marriage should not be terminated, except by death, was a basic Church tenet. The very words of the Church's regular marriage ceremony confirmed 'what God has joined together, let no man put asunder.' This held good into the twelfth century, even after one of the parties had died, resulting in some cases where the Church actually denied the blessing to any second marriage, on the assumption that the first one was indissoluble, even by death. This was obviously not good to hear for people whose marriages were less than happy, and who might be looking forward to widowhood and a chance of better luck next time.

However, the idea formed, albeit gradually, that second or even third marriages were just as desirable for the same reasons as the original one. That is, the production of children in accordance with God's word, the provision of a sex life for the laity which prevented casual fornication, and a companion for help and support (at least in theory) during one's earthly travail. Unfortunately, these aims were no more regularly fulfilled then than they are now.

The Church had no choice but to learn to accept flexibility, and seek to redress the balance that had been tipped by the strictures. It could use the power of annulment in those cases where a genuine mistake had been made or indeed in cases where the people concerned were important and influential enough to be in a position to command the Pope's attention. Some could pay for the privilege of ridding themselves of an unsuitable or unfruitful marriage, or obtain a dispensation to make a marriage to someone who might otherwise be considered unsuitable, by being connected too closely by a marital or blood relationship. Such dispensations were given regularly, if not routinely, for noble or royal persons where the number of potential marriage partners was not merely small but actually shrinking. They gradually all became related to each other, either by blood or marriage, and in such a situation it was almost impossible for a person of rank to find a mate of equal rank without their prospective union being subject to the laws of consanguinity. The Pope was obliged to permit such marriages, despite the Church's regulations, to allow important people to marry at all. This meant that some relationships were complicated in the extreme.

Consider the positions of two of the daughters of Queen Isabella of Castile and Ferdinand of Aragon. Their eldest daughter, also Isabella, was married to Alfonso, the only son and heir to John II of Portugal in 1490. He was killed in a riding accident in 1491, aged only sixteen and his young widow returned home to Spain. After the death of King John in 1495 his brother, the uncle of Alfonso, became king as Manuel I and after some negotiation[13] Isabella was married to him in 1497. The following year she died in childbirth, after bearing a son, Miguel, who became heir not only to the throne of Portugal but also Spain, by right of his mother.[14] This death left Manuel in need of a new wife, and in 1500 he married Maria of Castile and Aragon, who was his sister-in-law as she was his late wife's younger sister. Their marriage managed to break the poor Spanish royal record for breeding, and Maria produced ten children, eight of whom survived to adulthood, including a male heir, to general relief. This convoluted marital record would have been well-nigh impossible for any families of less importance, but the necessary dispensation was given, even if negotiation with the Pope was required to obtain it.

Another famous medieval marriage, though from a rather humbler sphere of life, was that of Margery Kempe. She was born in 1373 in Norfolk, a member of the Brunham family who were comfortably placed in King's Lynn, then known as Bishop's Lynn. When she was about twenty years old, she married John Kempe and they produced a family of at least fourteen children. Just after the birth of her first child, Margery began to experience what she called 'mystical visions'. She went to confession very regularly, which was unusual, as most people felt that one's religious duty was fulfilled if such rituals were performed two or three times a year. She began to wear a hair shirt, and prayed constantly. She tried to convince her husband to lead a celibate life with her, but did not succeed. Her visions apparently told her that God wanted her to turn away from the world, and she indulged in frequent loud displays of weeping and crying. She must have become a nuisance to her neighbours, as well as to her long-suffering husband. In the book she dictated in the 1420s she paid him the compliment of saying he had been a kind and good husband to a very emotional and melodramatic wife. Her religious ecstasies often proved embarrassing and suspicion fell on her more than once, as the period was one in which the clergy were on the lookout for heresy. She was able to defend herself when questioned, though her rather bizarre behaviour did not endear her to others. She went on several pilgrimages, a testimony not only to her husband's forbearance but also to their financial stability, though it might also suggest that her husband was eager to have some respite. In 1413, after the death of her father, she went on pilgrimage to the Holy Land, spending thirteen weeks in Venice on the journey during the winter season, and later moving on to see Jerusalem and its holy sites. She recounted how she had almost fallen from her donkey with emotion when she had her first sight of that city. On her return journey she again stayed in Italy, visiting Assisi, before moving to Rome until the Easter of 1415. This was a very long time for any married woman to be away from home. But in 1417 she was off again, visiting Compostela, returning home only to continue her travelling in England. She was actually arrested by the mayor of Leicester and interrogated, as the idea of a respectable married woman riding around the country, let alone abroad, was uncommon and therefore suspect. This was the general 'gadding about' that medieval males were usually so opposed to, leading to everything from suspicions of heretical leanings to the more general accusation of being a loose woman. By the 1420s she was living apart from her husband, but she returned to Lynn to nurse him when he fell ill. Both her son John and her husband died in 1431, Margery lived until 1438.[15] In her book she described her mystical experiences, her travels, and her 'temptations towards lechery' with astonishing freedom. The original manuscript of her book was copied before 1450 and the first page contains the inscription *Liber Montis Gracie* or 'the book of Mount Grace' referring to Mount Grace Priory in North Yorkshire. The only surviving copy of this fascinating book is now in the British Library.[16]

The most interesting aspect of her book to the twenty-first century reader is not the mystical visions she is said to have experienced, so much as its proof of her astonishing freedom to travel, despite her several brushes with the authorities who had serious concerns about her motives. Her husband's unusually tolerant behaviour towards her seems to have covered the fact that many people, including those who were her travelling companions from time to time, found her tiresome. She freely admitted that she seemed to get on better with poorer people, towards whom she was able to act charitably, while her own social class may have considered her attention-seeking. Certainly her frequent storms of tears, her overly ecstatic response to anything religious and her apparent lack of desire to go home to her family would appear to them to be unwomanly. Had she entered a religious house instead of marrying, she may have been revered as a great mystic, even a saint. For all her devotion, however, she was a woman out of her place, trying to be one thing while actually being another, doing neither of them at the right time and by her lack of control causing disturbances that irritated her contemporaries. She must have been a very demanding creature to deal with and it is her husband, John Kempe, who evokes the most sympathy.

Another well-known woman of the time was Christine de Pisan, (or Pizan). She was born in Venice in 1364, the daughter of Thomas de Pisan, and she moved to Paris at the age of three when her father was appointed doctor to Charles V. She did not have a vast amount of education, but she was taught to read and write by her father, who insisted that she be educated as a boy. She was naturally intelligent and was fascinated by books, which earned her the privilege of being permitted to use the king's library of in excess of 900 volumes. It was at that time one of the largest in the world. She wrote with obvious delight that 'one day I was surrounded by books of all kinds.' She was married at the age of fifteen to Etienne de Castel, one of the king's secretaries. It was to prove an unexpectedly happy marriage, and started off well with her new husband's forbearance towards her. She was to write lovingly of him in later life, saying that he did not force her to make love with him on their wedding night, realising that the frightened girl needed time to get to know him first.[17] She was clearly grateful for his understanding, which cemented their later relationship. She referred to Etienne as 'a man whom no other could surpass in kindness, peacefulness, loyalty and true love.' Unfortunately, both her father and her loving husband were to die when she was twenty-five, leaving her financial affairs in a mess, which took thirteen years of struggling in the courts to sort out. She did eventually regain her inheritance. At court she had already begun to grow into a strong supporter of women's rights, and was infuriated by the way women were portrayed in literature as being inferior to men.

No matter which way I looked at it, and no matter how much I turned the matter over in my mind, I could find no evidence from my own experience to bear out such a negative view of female nature and habits. Even so, given that I could scarcely find a moral work by an author, which did not devote some chapter or paragraph to attacking the female sex, I had to accept their unfavourable opinion of women. It was unlikely that so many learned men, who seemed to be endowed with such great intelligence and insight, could possibly have lied on so many different occasions.

This nicely satirical observation is from her book *The Citie of Ladies*, in which she also wrote:

Thinking deeply about these matters, I also began to examine my own character as a woman. Similarly, I then considered other women, whose company I frequently kept, princesses, great ladies, and women of the middle or lower classes, who told me of their private lives and their intimate thoughts. No matter how long I studied the problem, I could not see how the claims could be true, when compared to the natural behaviour and character of these women.[18]

She turned herself into a writer, studying history, science and poetry, and in 1393 she began to write songs, ballads and love poems. By the late 1390s she had succeeded in earning her living as a writer. *The Citie of Ladies*, which was published in 1405, is the work she is now most famous for, and in which she begins to make her feelings and frustrations clear.

> I am amazed by the opinions of some men, that they do not want their wives and daughters to be educated, because they would be ruined as a result. Not all men, especially the wisest, share the opinion that it is bad for women to be educated. But it is very true that many foolish men have claimed this, because it upset them that the women knew more than they did.

Her next book, *The Three Virtues*, published in 1408, tried to deal with the problem of the male-dominated society preventing women from reaching their full potential. It also gave advice to women how they could improve their lives. Christine wrote several other books, including a biography of Charles V of France and, surprisingly, a book of military law. This book had to have her name taken off the cover, for fear that men would be unwilling to read such a work written by a woman.[19]

Women did, of course, write more mundane things. There are many medieval letters still extant from educated women of the noble or gentry class writing to family members, including other women. One of the earlier ones is from Lady Hawisa de Neville, to her son Hugh de Neville, dated 1267. This letter describes the ongoing difficulties faced by many families who were divided in their allegiance. Hugh's mother had remained loyal to Henry III but Hugh had thrown in his lot with Simon de Montfort the Younger, and had had some lands confiscated as a result. Hugh submitted to the king in 1266 and received back two of his manors, but was obliged, as the price of his submission, to confirm

Robert de Walerand (who had been given them by the king) as the owner of the others. Hugh eventually left for the Holy Land after making his mother and younger brother attorneys to manage the lands while he was away. The fact that he was engaged in the Crusades gave the family hope that the Pope would look favourably on their claims. He actually received only his crusade expenses and his mother's anxious letter urges him to try for a more substantial reward.[20]

> ... wherefore your father-in-law and I and all your friends agree that you should come to England, but we pray and entreat you, by all the faith and love you owe us, that you will not by any means fail in this ... for we know it would be a very great dishonour and we consider it a great sin, to suffer us and ours to be disinherited by your indolence. Therefore I anxiously pray you, dear son, that you will travel with all possible haste, to go to the court of Rome, and procure if you can the letter of the Pope, express and stringent, to the King of England, that he should restore your lands...

There is a good deal more in this vein, with his mother applying desperate pressure on him. It would seem that, fond though she was, she had little faith in his ability to act quickly.

> ... but do not ever cease, as you love me, for any waiting for money, to borrow all that you can, and go to the court of Rome to acquire for our necessities and hasten to come to England to accomplish our needs...

Other families also wrote of their domestic concerns, notably the Stonors. They, like the famous Pastons, were a gentry family, but much richer and of far higher social status. Jane Stonor wrote to her daughter (she had two, Mary and Elizabeth, though the letter does not make clear which one is referred to). The girls were away from home in the manner of the times, in the household of Elizabeth, Duchess of Suffolk. The Duchess was the elder sister of Edward IV and was also half sister-in-law to Jane Stonor, as Jane was probably the illegitimate daughter of William de la Pole, the previous Duke of Suffolk. Queen Elizabeth Woodville seems to have been involved in negotiations to place the girls with her sister-on-law and the Stonors feared to offend her by taking them back home without her permission. Several notable people had offended Elizabeth Woodville with unfortunate results,[21] so Jane Stonor was treading very carefully:

> ...I understand that you would have knowledge how you should be demeaned. Daughter, you know well you are there as it pleased the Queen to put you and what time you came first from mine, albeit my husband and I would have had ... wherewith the Queen was right greatly displeased with us both. Albeit we know right well it came not of herself. Also methink they should not be so weary of you that did so great labour and diligence to have you and that whereas you think I be unkind to you, verily I am not ... So that my husband and I may have writing from the Queens' own hand, or else he or I neither dare nor will take upon us to receive you. Seeing the Queen's displeasure before, for my husband sayeth he had not willingly disobeyed her command before, nor will he begin now...[22]

Elizabeth Woodville, though looking like an angel, must have wielded enormous power to have caused people to live in such fear of her displeasure that they dare not receive their own daughter at home without her written permission.

Some other examples of fifteenth century family problems are shown by the Plumpton correspondence. The Plumptons were of Plompton (formerly known as Plumpton) near to Knaresborough in Yorkshire. They are rather less well known than other families whose letters are now in print. During the Wars of the Roses, William Plumpton (1404–1480) supported Lancaster, being captured at Towton where his benefactor Henry Percy, 3rd Earl of Northumberland, lost his life. William Plumpton was later able to regain his estates and offices after being pardoned by Edward IV. The following letter dates from April 1506 and is from Edith, Lady Neville, to Dame Isabel Plumpton, who was her daughter and the second wife of Sir Robert Plumpton. Upon her marriage Isabel found herself enmeshed in Sir Robert's financial disasters, and Lord Darcy of Templehurst, the second husband of Edith Neville, had agreed to forego a debt owed to him in order to help.[23] Lady Neville's letter shows sympathy for the situation in which her daughter found herself.

My own good Lady Plumpton. I recommend me to you and your good husband and right sorry I am of his and your troubles. If I could remedy it, but God is where he was and His Grace can and will purvey everything for the best and help his servants at their most need. My Lord my husband recommends him unto you both and sends you your obligation, and has received but £4 and a mark of the £20 and £2. The remnant my good lord gives to your good husband and you. I pray Almighty Jesu send you both well to do, as your own hearts can desire...[24]

There are several similar letters, showing that families helped each other out when they could. What is particularly interesting is that women often relied upon their brothers for help and advice even after they were married.

The first of the following letters concerns Katherine, the daughter of Sir William Plumpton, who had married a Chadderton of Chadderton Hall in Lancashire. The family was in a comfortable financial position and had just built a new chapel at their home, when Katherine asked her brother, George Plumpton, for a gift for their altar. Katherine's sister Isabel, who was married to Sir Stephen Thorpe of Lincolnshire, was in a far more difficult financial situation. This was so bad that Isabel could not afford to employ the usual female servant or companion for her own use. Yet Katherine, far better off, was still tactless enough to not only ask for gifts from her brother, but also ask that her brother look out for a young woman for her own household. This was a request that was taken amiss. A second cousin was Lord Scrope of Masham, but Katherine and the Scropes did not appear to get on at all well, and Lady Scrope had recently refused to see Katherine. As the Scropes were also not particularly well-off, Katherine's constant boasting about her household, along with her apparent greed for gifts and other courtesies, may have rather set their teeth on edge. Her letter shows a certain indifference to the woes of others, of which she may have been unaware, but her remark at the end of the letter is a rather unpleasant example of the innate selfishness of Katherine Plumpton.

My best brother. I am sorry, by my troth, that I shall not see you and have come thus far to York ... my husband had said, half at play 'pray my brother to get somewhat to my new chapel'. God knows, he meant neither gold nor silver, but some other thing for the altar. Had I known that you would have been displeased I would not have written, forasmuch as I have now displeased my best brother.

My sister, Dame Isabel, lives as heavy a life as any gentlewoman born, for which cause I fared never well since

I saw her last month ... She has neither woman nor maid with her, but herself alone ... Also brother, I beseech you entirely that if there be any goodly young woman, that is a good woman of her body, and pay four and twenty pounds or more, and I would have one of my own kin, as there were any, for myself. Dear brother, an you or any for you can espy, I beseech you get her for me, as hastily as you may, soon upon Easter, an it may be...

And brother, I goed to the Lord Scrope to have seen my lady and by my troth I stood there a large hour, and yet might see neither lord nor lady, and the strangest cheer that ever I had of my Mistress Darsie.[25] Yet I had five men in a suite, there are no such five men in his house I dare say...

To Master George Plumpton at Bolton Abbey.[26]

Katherine's indignation fairly bounces off the page, so annoyed is she at the Scropes' refusal to give her their attention, which she believed that her household of retainers entitled her. The Scropes, and others, seem to have been thoroughly tired of her, and her mention of her sister's obviously severe financial difficulties did not inspire her to offer any help in that direction, which it appears she could well have afforded. This gives the clue to her character, and explains why her family connections, even her own brother, were very unwilling to spend time with her.

The Paston family are rather more well-known, due to the large amount of extant correspondence.[27] The marriage of William Paston and Agnes Berry in 1420 was to set the family onto the road to success. He was forty-two years old and Agnes was only eighteen, but she and her sister were co-heiresses of Sir Edmund Berry. When he died, she brought three good manors to her husband. It was probably not a love match, and William was to die in 1444 but, for the next thirty-five years, Agnes held onto £100 a year's worth of property, including her inheritance, her jointure, and her dower. When she died, she was buried with her parents at the White Friars in Norwich, rather than with her late husband, leaving their son John (known as John Paston I.) He was born in 1421 and married the heiress Margaret Mountby, who in her turn had brought the family eight manors situated mainly in Norfolk, where the Pastons already held land. It was concerning this marriage that Agnes Paston had written her only surviving letter to her husband William, on 20 April 1440.

> Dear Husband. I recommend me to you. Blessed be God, I send you good tidings of the coming and the bringing home of the gentlewoman that you know of from Reedham this same night ... As for the first acquaintance between John Paston and the said gentlewoman, she made him gentle cheer in gently wise and said he was verily your son. So I hope there shall need no great treaty between them....
>
> The parson of Stockton (Norfolk) told me that if you would buy her a gown, her mother would give thereto a goodly fur. The gown needed for to be had, and of colour it would be a goodly blue, or else a bright sanguin (red)...[28]

The Pastons are largely famous for their tangled matrimonial affairs, particularly in the matter of Margery Paston. She was the daughter of John Paston I and Margaret Mountby and made the mistake of falling in love with Richard Calle, the Paston's chief bailiff. This attachment met with the strongest possible opposition from the family, despite the solemn pledge the pair had made to each other. Every effort was to be made to separate them. As we have already seen, the making of vows between a couple was a serious matter and could create a legal bond. The family chose to ignore this, and the fact that Margaret Paston and Richard Calle considered themselves betrothed, if not actually legally married. While Richard Calle was a trustworthy person – indeed as their chief bailiff he was required to be both accomplished and highly responsible – in the eyes of the ever-rising family he was very far from being suitable marriage material for a Paston daughter. They had definite social aspirations so the idea of a bailiff, however decent, marrying into the family was not to be considered. Margery's older brother, John III, wrote angrily to his parents that 'Richard should never have his goodwill to make his sister sell candles and mustard...'[29] This was a reference to Richard Calle's own family background, which was shop-keeping. The Pastons were concerned with Richard's motives, believing that he intended to raise himself up by the proposed marriage to Margery, much as they had done with their own earlier marriages, in fact. However, the loving correspondence between Margery and Richard bears out the real affection between them.

> My own lady and mistress before God, my true wife. I with heart full sorrowful recommend me to you as one that cannot be merry, nor shall be, until it be otherwise with us than now. For this life that we lead now is no pleasure to God or the world, considering the great bond of matrimony between us, and also the great love that has been and I trust yet is between us, and on my part never greater...

The family had dismissed Richard from their service as soon as the situation came to their attention, but they found that they could hardly be without him. He had dealt with all the complicated finances of their many properties honestly, and was not easy to replace, nor could they manage to deal with such matters themselves. On leaving, to go into hiding to escape their wrath, he had taken with him some of their documents. He made it perfectly clear that he would not use them to obtain money, but neither would he collect the rents owed to them, on their behalf. He merely wished to use them as a form of security against any of the acts taken by the family to his detriment. The family determinedly tried to have the marriage put aside, bringing in the Bishop of Norwich (Walter Lyhert) in the hope that he would declare the union invalid. However, they had reckoned without Margery, who stoutly defended herself and Richard, affirming at all times that they had made vows to each other in the proper way. The question of consummation of the union was another important point, and one that Margery testified to the Bishop. As a result of her testimony, he had no choice but to declare Margery's marriage with Richard Calle to be legal and valid. In a long letter to Sir John Paston, Margaret Paston gives him the full details.[30]

...my lord of Norwich ... charged me in pain of cursing, that she should not be deferred, and should appear before him the next day and I said plainly that I would neither bring her nor send her, and he said that he would send for her himself. He charged that she should be at liberty to come when he sent for her...

The Pastons had obviously been trying to prevent Margery from giving her full evidence to the bishop, who had grown irritated by the delays.

...on Friday the Bishop sent for her ... and said to her right plainly ... he said he had heard her say that she loved such a one as her friends were not pleased that she should have, and therefore he would have her be right well advised how she did. He said that he would understand the words she said to him, whether that made matrimony or not. She rehearsed what she had said, and said that if those words made it not so, she said boldly she would make that sure before she went hence, for she said she thought she was in conscience bound whatsoever the words were. These lewd words grieved me and her granddam as much ... Then Richard Calle was examined, by himself, that her words and his accorded and the time where it should have been done. When I heard say what her demeaning was I charged my servants that she should not be received in my house ... and so my lord of Norwich hath set her at Roger Bests, to be there til the day beforesaid. I wot well it goes right near your heart, and so doth it to mine, but remember you, and so do I, that we have lost of her just a brethele[31] and set it the less to heart ... For an he were dead at this hour she would never be at mine heart as she was. As for the divorce that ye write to me of, I discharge you upon my blessing that ye do not, or cause another to do ... God would take vengeance thereupon and should put yourself ... in great jeopardy.

It certainly seemed that the bishop's decision, though final and not to be argued with, was an extremely unpopular one with the family. There had been some talk of a 'divorce' in the matter, and the letter ended with Margaret saying that no further mention should be made of it: 'would ye took heed if there were any labour made in the court of Canterbury for the lewd matter aforesaid...'

Poor Margery and poor Richard, who would never be considered acceptable to his new in-laws, who always thought of him as a fortune hunter. Nevertheless, Richard and Margery had to be acknowledged as legally married, however much her family hated the idea. In fact, with astonishing pragmatism, they reinstated their unwelcome son-in-law as their bailiff because they needed him to sort out their muddled finances. Margery Paston Calle died in 1479 after only ten years of the marriage she had so wanted, with the man for whom she bravely fought her family. Another, more highly born lady from the later medieval period, was to find her marriage to be both longer and unhappy, though it started without the opposition faced by Margery Paston, as Margery Paston and Elizabeth Stafford were almost opposites of each other.

Elizabeth Stafford was the eldest daughter of Edward Stafford, 3rd Duke of Buckingham and his wife Lady Eleanor Percy. The Duke of Buckingham was the son of the Duke who was executed by Richard III in 1483, and would in his turn be executed by Henry VIII in 1521. Execution was one of the hazards of being close to the throne in the late medieval period, and came almost to be a mark of one's family status. All the most noble and powerful families walked the tightrope between success and failure, which could change from one to the other with dizzying speed.[32] Elizabeth was probably born around 1497 as we know that she was fifteen years old when she was married to Thomas Howard, in early 1513. She had lived with her parents until her marriage, however, by her early teens she had formed a close emotional attachment to Ralph Neville, who was a ward of her father and lived with the Staffords. Ralph returned her affection and this would prove to be a tragedy for them both. It was commonplace for great families to marry those they held in wardship back into their family, so as to keep the inheritance within their own circle. So perhaps Elizabeth and Ralph, as they grew, began to hope that they might be lucky enough to marry the person they favoured, but they were not. When Elizabeth was nubile, a marriage was arranged for her with Thomas Howard, who was then Earl of Surrey.[33] It must have seemed to her father to be an opportunity far too good to miss, despite the presence of the Neville youth, already a part of their household. Elizabeth would later write, very poignantly, that he and she had 'loved one another above two years' at the time of her arranged marriage to Thomas Howard. He was a widower,[34] aged thirty-three, whose three sons with his first wife had died in childhood, therefore, it was necessary for him for remarry. Despite Elizabeth's known attachment to Ralph, her objections to the proposed match were discounted and although he had the choice of more than one of the daughters of the Duke of Buckingham, Howard wanted Elizabeth. This may have been more a testimony to her childbearing potential than any emotional attraction, but also the eldest daughter, like the eldest son, had a certain status that the other children lacked. Her real love, Ralph, actually went on to marry her younger sister, Katherine, which must have been particularly painful for her. He later became the Earl of Westmorland and his brother George became Baron Abergavenny and was eventually married to yet another of Elizabeth's sisters, Mary. Through these arrangements Lord Buckingham succeeded in keeping the Neville inheritance in his family, while still securing the Howard match for his eldest daughter.

The marriage between Thomas Howard and Elizabeth Stafford took place in 1512 and at first they seemed to settle down together well enough. Medieval nobility and gentry had to learn early the art of pragmatism. Elizabeth was to bear five children to Thomas: Henry, who became Earl of Surrey when Thomas Howard acquired his Dukedom back in 1524; Mary, who married Henry VIII's illegitimate son Henry Fitzroy and became the Duchess of Richmond; Thomas who was the 1st Viscount Howard of Bindon, and two other girls, Katherine and Ursula, who both died young. It was a respectable score for the time.

Elizabeth had been well educated and became a friend and lady in waiting to Queen Katherine of Aragon, the first wife of Henry VIII. This was during the period when Henry's eyes turned elsewhere in dissatisfaction at his own lack of a male heir. He had become involved with Anne Boleyn, the daughter of Sir Thomas Boleyn, who was actually brother-in-law to

Thomas Howard through his marriage to Elizabeth Howard, his sister. Unfortunately, around this time, Thomas Howard also seemed to take a leaf out of the king's book, and began a close relationship with Elizabeth Holland, who was the sister of Howard's steward. The duchess hated her and always referred to her as 'Bess' and said she was merely a laundress. Possibly she had worked in the children's nursery at some point, but she managed to exert a powerful influence over the duke who absolutely refused to give her up, or even to conduct their affair discreetly. The relationship between the Duke and Duchess of Norfolk was to deteriorate rapidly after the affair with Bess Holland became a fixture in the duke's life. The duke was, in 1533,[35] obliged to write to his brother-in-law Henry Stafford, asking him to 'take her in' but Henry Stafford refused to do so, due to his sister's loud criticisms of mistresses in general and Queen Anne Boleyn and Bess Holland in particular. Such criticism of the new queen was likely to disrupt the peace of his household at best, and possibly involve him in serious trouble if the king should hear of it. He said in his letter of refusal to Thomas Howard, 'She would be my utter undoing, due to her accustomed wild language which is not in my power to stop, whereby so great danger might issue to me and all of mine.'

As Elizabeth had already refused to be the trainbearer to Anne Boleyn at her coronation, an honour to which her rank had entitled her, her brother was probably being sensible in wishing to have nothing to do with her thoughtless and potentially dangerous public remarks. Back in 1520, she and Thomas had been in Ireland as a family, when he was made Lord Lieutenant there. During that time, Henry VIII accused her father Buckingham of 'imagining and encompassing the king's death' which was most probably a trumped-up charge aimed at lessening the duke's power. However, Elizabeth was left with the belief that her husband had not done enough to try to help her father, who was executed in the following year. She may well have been right in her estimation of her husband's true feelings, for shortly afterwards Thomas Howard was quite happy to accept from the king six manors, which had been the property of Elizabeth's father.[36] This created another area of resentment between the married pair, and later, when her husband's open preference for Bess Holland became obvious, their relationship fractured completely.[37] Despite Elizabeth's sharp tongue and too-quick temper, it is still possible to feel some sympathy for her predicament. She had been obliged to give up the man she loved, to be married instead to a man eighteen years her senior who had been married already and had a brusque way of dealing with a wife's complaints. Her grief at the loss of her real love was compounded when he was married to her sister. Later her own husband failed in loyalty and support for her family, both when her father was in danger of his life, and also when he took a mistress blatantly, causing her humiliation. She considered that her husband had ruined her life, by first insisting on marrying her when she clearly was attached to someone else, then later by abandoning her completely, to live with Bess Holland, whom she called his whore.[38]

All came to a head in Passion Week of 1534. Elizabeth was at Kenninghall, their principal residence, and was in a rage about Thomas and Bess. There were apparently many scenes and she later was to claim that she had been held down by Thomas' servants until her fingers bled, and she spat blood. He had then locked her up and gave her clothes and jewels to 'that drab, Bess Holland.' The duke finally offered the duchess a separation, and she went to live at Redbourn in Hertfordshire with twenty servants and an allowance of £300 per year. She was to write to Thomas Cromwell in 1534,

...the Duke came riding all night and locked me in a chamber and took away all my jewels and apparell. He then sent two of his chaplains to me, Master Burley and Sir Thomas Seymer, to say that if I would agree to be divorced from him, he would give me back all my jewels and apparell, and a great part of his plate and household stuff, but I rebuked his priests.

She was to send a further letter to Cromwell, claiming 'Redbourn is uninhabitable for one brought up daintily…' She complained of having received no visits from her children: 'Never did a woman bare so ungracious an elder son (as Surrey) and an ungracious daughter so unnatural.'

Henry VIII finally commanded her to 'write gently' to her husband, as the duke was again thinking of a divorce, but needed her consent, which she absolutely refused to give. By 1539 Cromwell was tired of them both, and advised her to return to her husband and to try to live in peace with him. However, her reply was firm:

I can never go to my lord my husband for no fair promises nor cruel handling, I had rather be kept in the Tower of London during my life, for I am so well used to such imprisonment I care not for it. He will suffer no gentlemen to come to me, and very few gentlewomen.

The duke was to deny that he had ever 'pulled her out of childbed and dragged her around the house' as she had claimed, and also that he had ever wounded her with a dagger on the head. This was supposed to have taken place shortly after the birth of their daughter Mary, but all the time that the duchess was effectively in exile at Redbourn, he was living openly with Bess at Kenninghall.

Elizabeth had also objected strongly to the marriage of her daughter Mary to the king's bastard son Fitzroy, though this was very likely due to the match being promoted and encouraged by

Queen Anne Boleyn. The queen wished to draw the Howards (to whom she was closely related) nearer to the throne by the form of a marriage with the king's beloved illegitimate son. Elizabeth had been ignored and the marriage had gone ahead despite her protests and anger.

Elizabeth resolutely refused to allow Thomas to divorce her, fearing that Bess would take her place, yet to her credit, she did try from time to time to become reconciled with him. However, he was to remain deeply influenced by Bess and all Elizabeth's attempts never lasted, though she made the effort at least three times.

She was eventually reconciled with her brother Henry, who sent one of his daughters to live with her. Edward Seymour, then Earl of Hertford, and the Parr family influenced Henry VIII in her favour, so eventually it was Thomas who became isolated. Her son Surrey's arrogance and pride in his lineage and the uses of his coat of arms irritated the king greatly, probably because his own lineage was less credible. This caused further trouble for Thomas Howard. The duchess had at one point attempted to plead with the king while he was on a hunting trip nearby, but he merely counselled her to behave towards her husband with wifely duty and submission.

Thomas had made his own attempts at defence against his wife's accusations of brutality, notably the claim that he had 'dragged her about the house' after childbirth. In an undated letter to Thomas Cromwell, he says:

> ... Finally, my lord, I require you in no wise to send her where I am, for the same should not only put me to more trouble than I now have, whereof I have no need, but might give me occasion to handle her otherwise than I have done yet.

There was an implied threat there and one is left wondering exactly what their real relationship had been like and whether there was any truth to Elizabeth's claims. What had changed the 'passably pretty' girl into a shrew? Thomas Howard was known to be a hard man; his usage of his nieces Anne Boleyn and Katheryn Howard made clear that he had little sympathy with disobedient women. Even the mistress he favoured for so long failed to support him when he was himself endangered, so that may also give a clue to his rather difficult and ultimately unlovable character.

Henry VIII put both Thomas and his son Henry in the Tower in December of 1546. Bess Holland, the woman for whom Thomas had wrecked his marriage, spoke against them both, despite her close association of more than fifteen years. The king had Surrey executed in January 1547 but later that same month the king himself died, and nobody dared to kill Thomas Howard once he was gone. Howard remained a prisoner in the Tower until the accession of Mary Tudor in 1553, when he was finally pardoned. He died the following year, at Kenninghall, aged 80 and did not mention his estranged wife in his will. The duchess died in November 1588 and although both their effigies are on the tomb of the duke at Framlington, she was actually buried at Lambeth. Her epitaph, written by her brother, says 'she was a mother, a sister, and a friend most dear.'[39]

The marriage of the Duke and Duchess of Norfolk is one of the famous examples of a relationship going badly wrong and it is easy to read the reports of Elizabeth's behaviour and consider that the duke had made an unwise choice of wife. However, the duchess is also to be pitied. She had had no choice at all in her marriage partner, and had to marry her father's choice for her, despite her love for another man who returned that love. Their separation must surely be the foundation of the bitterness and unhappiness of the years ahead. The duke, finding that the pretty girl he had chosen was not dazzled or flattered by being his choice, became cool and distant towards her. He also let her down when her father was in danger, although there may have been little he could actually have done to save Buckingham without endangering himself. His subsequent long-standing affair, conducted openly, ruined their marriage although even his mistress seems to have developed no real loyalty for him. All the people concerned may have been unhappy in their situation, and even the Norfolk's children seemed to be distant and uncaring – a dysfunctional family indeed.

Nobody could pretend that the modern idea of marrying where one chooses is not sometimes equally disastrous. People still make unwise choices, or merely grow apart as the years move on. In some cultures a marriage partner needs to have parental approval and it may be argued that then the couples often enter into marriage with less frenetic expectations. Certainly the modern demands of deep love, firm support, abiding loyalty, frequently fail to materialise, but humans still have the need to find that 'spark' with someone who hopefully feels the same way.

We are bound to wonder how Elizabeth's life might have unfolded had she been able to marry Ralph Neville. Her letters to Cromwell show that there was a desire for what might be termed a 'normal' family life, though her husband's knowledge that she had preferred someone else might also have corroded the relationship. Perhaps if Thomas had married Mary Stafford, and Elizabeth had been able to marry Ralph, several lives would have been happier.

IO

GENDER PREJUDICE AND HOME CORRECTION

The study of the medieval period, in which the lives of women were in many ways circumscribed, may lead us to assume that modern women are far more fortunate. The feeling that time is an arrow stamped 'progress' comes naturally to us. But although in modern times the law appears to intervene in domestic matters, the results of such intervention are often sketchy. Even in the medieval period there were laws designed to prevent abuse from becoming too dangerous, while still acknowledging a need for recalcitrant females to be 'corrected'. The modern mind is apt to rebel at the idea that a woman needs to be 'corrected' by her husband at all. Even so, it still goes on. We might also be repelled by the idea of physical or mental torture, and that still continues, often behind closed doors. So where is the difference between the lives of the women of the fourteenth or fifteenth century and our own?

In so many ways, there is little real change. Our present laws give lip-service to the idea of a woman being able to leave an abusive man at will, yet still deny her monetary aid with which to bring a divorce action, unless she can prove that physical or mental abuse has already happened. In too many cases, it has to happen repeatedly before she decides, or is able, to leave, realising that enough is enough.

The statistics show that, even now, ninety-four per cent of women who have been killed in a domestic situation were attacked by a man they already knew well, had a relationship with, and the husband or partner is still the first suspect in any domestic murder investigation. In 2014, 4,000 women in the USA died as a result of domestic violence and seventy-five per cent of those homicides happened as they attempted to leave the abusive relationship, or some little time after the relationship had ended.[1] The statistics for the UK are equally horrifying, there are two women killed every week by a current or former partner.[2] One woman in four in England will experience domestic violence at some time in their life (Crime Survey of England and Wales 2013/2014) and on average a woman is assaulted thirty-five times before she makes her first call to the police.[3] Although this statistic has been questioned by some writers, it still begs the question of how many such offences are never reported at all, and also how many have already ended tragically before any kind of help could be reached. It does not appear to give any woman confidence that things have actually changed appreciably since medieval times.

During the medieval period there were the same problems regarding the issue of marital abuse as being taboo. A prevailing attitude existed, and sometimes still does, about the sufferer having made her bed and being obliged to lie in it. Although in earlier times there was a far greater percentage of marriages made by the family, rather than from personal choice. There can surely be no greater shock than to find out, in the most unpleasant way, that the person one is expected to trust is not in fact to be trusted; that the person who is one's natural protector offers no protection at all, and that the home, which should be a haven of safety, has become the setting for acts of violence and verbal abuse. Many women stay far too long in a situation where denial, not affection, rules the household, at least until the situation becomes so bad that permanent damage is likely, in which case outsiders may be forced to intervene in some way. This happened in more than one of the medieval cases described, when neighbours felt themselves obliged to step in, and even braved the courts to act as witnesses on behalf of a woman who had been hurt too severely.

Legal systems are usually dependent upon laymen playing their part. Therefore, the beliefs and prejudices of the people who are likely to form juries and appear as witnesses are instrumental in influencing judgements over time. The opinions of the community in which abused and abuser both have to live have a real bearing on the cases. Where 'correction' however mild, is condoned, then there can be no fair treatment of the weaker party. This is shown by the case of Nesfield and Nesfield in 1394,[4] which was discussed in chapter five. However, to recap, Margery Nesfield had been attacked by her husband Thomas with such severity that her arm was broken. Thomas was able to bring witnesses to testify in court that Margery had in temper threatened him, which was surely a defensive measure and an attempt, however futile, to stand up for herself. However, her defiance of her 'natural master' meant that in not one but two court hearings Margery was held to be at fault, and the decision was made that her marriage to her abuser was valid, and must remain in place. In the evidence given, Margery's cry for help was real: 'He surely would have killed her if he had not been pulled off her by the witnesses.'[5] How terrible for that woman to be obliged to return to live with the man who had so little concern, not only for her physical well-being, for also for the opinion of the courts, that he must be physically restrained in public, otherwise he was likely to have killed her. It was the fact that she shouted back, called him names and made silly threats which were obviously meaningless against such a man, which turned the court against her. His very real attack on her was discounted, the actual bodily harm he had inflicted on her and from which it took her a full two weeks to sufficiently recover to be able to leave her home, was ignored. Her refusal to accept his complete dominance over her was the only factor in which the court was interested. Certainly, the court then required a 'surety' that her husband would in future 'treat her well' but once the relationship was beyond repair such a verbal promise meant little or nothing. Margery must have been in despair, and made another attempt to have her case heard, but the court would not consider it, refusing her appeal. It is plain that by not acting the part of the quiet and obedient wife, she had lost the sympathy of those who could have helped her. Only the man was considered, in that he had been shouted at and threatened in public by a crying wife. Her attitude of refusing him her obedience and respect had reduced him in the eyes of others, and therefore his treatment of her, even if it did occasion actual bodily harm, amounted to no more than 'home correction'. This was condoned, not only by the other males who knew the family, but also by the court to which Margery had appealed for help. Such female defiance was not to be tolerated, and her injuries were considered no more than she had deserved.

A broad presumption in favour of maintaining existing marriages and a strong preference for supporting the status quo unfortunately runs through the evidence preserved in the Court Papers.[6] The personal cost is far less important in the scheme of things than the idea of promoting respectful and obedient conduct within the marriage, and the endurance of the legal tie itself, at whatever cost. Alison McRae Spencer argues[7] that there were levels of violence that were then considered to be intolerable, though it is sometimes difficult to see where this line is drawn.

In the matter of the dispute between Thomas Assholf and his son-in-law John de Scholes that came before the Manor Court of Wakefield[8] there is marital violence involved. However, in this instance the disputing parties seem to be far more concerned with a breach of contract that was also a part of the matter. The sufferings of the wife took very much a second place to the demand that Scholes should keep his side of the bargain the two men had made. Ellen's problems did provide her father with a reason for bringing the son-in-law into court, but in the process Ellen's problems took on a secondary and lesser role. That may not have originally been her father's intention, but it still happened.

In a case before the Consistory Court at York, that of Devine and Scot[9] in 1348 and 1349, adultery was set alongside marital violence as being the reasons for the requested divorce. Adultery was considered apparently to be more important to push the case through, where physical violence alone, so commonplace, may not have been considered sufficient. In the matter of Wyatt and Venables (Court Papers F56) the same preference applies.

In the case of Ireby and Lonsdale[10] the poverty of the battered wife Joan Ireby was discussed. It was alleged that her husband had full control over her money and had left her desperately poor, so much so that she had to borrow money to take her case to court. This is a situation that may be recognised by any modern woman who finds herself suffering what is now termed 'financial abuse'.

The one thread running continually through all of these cases of marital dispute is that a certain amount of violence was actually expected. The male was induced to 'keep his wife under control' to prevent her from causing disturbances and the wife was, nominally at least, meant to obey and respect him. She was certainly not to cause him severe embarrassment by telling all the neighbours what had gone on between them behind closed doors. 'Controlling an unruly wife'[11] was a definite part of any man's duty and he was frowned upon if he could not, or would not, make her behave.

The cases of women such as Margery Nesfield must elicit sympathy from any reasonable person, as the husband did not appear to be long-suffering, as he had perhaps intended to appear, but rather violent in the extreme. He was obviously not the only man who could not control his temper when riled by his wife, and whose reactions were greatly in excess of what was needed. However, it must be said that the Wakefield Court Rolls have also shown that some of the women could be very confrontational with each other, if not so much towards the men. They were also perfectly capable of behaving in a manner not conducive to good order. As no man could expect to get a divorce because he had found that the sweet and gentle maiden he had married so hopefully had gradually shown herself to be a harridan, he was left with the age-old male defences. These were either to be out of the house for most of the time, or to be driven to reacting to his wife's worst excesses with a punch. Even this was not always effective, as was shown by Chaucer in *The Wife of Bath's Prologue* where the erring wife fakes a collapse in order to draw her husband close enough to give the knock-out punch herself![12] On the other hand, Chaucer shows the husband's authority over the wife clearly in *The Clerk's Tale* because of the legal power men had over women, in almost every aspect of their lives. Far from being acknowledged and accepted by all women, it seems to have produced great resentment and caused domestic arguments in many families, from which only a kindly husband married to a charming wife might find themselves exempt.[13]

It is too simplistic to claim that a violent society breeds domestic violence. It does not seem to be entirely the case that medieval society was more likely than others to tolerate physical violence within the marriage. Unfortunately, that it was only intolerable if it was perpetrated against an otherwise meek and obedient spouse may well have been an offshoot of the general control scenario, in which women were always expected to be amenable. If a man lost control of his wife he was effectively unmanned, which was a far more serious matter socially than if he had attempted to try to control her by a blow. In the fifteenth century a young man consulted a doctor about his difficulties in controlling his disobedient wife, and was told: 'to beat his wife until she bleeds, then rub ashes into her wounds, and sew her inside a salted horsehide for three days and nights.'[14] The wife's attitude towards her husband was expected to be transformed by this treatment, as well it might be.

The Church, aided and abetted the control of women, out of a deep-seated fear of any kind of feminine interference. Women could not be allowed to 'gad about' when they could be far better employed at home, breeding children and embroidering altar cloths. The very early idea of double monasteries would quickly come under attack. These had been large establishments, with accommodation quite separate for the monks and nuns, yet they were usually ruled by an abbess of impeccable respectability. She was very often a widow and a lady of high birth. St Hilda of Whitby Abbey is the one who springs most easily to mind in this context. St Hild, or Hilda (614–680) was the founding saint of Whitby Abbey and was the daughter of Hereric, the great-nephew of King Edwin of Northumbria. Her elder sister Herewith had married the King of East Anglia. Hilda was among the nobles who accepted Christianity and were baptised with Edwin. It seems that when Edwin was killed in battle in 633 she went to live with her sister at the Anglian court. When her sister became a widow she contemplated joining a convent in France, and Hilda was asked by Bishop Aidan of Lindisfarne to return to Northumbria.

In 657 she became the foundress of Whitby, (then known as Streonshalh) and she remained there until her death in 680, at sixty-six years old. Whitby was the venue for the famous Synod, and Bede described her as 'a woman of great energy, as well as being a skilled teacher and administrator'. She had a reputation for wisdom that embraced people of all classes, even though her advice was sought by kings and princes. She was a very important figure in the conversion of the Anglo-Saxons to Christianity.

However, even a lady of such probity can come under fire from a churchman, and in the seventh century Archbishop Theodore wrote to St Boniface regarding his increasing disapproval of the double monasteries, however holy and sexually segregated they were. He presumably believed that any monks and nuns living within half-a-mile of each other would be climbing the walls to get at each other, rather than attending to their devotions, which was an insult to both sides.

St Boniface also sent a letter to the Archbishop of Canterbury, after he had received another letter, this one from Abbess Eangyth, in which she asked for his support for a pilgrimage to Rome she wished to make, accompanied by her widowed daughter. She declared that she was drained and tired by pastoral responsibilities and worn down by taxation and harassment. Boniface, however, was quite unsympathetic and considered that she and her daughter simply wanted to have a holiday. He believed that she should stay at home and devote herself more stoutly to her duties. His letter[15] was strict and censorious and in it he made it clear that he thought that even a holy abbess and her widowed daughter would end up being little more than courtesans if they undertook such a perilous journey.

> ...it would be well and favourable for the honour and purity of your church ... if your synod and priests would forbid matrons and veiled women from making frequent journeys back and forth to Rome. A great part of them perish, and few keep their virtue. There are very few towns in Lombardy, or in Frankland, or Gaul, in which there is not a harlot of English stock. It is a scandal and a disgrace to your whole church...

It seems to be an hysterical response regarding a pilgrimage to be undertaken by two respectable ladies of a certain age, who were hardly likely to throw off their veils and end up as inmates of some seraglio. But to him, these women had become 'veiled' and had therefore given their lives, in entirety, to God. To the abbey they had gone and there they should certainly stay and be content with it. It was quite incomprehensible to him that they might want, let alone need, some change of scene, even to visit the Holy City and see the Pope. Any idea of such a thing was to be firmly discouraged.

The Church's attitude towards women in general was strict enough, but it was only to get worse. The essence of the problem in the eyes of the clergy was that women were a nuisance. They tended to be silly, misguided creatures, easily distracted and as easily led astray. If not held by the bond of matrimony and kept under the control of their men, they should be in a religious house, although even there they could present problems, as the Abbess Eangyth had. Women were altogether too flighty, too much in need of little pets, friends to chat with, and all forms of entertainment. He sounds such a miserable misogynist that it is easy to sympathise with the poor abbess, who was probably desperate for a change of scene, but was unable to have even what amounted to a buswoman's holiday unless her male superiors permitted it.

The approach she found herself up against was not confined to a few elderly men, living frugally and finding fault, it was endemic. St Augustine, in asking advice from Pope Gregory the Great (540–604) questioned whether any woman could be allowed to even enter a church if she was menstruating, and whether that condition would prevent her from taking communion. The Pope, sensibly, replied that it should be entirely a matter of choice. However, the eighth-century *Penitential of Theodore* had a different view on the subject.[16] Theodore was far stricter with regard to women, and the very presence of them in a church offended his sensibilities, as they were considered to be regularly 'unclean'. His *Penitential* contained proscriptions against them, centring on their times of menstruation, when they should not be allowed to enter the holy building at all, let alone take the Holy Sacrament.

> Women should not, in times of impurity, even enter into a church, or communicate, either nuns or laywomen. If they should presume to do this, they shall be obliged to fast as a penance, for three weeks.[17]

Theodore was equally intransigent when it came to the uncleanliness of childbirth: 'If not purified after a birth (usually known as churched) they cannot enter a church and if they do so, they must fast and do penance for forty days.'

His other major vexation was that women, those disgustingly defiled creatures, should actually aspire to the priesthood. It was an idea that horrified him. In this he was well supported by other clerics, equally fearful for their places and hating the idea of any female competition. It is an argument that goes on even now, when there are many devoted Church of England vicars who are female, but even with that milestone there is still opposition to them taking the places of men. In the Catholic faith, their participation in such a way still cannot be countenanced at all.

The prohibition on 'unclean' women was a matter of 'ritual purity'.[18] But before Christianity took hold, there were many priestesses in all the main religions who were respected and who continued to perform their offices without being considered in any way inferior. Only when Christianity became the state religion were women marginalised in this way and that influence affected the lives of other women for centuries. Even the prohibition against nuns entering the church, if in an 'impure' state, must have created great inconveniences to the running of any convent. Groups of women living together tend to synchronise in their monthly cycles after being together for some time, as do other mammals.[19] To have had most of the inmates of a convent refused admission to the church at the same time must have caused logistical problems.

It was unlikely that the men had any real fear of the female menstrual cycle. Their fear was not concerned with women's physical manifestations. The real fear was of the intellect of women, one like that of Hilda of Whitby, whose own intelligence was formidable. Throughout the history of Europe, female rulers have had to walk a very fine line in order to avoid being accused of immorality, which was a far easier accusation to make than to admit to a dread of feminine capability. Men could, of course, do much as they liked in a physical sense, and end up by being considered a Jack the lad, but if a woman behaved with anything less than perfect propriety she was considered to be loose. She was then treated accordingly, and her behaviour held up as being an example of female weakness in general.

The emphasis on female cycles, and the restrictions they are supposed to impose, focussed on the one thing that women cannot help or avoid – a perfectly natural function, yet one that was considered to be generally unclean and even in some way sinful. Even the virgin nuns who were supposed to be the brides of Christ were not immune from that appalling attitude. Virginity was so highly prized, yet even the virgin, clean, pure and right-thinking though she may have been, was brought down to an animal level every month. As the nuns were already living what might be termed a holy life, they were presumably beyond chastisement for any other offence, and it can be considered as a way of keeping them in subjection when they would otherwise be beyond reproach – judging them not by the quality of their lifestyle, but by a bodily function. This could reduce the most decent and highly educated abbess, the pious and high-born queen, the devoted mother, and define them all by that one aspect of their lives, rather than by any real achievements, qualities, or abilities.

Boniface had not always been so intransigent in his opinions, and in an earlier letter to Abbess Bugga, who was intent on making the lengthy and arduous journey to Rome, he had merely said, 'Do what God's grace shall inspire you to do.' Yet later on he would fire off that anxious and wholly disapproving letter to the Archbishop of Canterbury, counselling the refusal of permission to Abbess Eangyth and her daughter, when they hoped to do the same.[20] It would appear that under Archbishop Theodore there was to be a new and far stricter perception of the faults of all women, and this was used against them to justify greater levels of control over their activities. This further marginalisation was an insult to all the very many women who continued to live decently, whether as wives, mothers, widows or nuns. The women living in the world were reduced to child bearing servitude, subjected to the whims of fathers or husbands.

For women living in a religious community, the new harsher strictures prevented them from assisting at the Mass, and excluded them from the central ritual of the Church to which they had given their lives. Many of these women, both clergy and laity, proved themselves worthy in their daily lives, needing no further challenge to their motives. But they were all reduced alike, along with the women of the lowest morals, as mere female flesh, as if they were unable to rise above the purely physical constraints of their bodies.

When the stories of the early saints came to be rewritten for the Normans, they were closely edited to suit more severe Norman tastes. They much preferred to hear not the tales of great co-operation between the sexes, with men and women working together and supporting each other towards a general aim, but grim tales of conflict, temptations and betrayal. Even St Cuthbert, that mildest of saintly men,[21] who had been laid to rest at the age of fifty-three wearing a shroud that had been lovingly made for him by an abbess who was his very good friend, was altered to suit the new and more warlike stamp. He became, in the process, transformed into a man whose supposed hatred of women was so great that they dared not approach his tomb, for fear of being cursed by his spirit. That was an image that would have not only surprised but also dismayed him.[22]

The Normans were, in the early days at least, expected to be Philistines, and as Northmen who had only been settled in France since the tenth century, they had good reason to be a little touchy about their antecedents. Strangely, while they continued the Norsemen's warlike lifestyle, they had retained little or nothing of the Norse sense of equality and fair play. They were eager at that stage only to confirm and validate their military might, before having time to settle down to recreating a cultural identity. This they gradually did by appropriating all they could of the Anglo-Saxon past, rewriting its history where it was considered necessary. They then housed the old Anglo-Saxon saints in great cathedrals, even as they altered their character. They also tried to replace the Anglo-Saxon literary culture with one of their own, written in their own vernacular, Old French. In this way they attempted to create bonds with the people they had conquered, who already had a rich heritage of their own. Once the fighting had stopped, and the years had passed, making the realities of the Conquest less raw, there was time to attempt cohesion that was aided by intermarriage. Eventually, Old French was to move over to allow room for Anglo-Norman, the new dialect that would emphasise and ease the joining of the two disparate cultures. The court of Eleanor of Aquitaine and Henry II would come to overshadow the earlier patrons of literary works, but the foundations had already been laid. It reached its apogee during those years, making England into a centre of new culture, gradually permeating downwards. Unfortunately, the personal relationship between Eleanor and her husband suffered problems, caused mainly by their greedy and warring sons, and this fractured the family that had earlier been an example of amity and harmony.[23]

Though the medieval women had lost the freedom of their earlier counterparts, some might argue that they had lost the fighting spirit also. No longer was a woman expected to fight alongside the men, as the earlier tribes had done, at the very least supporting and exhorting them to greater efforts. While she had gained some aspect of physical safety in warfare, unless she became part of general collateral damage, she had also lost her position of equality and respect. The new heroine of literature was not to be revered for her battle skills, or her unhesitating support of her men, as ready to make battle as make love. Instead she would derive her identity only from her beauty, piety, or submissiveness. With a function reduced only to obedient sexuality, she easily became a victim of rape, or merely desire, an object of religious devotion if pious, but certainly a distraction from the real business of men's lives, always on the edge of their reality. This makes her easy to blame for all the ills to which men are subject, and gives her the reputation as being nothing but a nuisance. She becomes the temptress taking the minds of men away from their more important duties to family, Church or State, and the literature of the times begins to reflect that new status.

In *Sir Gawain and the Green Knight* the hero naturally blames all his failings on a woman,[24]

If a dullard should dote, deem it no wonder,
And through the wiles of women be moved into sorrow,
For so was Adam by one, when the world began,
And Solomon by many more, and Samson the mighty.
Delilah was his doom and David thereafter was
Beguiled by Bathsheba and bore much distress.

Now these were vexed by their devices, were a very joy,
Could one but learn to love and believe them not.
For these were proud princes, most prosperous of old,
Past all lovers lucky, that languished under Heaven bemused,
And one and all fell prey to women they had used,
If I be led astray methinks I may be excused.

Chaucer's Wife of Bath also speaks of the reading matter of her husband Jankyn. He too has a book of tales of 'wicked wives' who were not only harridans who made the lives of men a misery but who became a standard for real wives. Stories in which men were cozened and defeated by the wiles of women abounded, in which life became a battle. Chaucer, always at grass roots level with his characterisations, has the wife tearing the book from her husband's hands and destroying it, before striking him a blow in temper. Of course, Chaucer was writing fiction, however lifelike it appeared to be at times.

An earlier, female writer, Christine de Pisan, was able to feel exasperation at the usual depictions of women by male writers.[25] As already mentioned, she was one of the earliest of female activists and her writing in *Citie of Ladies* was directly influenced by the misrepresentations of women, exasperated 'that so many men and learned men among them, have been and are so inclined to express, both in speaking and in their treatises and writings, so many wicked insults about women and their behaviour...'[26]

This begs the question, were men generally afraid of showing that they could have a more sensitive side? Did the idea of emotional closeness with women make them anxious? Did they really believe all the garish stories of women's wiles and fear that some woman would similarly enslave them? After all, most of them may well have had perfectly reasonable relationships with mother and sisters, who were obviously neither wicked nor wanton. Was their fear of the feminine more centred on losing their masculinity if they showed anything other than the most obvious machismo? By treating women roughly, or with disdain, were they affirming their perceived superiority over those baffling and contrary creatures, people that they needed, desired, manipulated, but could never fully understand?

There was also a resentment at being caught by those 'women's wiles', as many were at some point. The necessity of putting one's head into the matrimonial noose in order to provide family heirs, yet remaining aware that any close relationship with women, on anything other than the most basic sexual level, was something they might not have been able to cope with. Marriage was a frightening partnership, where despite changing fashions in behaviour, the basic needs remained the same. Everyone needs to feel wanted and cared for, and in a nurturing relationship children grow and thrive much better. But many marriages must have failed to achieve anything like the ideal. The people involved in such marriages found themselves doing their duty, but no more. Once they had lived together long enough for the novelty to wear off, they effectively went their separate ways, the men to the camaraderie of other men, and the women to devote themselves to children, or finding their friendship and support with other women. This did not make domestic life impossible, as for most people the pragmatic view of the realities of married life prevailed, and they were able to simply make the best of what they had. They lived a reasonable life, like many of their contemporaries, but perhaps without the spark that makes it all so worthwhile.

For the elderly person of means there were several options if no children existed to take over. If there was no possibility of a relative moving in to care for the aged, a corrody[27] could be purchased at the local monastery or nunnery, where the elderly could retire to live out their days in peace, and with some physical care allowed for. The position of single ageing people was naturally far more worrying than those who were married, providing that they still had some means, land or other property, to use as a negotiating tool. The contracts show that such arrangements tended to be left until the last moment when, usually after the death of a spouse, the retiree decided that they could no longer cope alone.[28] Two to three acres of land was considered to be the minimum amount on which to support one person but for many, even that would represent real riches. The poorest would still be left with nothing at all, once their strength failed them and they could no longer hire themselves out for physical labour. People of the peasant class would have had no access to monasteries or nunneries to be cared for when they became too old or frail to support themselves. The impoverished elderly were often reduced to begging, even if they had children still living in the same village, as is shown by one pitiful case from Bedfordshire.

> On 14 January 1267 Sabina, an old woman, went into Colmworth to beg for bread. At twilight she wished to go back to her home, but fell into a stream and died, by misadventure. The next day her son, Henry, searched for her, and found her drowned.[29]

In another case, that of Alice Berdholf, of Donyngton, a beggar of seventy years, she was found drunk near to a well in the highway. She saw a straw, and while reaching for it, fell in and was drowned.[30] At least Alice was known, and not an indigent, as so many of the poor and elderly unfortunately became. An old person found dead of cold and exposure in a cowshed in December of 1362 was merely described as 'an old stranger'. These were not isolated incidents, as the court records show. Wandering people, with no homes of their own, were entirely dependent on charity for their food and also on the hope of finding some dry shelter on cold winter nights. Any such old person, who was already known to the local community, was usually tolerated and may have been able to survive for a time in this manner. Strangers were viewed with more suspicion.

Religious houses and parish priests could usually be expected to make some provision for food for the desperate, and many people were generous with their alms giving. However, the problem was a large one, in times of general hardship, such as a poor harvest, many otherwise kindly people might also find it difficult to make regular donations; therefore, the relief given to the poverty-stricken could be sporadic at best.

Many old people suffered accidents around their homes, just as they do today. Local streams and rivers seemed to take more than their fair share of elderly lives, and trying to obtain water from a local stream, possibly in spate, with the banks steep or muddy, must have been a hazard for anyone, even the able-bodied. Many of the elderly still tried to make themselves useful, and there are records of old women baby-sitting while the rest of the family worked in the fields at harvest time. Unfortunately, in one case the child in her charge was drowned.[31] While the elderly may have been more at risk of drowning than anyone else, many of them were reported to have been drunk at the time of their accident. Perhaps only a little ale would be required, added to the general lack of physical stability, rather than a general assumption that people became alcoholic as they aged. They naturally also had higher mortality figures during the winter months, only to be expected when cold and hunger become a factor. Surprisingly, however, the records also show an increase in aged mortality during the month of August, when many elderly people died from their exertions in the harvest fields.

Not only were elderly people more susceptible to falls into water, but there are records that several even fell from trees while attempting to collect fruit. Some died in fires, either by falling into them or by knocking over or forgetting to extinguish candles or tapers. These are people who generally still retained their mental faculties, despite bodily weakness, but senility also took its toll. Margery Kempe wrote of having to look after her husband when his mental state declined. He had been 'of great age, more than threescore years and ten' when he hurt his head in a fall downstairs. After the accident he was unable to look after himself and she wrote, 'In his last days, he turned childish again, and lacked reason. He could not do his own easement to go to the latrine, or else would not, but as a child voided his natural digestion onto linen cloths.' She complained that she had to wash everything and also had to keep a fire going constantly, so that he was warm enough.[32]

The elderly who were still compos mentis had concerns for the state of their souls. Most people still died at home, in their own beds. If they had anything worth leaving for their remaining family and friends, they would then make a will. For the illiterate this could be a spoken one, dictated in the presence of the priest, who would also offer the Last Rites to speed the soul on its journey when the time came. Then, as now, the ceremonies attendant upon a death could be expensive. The lord would first of all need to be considered, as he would require the best beast as his heriot payment. The second best beast went to the church for the mortuary fee. If the family were townspeople and owned no livestock, the fee would be demanded in money or equivalent goods. These payments could be onerous, but some kind of funeral feast would still have to be provided, with the family holding a wake. The church, naturally enough, tried to discourage any revelry, but prayers and Masses would have to be paid for to attempt to assist the soul towards Heaven and out of Purgatory. For more fortunately placed people, the funeral bills could be very large. The will of a guild chaplain shows that even a village funeral could be fairly lavish.

To the rector and high altar 3s. 4d.
For the fabric of the cathedral church 6s. 8d.
The upkeep of St John Baptist's altar 3s. 4d.
Altar of the Holy Trinity 3s. 4d.
St Mary's 3s. 4d.
Parish church of Lympe in Kent 40s
For each chaplain attending 8d.
For each clerk attending 4d.
For each clerk reading a lesson 2d.
For each poor scholar 1d.
For each bell ringer 2d.
Fee for the ringing of the bells 12d.[33]

Some people went so far in ordering prayers and Masses for the repose of their souls that they practically beggared their families. Many people were anxious that their executors would not abide by their last wishes, and declared that the bequests would not be forthcoming unless their intentions were honoured. These bequests would often cause some considerable friction within the family. The person on his or her deathbed was anxious to ensure their future in Paradise, but the next-in-line were often far more concerned with making sure that the church did not pocket the whole legacy, and leave the family destitute.

Friends often played a large part in wills, receiving personal belongings, money, animals and household goods, while some even received land or property. It shows that friends and neighbours formed an important part of the average person's daily life and also that bonding was usual between a wide variety of people. These may well have proved to be among the closest relationships formed, the people to whom one turned in times of trouble, as well as becoming responsible for performing, or helping to perform, the rites of passage at times of births or deaths.

Despite the failures when poor people could find themselves indigent and helpless, the strongest bonds for the medieval woman still appear to have been forged with her neighbours and her friends. These were her 'gossips' and the women she would help, or who would be likely to help her, through the difficulties of life. For the twenty-first century woman, perhaps living in a large city, with little knowledge of her neighbours and possibly with family and old friends at a distance, it is a loss we can barely begin to understand. Despite the many problems of her life, the medieval woman who had to deal with male superiority, the interference of the Church, poor health care and high infant mortality as a part of her daily lot, nevertheless had this support network – the bonding with other women and the mutual dependence and support, in the sure knowledge that within the village there would always be other people who could be turned to. Probably these people would have known her all her life, and also knew her family situation and her relatives. They would also be fully aware of the state of her relationship with her husband. This intimacy may now seem to us to be perilously close to an invasion of personal privacy, and no doubt it did sometimes become that. But it also meant a real help when trouble threatened, and a form of companionship that must have made up for much of the hardship of life. Despite our modern benefits, which are many, we have largely lost this network, so perhaps we are ultimately the losers.

The study of the lives of the women of the medieval period remains a fascinating one, and the evidence to be found regarding the lives of the ordinary people is still there to be read and pondered over. These were real lives, not fiction, and real problems, not a script. As such, they need to be viewed with sympathy and some understanding of the pressures and constraints placed upon our ancestors.

As Howell said,

History is the great looking glass through which we may behold with ancestral eyes not only the various actions of ages past, and the odd accidents that attend time, but may also discern the different humours of men, and feel the pulse of former times.[34]

NOTES

CHAPTER 1

1. *The Sarum Missal*, or 'use of Salisbury' was a variant of the Roman rite established by Bishop Osmond in 1078. It was widely used for public worship, Mass and divine office. It was prevalent until the reign of Queen Mary I and contained revisions of the extant Celtic and Anglo-Saxon rites.
2. Paul Hill. *The Age of Athelstan*. The History Press. 2004.
3. The Danelaw was the northern and eastern area of England, which was occupied by the Danish settlers between the Battle of Edington in 878 and the driving out of Erik Bloodaxe from Northumbria in 954. However, even when direct Danish control had gone, the laws were retained and many northern place names still have Danish roots.
4. Henrietta Leyser. *Medieval Women*. Weidenfeld & Nicholson (1995).
5. Christine Fell. *Women in Anglo-Saxon England*.
6. *Oxford Dictionary of National Biography*, regarding Edyth Swannesha (Edith Swan Neck.)
7. Christine Fell. *Women in Anglo-Saxon England*.
8. Ibid.

9. Carol Hough. 'Marriage and Divorce.' Article in *Blackwell's Encyclopaedia of Anglo-Saxon England*, ed. Michael Lapidge.

10. James Campbell, ed. *The Anglo-Saxons*. Penguin Books, London.

11. John Blair. *The Anglo-Saxon Age*.

12. Christine Fell. *Women in Anglo-Saxon England*.
    An 'oblate' is a young person offered to the service of God, though not professed. In the early medieval period, boys could enter into a monastery on the understanding that they could leave at puberty if they did not then wish to continue with monastic life.

13. Helen Jewell. *Women in Medieval England*. Manchester University Press, (1996).

14. Christine Fell. *Women in Anglo-Saxon England*.

15. Aethelbert of Kent died in 616, twenty-one years after his conversion to Christianity.

16. Henrietta Leyser. *Medieval Women*.

17. Ibid.

18. Laws of Aethelstan, Clause 31, 'Adultery.'

19. Margaret Clunies Ross. 'Concubinage in Anglo-Saxon England.' Article in *Past and Present No. 198* (1985)

20. Christine Fell. *Women in Anglo-Saxon England*.

21. Laws of King Alfred. Clause 42.

22. Laws of King Cnut II. Clause 53.

23. Terence Wise. *1066 the Year of Destiny*

24. T.J. Olsen. 'Edward the Confessor's promise of the throne of England to Duke William of Normandy.' Article in the *English Historical Review. LXXii.*

25. *The Anglo-Saxon Chronicle.* (Trans.by G.N. Garmonsway). The 'E' version was compiled at Peterborough and is known as 'The Laud.' It was copied in the twelfth century from the Kentish Chronicle, which is now unfortunately lost.

26. Richard Brookes. *The Knight who Saved England*.

27. Norah Lofts. *Domestic Life in England*.

28. Richard Brookes. *The Knight who Saved England*.

29. Norah Lofts. *Domestic life in England*.

30. Richard Brookes. *The Knight who Saved England*.

31. It took over 800 years until the Married Women's Property Acts of 1870 and 1874, which were the first legal attempts to safeguard women's property rights. Throughout the intervening years concerned families engaged in many shifts and contrivances to protect the family property from the depredations of prospective sons-in-law, often without any real success.

CHAPTER 2

1. Norah Lofts. *Domestic Life in England.*
2. Barbara A. Hanawalt. *The Ties that Bound.*
3. Maurice Beresford and J.G. Hurst. *Deserted Medieval Villages.*
4. Barbara A. Hanawalt. *The Ties that Bound.*
5. *Court Roll of Chalgrove Manor (1278–1313)* Ed. M.K. Dale. Bedfordshire Record Society (28).
6. Heriot. This was essentially a death tax, one of the many extortions to which the peasant family was subject. It usually consisted of taking the best beast belonging to the deceased, which became the property of the landlord. Only if the tenant was killed in battle, in the service of his lord, was the payment remitted. For townspeople, payment would be demanded in cash or in kind, often by the church, as in the case of Richard Hunne, when a dispute arose with the parish priest regarding payment of the tax.
7. Norah Lofts. *Domestic Life in England.*
8. Dieter Podlech. *Herbs and Healing Plants.*
9. J.J. Bagley. *Life in Medieval England.*
10. Norah Lofts. *Domestic Life in England.*
11. Garrett Mattingly. *Catherine of Aragon.*
12. Henrietta Leyser. *Medieval Women.*
13. Paul Murray Kendall. *The Yorkist Age.*
14. Henrietta Leyser. *Medieval Women.*
15. Lynda Telford. *Tudor Victims of the Reformation.*
16. Henrietta Leyser. *Medieval Women.*
17. Frederik Pedersen. *Marriage Disputes in Medieval England.*
18. Barbara A. Hanawalt. *The Ties that Bound.*

19. Judith Bennett. 'Medieval Peasant Marriage: an examination of marriage licence fees in the Liber Gersumarum.' From *Pathways to Medieval Peasants* ed. J.A. Raftis.
20. Margot A. Adamson. Ed. *Treasury of Middle English Verse.*
21. Henrietta Leyser. *Medieval Women.*
22. P.J.P. Goldberg. *Women, Work and Life Cycle in a Medieval Economy.*
23. P.J.P. Goldberg. *Women, Work and Life Cycle in a Medieval Economy.* Quoting from the York Cause Papers at the Borthwick Institute of Historical Research. The papers record the individual cases of the church courts. The Borthwick Institute is one of the largest archive repositories outside London. The papers contain more than 13,000 cases and are of great importance for social, economic and legal history. Re-cataloguing was funded by the Andrew W. Mellon Foundation. This made it possible to update the manual indexes and make these important archives available for wider research.
24. J.P.V.D. Balsdon. *Roman Women.* The Roman way of life was often revered, if rather imperfectly understood, in the medieval period. It was seen as being an ideal with regard to law, and the position of the Paterfamilias within the family. Much of church law and perceived wisdom stemmed from it.
25. A virgate (or yardland) was a measure of land of approximately 30 acres, though as with many medieval land measurements it varied with the fertility of the soil, areas of poorer production being awarded a few more acres in compensation. Similarly, the term 'bovate' (or oxgang) shows its origins in its name, being the amount able to be ploughed by oxen in one day. This usually measured around 15 acres. A carucate was much larger, averaging 120 acres and being the amount able to be ploughed in one season by a full team of eight oxen.
26. Barbara A. Hanawalt. *The Ties that Bound.*
27. Colin Platt. *The English Medieval Town.*
28. Kenneth Stevenson. *Nuptial Blessing – A Study of Christian Marriage Rites.*

29. Barbara A. Hanawalt. Quoting W.O. Hassell, *How They Lived, An Anthology of Original Accounts Written Before 1485.*
30. Norah Lofts. *Domestic Life in England.*

CHAPTER 3

1. Galen of Pergamon. His real name was Aelius Galenus (or perhaps Claudius Galenus) and he was born in Pergamon in modern-day Turkey, of Greek parents. He developed his theory and practice of medicine and died in Rome in 216 AD.
2. Leonardo di Ser Piero da Vinci's notes appear to have been intended for publication as in many cases, such as the study of the human foetus, the drawings and text are together. His works on anatomy were started under Andrea del Verrochio who expected his students to understand it. He was given permission to dissect human corpses at the Hospital di Santa Maria Nuova in Florence, making 240 detailed drawings, and writing about 13,000 words towards the production of a treatise on anatomy. He died in France in 1519.
3. Infertility. Unfortunately, royal women were just as likely to be blamed for a lack of sons, or any children at all, as lesser women – medical knowledge being as poor as it was. Even Eleanor of Aquitaine was blamed, in her first marriage to the King of France, for producing no male heir. In her second marriage, to Henry II of England, she produced a brood of sons and daughters. Humbler women might have to go through their lives being reproached for the lack of children.
4. Nigel Cawthorne. *The Cures of Old England.*
5. Angus McLaren. *Impotence: A Cultural History.*
6. Stoned horse. The term 'stoned' horse is one commonly used in medieval times to differentiate between a stallion and one that had had its stones removed (a gelding). In the Yorkshire Dales there are still areas such as Stonehorse Pasture, referring to the field where the stallion was grazed.
7. Norah Lofts. *Domestic Life in England.*

8. Baptism has always been permitted by a midwife (lay baptism) if a child appeared to be *in extremis,* if a priest was not available, or if there was reasonable expectation that one could not be reached in time. It was considered preferable for a lay woman to baptise the child, than for it to die unbaptised.

9. Frances and Joseph Gies. *Life in a Medieval Village.*

10. 'Houses of Cistercian Monks – Rievaulx' from *History of the County of York. Vol 3.*

11. David Hoffman. *Complete Herbal.* Raspberry leaves (*rubus ideaus*) have been used for centuries to tone the tissues prior to childbirth. They also check any threat of haemorrhage during the birth. Common nettle (*urtica dioicia*) is also recommended (in a drink) as being a useful source of iron for the pregnant woman.

12. Norah Lofts. *Domestic Life in England.*

13. J.P.V.D. Balsdon. *Roman Women.*

14. Norah Lofts. *Domestic Life in England.*

15. David Hoffman. *Complete Herbal.*

16. Dian Dinchin Buchman. *Herbal Medicine, the Natural Way to Get Well and Stay Well.*

17. Anna Sawkins. (www.alhealth.com.uk) Internet article regarding the side-effects of antibiotics, particularly broad-spectrum types, some of which are capable of producing contra-indications far worse than the original ailment. They are also capable of building up immunities, which cause the rise of 'superbugs' and the return of the original problem, often in a more virulent form.

18. Alexander Fleming was Professor of Bacteriology at St Mary's Hospital, London. He developed the first viable penicillin in 1928. This was not immediately available for public use. In Austria in 1952 Hans Magreiter and Ernst Brandl produced the first acid-stable penicillin for oral administration. (Penicillin V).

19. Warning! No one should dose themselves with even garden herbs without prior knowledge of their effects and side effects. It is recommended that the advice of a recognised medical herbalist be sought.

20. Terry Pratchett. *Mort*.
21. Lacey Baldwin Smith. *A Tudor Tragedy*.
22. J.P.V.D. Balsdon. *Life and Leisure in Ancient Rome*.
23. Ovid. *Ars Amatoria Amores*.
24. Dieter Podlech. *Herbs and Healing Plants*. Hemlock contains the poisonous alkaloid C8H17N, which is fatal to livestock and humans. It is very similar to cow parsley, being a tall umbellifer plant, with creamy white flowers. Hemlock does have a rather different stem, showing blotchy purplish marks on the green, and tends to have a fetid smell, which is different to that of cow parsley. Cow parsley/Queen Anne's Lace (*anthriscus sylvestris*) is not harmful, although hemlock, which can be mistaken for it, is deadly. It requires only 0.1g or even less, to cause fatality in humans. The Ancient Greeks used it in a decoction as a means of execution.
25. Henrietta Leyser. *Medieval Women*.
26. Terpenes are a large class of organic hydrocarbons produced by plants. They are referred to as 'terpenoids' when denatured, that is when they have been oxidized by the method of drying and curing their seeds or leaves. These are the building blocks of plant resin or essential oils.
27. Tertullian. Quintus Septimus Florens Tertullian was the author of *Apologeticus* around 196 AD. He may have been the son of a Roman centurion or perhaps a resident of Carthage. His *Apology* refers to the unjust treatment of Christians under Roman rule.

CHAPTER 4

1. Norah Lofts. *Domestic Life in England*.
2. Ian Mortimer. *Time Traveller's Guide to Medieval England*.
3. Ian Mortimer. Ibid.
4. Barbara A. Hanawalt. *The Ties that Bound*.
5. Ian Mortimer. *Time Traveller's Guide to Medieval England*.
6. Paraphernalia is a Greek word meaning 'goods brought by a bride over and above her 'pherne' or dowry. To the Spartans it also meant the portion of the sacrificial animal reserved for the god.

7. Lesley-Wynne Davis. An article in the *Ricardian Bulletin* of Autumn 2005, entitled 'To my wife, her own clothes' from the Logge Wills Series. Richard III Society.

8. Logge Wills. *The Logge Register of Wills (1479–1486, 2 volumes)*. Eds. Lesley Boatwright, (later Lesley Wynne-Davies), Moira Habberjam and Peter Hammond. These are full transcriptions and translations of the 379 wills and testaments recorded in Latin or English in the Register of the Prerogative Court of Canterbury 1479–1486.

9. Lesley Wynne-Davies, 'To my wife, her own clothes.'

10. Agnes Blacston. This case of a runaway wife appeared in *Buckinghamshire Inquests and Indictments*. (Bucks. Record Society).

11. Barbara A. Hanawalt. *The Ties that Bound.*

12. John Myrc. *Instructions for Parish Priests* ed. Edward Peacock.

13. George Shuffleton. Ed. 'How the wise man taught his son' from Codex Ashmole 61 *A Compilation of English Verse.*

14. A 'dote' is an Irish colloquialism denoting a gorgeous or adorable person.

15. *Court Rolls of the Manor of Wakefield, YAS Series II*. Trans. Sue Sheridan Walker; also *Court Rolls of the Manor of Wakefield, YAS Series 109*. Trans J.P. Walker.

16. Barbara A. Hanawalt. *The Ties that Bound.*

17. *Court Rolls of the Manor of Wakefield, Series 109.*

18. *Court Rolls of the Manor of Wakefield, Series 57* also *Series 78.*

19. *Bedfordshire Coroner's Rolls, no 41*. Beds. Historical Record Society.

20. *Ancrene Wise, a Guide for Anchoresses*. Trans. James Morton

21. From a talk entitled 'Medieval Marriage' given by Lynda Telford to the Richard III Society Study Day, June 2016.

22. *Le Dite de Hosebondrie Walter de Henley*. Trans. Elizabeth Lamond.

23. Norah Lofts. *Domestic Life in England.*

24. Ian Mortimer. *Time Traveller's Guide to Medieval England.*

25. David Hugh Farmer, *Oxford Dictionary of Saints*.

26. Martin Whittock. *A Brief History of Life in the Middle Ages*.

27. Ibid.

28. William of Newburgh. The writer of the *Historia Rerum Anglicarum* in five 'books' or volumes, though it is believed that he died before his work was completed. Newburgh Priory is near Coxwold, in North Yorkshire.

29. Matthew Paris (1200–1259) was a Benedictine monk based at St Albans. He was the writer of the *Chronica Majora* and also famed as an illuminator and cartographer.

30. Angela Bourke. *The Burning of Bridget Cleary – a True Story*.

31. Angele de la Barthe (1230–1275). Scholars have cast doubt on the veracity of the Barthe story, as there is no record of her trial in 1275 in Toulouse. Without full court records, it is impossible to take a stand either way and many of the relevant records have been lost. However, it is not unusual for people to admit to all kinds of horrors under duress, so the story may well be based on a relatively simple heresy trial.

32. Mother Shipton. (aka Ursula Sontheil, 1488–1561). 'Mother Shipton's Cave', at Knaresborough in Yorkshire is a oldest surviving 'tourist attraction' as there has been a petrifying well open there since 1630. It stands in what was once part of the Royal Forest of Knaresborough. There are still many books available giving details of Ursula's uncannily accurate prophecies.

33. Benjamin Woolley. *Dee, the Queens Conjurer*. Dr John Dee, (1527–1608), studied at Cambridge and was known as a courtier, scholar, mathematician, scientist, alchemist and magician at the court of Queen Elizabeth I. He is famous for predicting a long and successful reign if she was crowned on 15 January.

34. Norah Lofts. *Domestic Life in England*.

35. Natalie Zemon Davis. *The Return of Martin Guerre*.

CHAPTER 5

1. Ian Mortimer. *Time Traveller's Guide to Medieval England*.

2. Petty treason, is the crime of killing or attempting to kill a person in authority. This included one's husband, considered to be a woman's natural master, but could also apply to one's employer. The penalty was intended to be so frightful as to discourage any attempts, though it created a very unfair situation for any woman having to defend herself against abuse.

3. Norah Lofts. *Domestic Life in England*.

4. Johannes Gratian was the author of the *Decretum Gratiani* also known as the *Concordia Discordantium Canonum* published in 1140. This was a collection of canon laws forming part of six legal texts, together known as the *Corpus Juris Canonici* used by canonists until 1918 when a revised code, promulgated by Pope Benedict XV in 1917, obtained legal force.

5. Frederik Pedersen. *Marriage Disputes in Medieval England*. Professor Pedersen has done a brilliant piece of work on the church courts in York, dealing with marital discord. The cases heard by the ecclesiastical tribunals show the only time that the voices of married women could be publicly heard, as they were unable to become litigants in any other legal form.

6. Frederik Pedersen. *Marriage Disputes in Medieval England*.

7. The Lateran Councils were so called because they were held at the church of St John Lateran. This is the Cathedral Church of Rome and the official seat of the Pope, not St Peter's Basilica.

8. The *Liber Extra* published in 11234, is the *Decretal* of Pope Gregory IX and was intended to clarify and revise the *Decretum's* canons on marriage issues. With its publication, marriage law was complete and remained static until the Reformation.

9. Frederik Pedersen. *Marriage Disputes in Medieval England*.

10. Richard A Helmholz. *Marriage Litigation in Medieval England*.

11. Other courts were the Archbishop's Exchequer, which dealt primarily with financial matters within the diocese, as well as the running of the Archbishop's household. The Archbishop's Court of

Audience dealt with criminal matters and also with spiritual ones, which included cases of heresy and apostasy.

12. Litigation documents of the Consistory Court are now held at the Borthwick Institute for Historical Research, part of the University of York at Heslington. It has been calculated that approximately ninety-eight per cent of the original documents referring to matrimonial cases have been lost over the intervening centuries. However, the remaining eighty-eight litigation files contain the depositions of more than 580 people. It is a tragedy when one considers what fascinating and illuminating archive material has been lost.

13. Frederik Pedersen. *Marriage Disputes in Medieval England.*

14. C.B. Firth. *Benefit of Clergy in the Time of Edward IV.*

15. Frederik Pedersen. *Marriage Disputes in Medieval England.*

16. *Cause Paper E.70 (1355–1356)* Schipyn and Smyth.

17. Richard A. Helmholz. *Marriage Litigation in Medieval England.*

18. *Cause Paper E. 215 (1394–1395)* Greystanes and Dale.

19. Consanguinity is the prohibition of a relationship within the forbidden degrees. These may be formed even by an illicit attachment, which could then form a legal tie, for instance if a man had a sexual relationship with one woman, then married her sister.

20. *Cause Paper E. 33–1 (1337)* Boton and Acclum

21. *Cause Paper E. 79 (1358)* Midelton and Welewyk.

22. Frederik Pedersen. *Marriage Disputes in Medieval England.*

23. Barbara A. Hanawalt. *The Ties That Bound.*

24. Richard A. Helmholz. *Marriage Litigation in Medieval England.*

25. A. C. Chibnall. *Sherington: Fiefs and Fields of a Buckinghamshire Village.*

26. Richard A. Helmholz. *Marriage Litigation in Medieval England.*

27. Ibid.

28. Barbara A. Hanawalt. *The Ties that Bound.*

29. J. Murray. 'On the origins and role of wise women in cases of annulment on the Grounds of male impotence.' *Journal of Medieval History No.16*

30. *Cause Paper E. 105 (1370)* Lambhird and Sanderson.
31. The Dean of Holderness was at that time Thomas of St Martin. Holderness is now an area of rich agricultural land in East Yorkshire, but it had been marshland until it was drained during the Middle Ages.
32. Frederik Pedersen. *Marriage Disputes in Medieval England.*
33. *Cause Paper E. 259 (1368)* Cantilupe and Paynell.
34. Frederik Pederson. *Marriage Disputes in Medieval England.*
35. Richard A. Helmholz. *Marriage Litigation in Medieval England.*
36. Michael M. Sheenan. 'The formation and stability of marriage in fourteenth century England, evidence of an Ely Register.' In *Medieval Studies No. 33.*
37. *Cause Paper E.114 (1372–1373)* Rowth and Stry.
38. *Cause Paper E.211 (1394–1395)* Partik and Mariot.
39. *Cause Paper E.37 (1337)* Forester and Staynford.
40. *Cause Paper E.76 (1357)* Aungier and Malcake.
41. Frederik Pedersen. *Marriage Disputes in Medieval England.*
42. Michael M. Sheenan. *Formation and Stability of Marriage in Fourteenth-century England.*
43. *Cause Paper E. 221 (1394)* Nesfield and Nesfield.
44. Deferring an appeal was indicated by a Memorandum added to the document of sentence. The reasons for such decisions were not usually given in the Memoranda.
45. *Cause Paper E. 257 (1348)* Devoine and Scot.
46. Frederik Pedersen. *Marriage Disputes in Medieval England.*
47. *Cause Paper E. 89 (1365–1366)* Marrays and Rowcliffe.

CHAPTER 6

1. Philip Zeigler. *The Black Death.*
2. Ian Mortimer. *Time Traveller's Guide to Medieval England.*
3. J. Thorold Rogers. *A history of Agriculture and Prices in England. Vol. 1.*
4. Philip Zeigler. *The Black Death.*
5. Ian Mortimer. *Time Traveller's Guide to Medieval England.*

6. Lynda Telford. *Sulla, a Dictator Reconsidered.*
7. Chris Given-Wilson. Ed. *'PROME', The Parliamentary Rolls of Medieval England. (1275–1504).*
8. The original measurement of an ell was similar to that of a cubit, being the measurement from a man's elbow (hence ell) to the tip of the middle finger, about 18 inches. The English ell, however, used as a measurement of cloth, was taken roughly from elbow to elbow, but became more standardised at 45 inches or a yard and a quarter. (114.3 cm).
9. Norah Lofts. *Domestic life in England.*
10. The codpiece was a padded and often decorated piece of clothing over the male genitals. This became larger and more ornate as time passed, reaching its apogee during the reign of Henry VIII (1509–1547). The construction was intended to give the impression of a permanent state of sexual arousal. 'Cod' was Middle English for scrotum.
11. St Thomas Aquinas was a doctor of the church, a Dominican friar, a philosopher and one of the most influential of the medieval thinkers. He was born in 1225 in Roccasecca in Italy, and died in March 1274. He was known as Doctor Angelicus and Doctor Communis. He was the foremost classical proponent of natural theology with great influence on western thought. He wrote *Summa Theologiae* and *Summa contra Gentiles*. The study of his work was long used as a basis for those seeking ordination.
12. Ruth Mazo Karras. *Common Women, Prostitution and Sexuality in Medieval England.*
13. Jacques Rossiaud. *Medieval Prostitution.*
14. Ruth Mazo Karras. *Common Women, Prostitution and Sexuality in Medieval England.*
15. 'Stews' were bathhouses, offering 'extras' to clients. There are drawings showing men sharing baths with their prostitute of choice, sitting with her in the water, even sharing food that was served to them there. Curtains offered a little privacy. This at least had the benefit of giving the female a relatively fragrant client. Interestingly, the prostitute is always wearing a headdress or veil, as the last bastion of modesty.

16. St Albertus Magnus, (1200–1280) was also known as Albert of Cologne. He influenced St Thomas Aquinas. A Dominican friar, he was one of the thirty-six doctors of the church. He was a prolific writer, author of the philosophical work *De Mineralibus* and the *De Animalibus* on natural science. His wide-ranging interests led him to produce many papers, including a treatise on 'friendship'.

17. St Peter Damien. (1007–1072), was a Benedictine monk and a cardinal. He was placed by Dante in one of the highest circles of Paradise, in his 'Divine Comedy" St Peter Damien also wrote the *Book of Gomorrah*, an ecclesiastical discipline of 1049.

18. Eleanor of Aquitaine was born at Poitiers in 1122 and died in 1204. She was the queen of Louis VII of France and later queen to Henry II of England. She was the mother of Richard the Lionheart (and others) and King John. She outlived all her children, except for John and one daughter, the Princess Eleanor, who became Queen of Castile. Eleanor of Aquitaine is buried at Fontevrault Abbey in France.

19. Ian Mortimer. *Time Traveller's Guide to Medieval England*.

20. F.G. Emmison. *Elizabethan Life, Morals and the Church Courts*.

21. Homosexuality was anathema to the medieval church. However, the clerical horror at the idea of sodomy may give the impression that this particular act was generally detested and was therefore rare. This, of course, was not the case, even though any practising homosexual would have been wise to keep his inclinations private as tolerance could be rare and official tolerance even more so.

22. John Gough Nichols, ed. *The Diary of Henry Machin*.

23. Lynda Telford. *Tudor Victims of the Reformation*. The crime of incest did not become a specific offence in England and Wales until 1908. Before that time it could be dealt with only by canon law and was punishable only by a penance imposed by a priest. (This does not apply to the Protectorate of the 1650s, when the offence was briefly punishable by death.) Queen Anne Boleyn and her brother George, Lord Rochford, were accused of incest during her trial in May 1536, and that was the only charge brought against George Boleyn at his own trial. Although he was executed, in the

sixteenth century the matter did not concern an ordinary court and did not carry such a penalty.

24. Ian Mortimer. *Time Traveller's Guide to Medieval England.*

25. F.G. Emmison. *Elizabethan Life, Morals and the Church Courts.*

26. Major excommunication was a far more serious matter, meaning exclusion from the entire Christian community, being unable to confess or take communion, being unable to marry or be buried in a consecrated place, if one died before the lifting of the ban.

27. Ian Mortimer. *Time Traveller's Guide to Medieval England.*

28. C. M. Woodgar. *The Senses in Medieval England.*

29. J.P.V.D. Balsdon. *Roman Women.*

30. Paul Murray Kendall. *The Yorkist Age.*

31. Toni Mount. 'Whores and Winchester Geese.' Article in *Ricardian Bulletin. 2016.*

32. Ibid.

33. Robert Fabyan's *Great Chronicle of London*, known as *Fabyan's Chronicle*. Robert Fabyan was a master draper, sheriff and alderman of London and the author of the Chronicle, which presented a history up to the death of Henry VII. Two manuscripts are extant: *Holkham Hall ms 671* and *B.L. Cotton ms Nero.C.Xi.* These are not believed to be in Fabyan's own writing, but the text is likely to be his.

34. Cock Lane, Grope Lane, Codpiece Lane, Slut's Hole, and Cuckold Court were among the common names used for 'red-light' areas.

35. Toni Mount. 'Whores and Winchester Geese' article in *Ricardian Bulletin 2016.*

36. Ruth Mazo Karras. *Common women, prostitution and sexuality in medieval England.*

37. Corporation of London Records (CLRO) L-BL Fol. 189v (Sharpe Cal.L-BL216)

38. Ruth Mazo Karras. *Common women, prostitution and sexuality in medieval England.*

39. Chris Given-Wilson. *PROME. Parliamentary Rolls.* 4:447

40. Ruth Mazo Karras. *Common women, prostitution and sexuality in medieval England.*

41. Robert Rypon. *Sermons* (14th century). *BL. Ms Harleian. 4894. Fol. 176v*

42. Ruth Mazo Karras. *Common women, prostitution and sexuality in medieval England.*

43. *B.L. Ms. Harleian. 1288. Fol. 35v.*

44. John of Bromyard (d. 1352). *Summa Praedicantium.* John Bromyard was an Influential Dominican friar and the compiler of many preaching aids. The *Summa Praedicantium* was printed in Venice in 1586. Many of his books are now lost.

45. Alexander Carpentarius. *Destructorium Vitiorum* Cologne 1485.

46. Ruth Mazo Karras. *Common women, prostitution and sexuality in medieval England.*

47. Owen, *The Making of King's Lynn.* Public Record Office SC2/191/56 m2 m2d.

48. A.H. Thomas. Ed. *Calendar of London Court Rolls. (Mayor's court roll), G.m.13, m14d.* Quoted by Karras in *Common Women* etc.

49. *Calendar of London Court Rolls, Rep.3 fol.40R.* Quoted by Karras.

50. *Calendar of London Court Rolls, L-BB fol.3R.* Sharpe. Quoted by Karras.

51. Toni Mount. 'Whores and Winchester Geese.' Article in *Ricardian Bulletin 2016.*

CHAPTER 7

1. Henrietta Leyser. *Medieval Women.*

2. Lesley Wynne-Davies. 'To my wife, her own clothes.' *Ricardian Bulletin. 2005*

3. Barbara A. Hanawalt. *The Ties that Bound.*

4. Mary O'Regan. LL.B Hons. Feoffees were persons who had been 'enfeoffed' with land or other property that they then held in trust for another. During the term of enfeoffment they would have jurisdiction over it and be effectively the owners for that period. The feoffee was said to hold the property *as opus* or 'to the use of' the beneficial owner, who was or could be named by

the feoffer. The use was begun as a device whereby the newly created orders of friars, vowed to personal poverty, could be effective owners of property in someone else's name. The right of the feoffee during the designated term was so firmly upheld in law that any dispute between the feoffee and the beneficial owner would have to be heard by the king. This would be through his chancellor, as common law would uphold the rights of the feoffees.

5. Mary O'Regan. *The Medieval Manor Court of Wakefield.*

6. The court of the manor of Wakefield began in the thirteenth century and continued its sittings until the twentieth century. It is very rare for a manorial court to have survived so long, ending only with the land law reforms of 1922 and 1925. Its records survive, with a few gaps, and are in the archives of the Yorkshire Archaeological Society.

7. The 'fine' or tax in this case was known as 'Gersuma.' The medieval peasant had to pay these exactions at every alteration in his life, and they were often considered to be a great burden.

8. H.S. Bennett. *Life on the English Manor.*

9. *Wiltshire Archaeological Magazine Vol.5. 7ff. CfXLI*

10. *Hales Rolls of the Manor of Hales (1272–1307)* Worcester Historical Society.

11. *Bedfordshire Historical Record Society. (1913) Vol. XIII*

12. *Durham Halmote Rolls. Vol. IX*

13. *Durham Halmote Rolls. Vol. X*

14. Seisin denotes the legal possession of a feudal feoffedom, transferring rights and control of property to another person.

15. H.S. Bennett. @Life on the English Manor.' *Law Magazine and review. Vol.XIII*

16. *Suffolk Institute of Archaeology and Natural History. Proceedings Vol.2. 227 ff.*

17. Geoffrey Chaucer. *The Canterbury Tales.* Trans. Raffel.

18. J.S. Hamilton. *The Character of Edward II.*

19. Rank was something that, once acquired, nobody wished to relinquish. When Henry VIII's sister, Mary Tudor, was widowed

from her marriage to the King of France, she retained her title of queen. Her marriage had lasted barely three months but she subsequently was referred to as Queen of France for the remainder of her life.

20. Ian Mortimer. *Time Traveller's Guide to Medieval England.*
21. Ian Mortimer. *The Greatest Traitor.*
22. Regine Pernaud. *Eleanor of Aquitaine.*
23. *Cause Papers E. 108 (1370)* Hiliard and Hiliard.
24. Frederik Pedersen. *Marriage Disputes in Medieval England.*
25. *Cause Papers E. 62. (1348)* Hopton and Brome.
26. Frederik Pedersen. *Marriage Disputes in Medieval England.*
27. The Married Women's Property Act of 1870 allowed women to be the legal owners of any property they inherited or earned and allowed each spouse to own separate property. However, this early Act had loopholes, in that any woman who had married before the Act became law could not recover property retrospectively. Also the law could be evaded, as any property not put into trust for the wife (i.e. by her father), was not covered and could still be seized by the husband. The Act of 1870 laid the groundwork for the amended Act of 1882.
28. *Logge Will No. 30.* (Warham).
29. *Logge Will No. 40* (Bifeld).
30. *Logge Will No. 177* (Stepham).
31. *Logge Will No. 277* (Tillys).
32. *Logge Will No. 9* (Lewkenor).
33. *Logge Will No. 256* (Brampton).
34. Martyn Whittock. *A Brief History of Life in the Middle Ages.*
35. *Chertsey Abbey Court Rolls.* (Quoted by Barbara Hanawalt).
36. Margaret Spufford. *Peasant Inheritance Customs and Land Distribution in Cambridgeshire from the Sixteenth to the Eighteenth Centuries.*
37. Margaret Spufford. *Contrasting Communities: English Villages in the Sixteenth and Seventeenth Centuries.*
38. Marian K. Dale. Ed. *Court Roll of Chalgrave Manor (1278–1313)* Bedfordshire Historical Record Society.

39. Barbara A. Hanawalt. *The Ties that Bound.*

40. Richard A. Helmholz. 'Bastardy litigation in medieval England.' In *American Journal of Legal History no. 13.*

41. Cicely Howell. *Peasant Inheritance Customs in the Midlands 1280–1700.*

42. The author knows personally of one case where this happened in the late twentieth century. The informal agreement broke down when the tenant refused to hand back to the widow's son the land he had cultivated for several years. He claimed that the length of time he had worked the land made it his by right and the widow could not afford to argue the case in court.

43. Elaine Clark. *Some Aspects of Social Security in Medieval England.*

44. Barbara A. Hanawalt. *The Ties that Bound.*

45. R.H. Hilton. *The English Peasantry in the Later Middle Ages.*

46. Judith Bennett. *Medieval Peasant Marriage.*

47. Henrietta Leyser. *Medieval Women.*

48. P.J.P. Goldberg. *Women, Work and Life Cycle in a Medieval Economy.*

49. M. Sellers. Editor of the *York Memorandum Book.*

50. E. Miller. *Medieval York*

51. British Institute of Historical Research. *Probate Registry 2. Fo. 278.*

52. P.J.P. Goldberg. *Women, Work and Life Cycle in a Medieval Economy.*

53. Barbara A. Hanawalt. *The Ties that Bound.*

CHAPTER 8

1. J.P.V.D. Balsdon. *Roman Women.*

2. Gabrielle Brown. *The New Celibacy.*

3. Norah Lofts. *Domestic Life in England.*

4. Mario Mazzuchelli. *The Nun of Monza.*

5. Sister Virginia was released in 1622 knowing nothing of her lover's end, or the survival of their daughter. She claimed to have visions and lived a saintly life, dying in 1650.

6. Martyn Whittock. *A Brief History of Life in the Middle Ages.*

7. Ibid.

8. David Hugh Farmer. *Oxford Dictionary of Saints.*

9. Lady Margaret Beaufort was styled Countess of Richmond and Derby due to her several marriages. During her final marriage, to Thomas Stanley, she took a vow of celibacy, with her husband's permission, before the Bishop of London.

10. St Augustine. *Treatises on Marriage and Other Subjects.*

11. Dyan Elliott. *Spiritual Marriage.*

12. Michael K. Jones and Malcolm G. Underwood. *The King's Mother: Lady Margaret Beaufort, Countess of Richmond and Derby.*

13. Dyan Elliott. *Spiritual Marriage.*

14. Margaret Beaufort kept separate rooms at her manor at Collyweston for the use of her husband during his visits to her.

15. Sean Martin. *The Cathars: Rise and Fall of the Great Heresy.*

16. Peter Lombard. *Sententiae in IV libris distinctae.*

17. James A. Brundage. *Carnal Delight: Canonistic Theories of Sexuality.*

18. Alan of Lille. *De planctu naturae.*

19. Huguccio. *Theories on the Formation of Marriage.*

20. St Bernard of Clairvaux. *Sermon 65 on the Song of Songs.*

21. Hildegard of Bingen (1098–1179) was a Benedictine abbess, writer and philosopher.

22. Dyan Elliott. *Spiritual Marriage.*

23. Peter the Chanter. *Summa de Sacramentis et Animae Consilis.*

24. Pope Innocent III. *On the Misery of the Human Condition.*

25. Jacqueline Murray. *On the Origins and Role of Wise Women in the Causes for Annulment on the Grounds of Male Impotence.*

26. Johannes Gratien. *The Decretum Gratien.*

27. Dyan Elliott. *Spiritual Marriage.*

28. Richard A. Helmholz. *Marriage Litigation in Medieval England.*

29. Papal infallibility was declared at Vatican I on 18 July 1870. It did not mean that a pope could do no wrong, merely that in matters appertaining to church law he would expect to be guided in his decisions by God.

30. Dyan Elliott. *Spiritual Marriage.*

31. Chaucer. *The Canterbury Tales*. The power of the man over his wife, even to his interference in her vows to God, is the core of *The Franklin's Tale*.
32. St Raymond de Penafort (d. 1275) was a professor of canon law in Bologna.
33. Dyan Elliott. *Spiritual Marriage*.
34. St Raymond de Penafort. *Summa de Casibus Poenitentia et Matrimonio*.
35. Thomas of Chobham. (1160–1233) *Summa confessorum*.
36. Dyan Elliott. *Spiritual Marriage*.
37. B.A. Windgatt. Ed. *The Book of Margery Kempe*.
38. St Bridget of Sweden (1303–1373) was a mystic and founder of an order of nuns after her widowhood. Her daughter also became one of the Scandinavian saints as St Catherine of Sweden. (1332–1381)
39. Dyan Elliott. *Spiritual Marriage*.
40. Andre Vaudez. *The Canonisation of Dauphine*.

CHAPTER 9

1. Christopher Brooke. *The Medieval Idea of Marriage*.
2. The councils were called 'Lateran' due to the church of St John Lateran being the Pope's church in Rome, his position being Bishop of Rome. It is still considered to be Rome's main cathedral and the Pope celebrates Maundy Thursday Mass there.
3. Pope Innocent II was Gregaroio Papareschi (1130–1143). His election had been controversial and his first eight years of rule were spoiled by his struggle against the claims of the Antipope Anacletus II.
4. P. M. Barnes. *The Anstey Case*.
5. A promise to wed was either *de futuro* or *de presenti* which was at some time in the future, or with immediate effect. Even a solidly legal marriage, with all church ritual and witnesses, still needed to be consummated to confirm it.
6. Christopher Brooke. *The Medieval Idea of Marriage*.
7. J. Barrow. *A Twelfth Century Bishop and Literary Patron, William de Vere*.

8. St Bernard of Clairvaux. (1090–1153) was the great reformer of the Cistercian order. His reforms had a great influence on western monasticism and Bernard led the foundation of 163 monasteries, which by his death had grown to 343. He was the author of many books and sermons and a promoter of the Second Crusade of 1146–1149.

9. Hugh of St Victor (1096–1141) was a Saxon regular canon and one of the great Medieval theologians.

10. Hugh of St Victor. *De Sacramentis. (Sacraments of the Christian Faith.)*

11. Christopher Brooke. *The Medieval Idea of Marriage.*

12. These apparent contrivances were due to the popes of the twelfth century trying to formulate an acceptable way of dealing with marriages for ascetic and celibate clergy. They did eventually raise marriage to the level of a sacrament, but its elevation made it more difficult to interpret and clarify.

13. During the marriage negotiations between Spain and Portugal, one of the conditions of the proposed union was that Portugal should expel all its Jews. This was complied with.

14. Miguel da Paz (1498–1500). The son of Manuel I of Portugal and Isabella of Aragon would have inherited the kingdoms of Portugal, Aragon, Castile and Leon. His mother, who died at his birth, was eldest daughter of Isabella and Ferdinand of Spain. When the only son of the Spanish sovereigns, Juan, Prince of Asturias, died as a youth his sister became heiress only of Castile, not Aragon, as Aragon had the Salic law which rejected female rule. Her son, on the other hand, could have become heir to all, but he died in 1500, aged only two years.

15. *The Book of Margery Kempe.*

16. *British Library Ms (additional)* 61823. Found in the private library of the Butler-Bowden family, in 1934, by H. E. Allen, it is now widely translated and reprinted.

17. Ian Mortimer. *Time Traveller's Guide to Medieval England.*

18. Christine de Pisan. *The Book of the Citie of Ladies.*

19. Christine de Pisan. *The Book of the Body Politic.*

20. *Public Record Office. DL. 34/2. Wood.*
21. One example is the case of Thomas Fitzgerald, Earl of Desmond, former Deputy of Ireland and friend of Edward IV. He was reported to have cast aspersions on the marriage of Edward and Elizabeth Woodville, who plotted his downfall as a result.
22. *Stonor letters (No. 120)*
23. Edith Neville's use of the title of her first husband was not unusual. It was common for a woman who had been married more than once to continue to use the title of the husband of highest social standing.
24. *Plumpton letters. (No. 2000).*
25. Mistress Darcy was daughter to Lord and Lady Scrope of Masham.
26. *Plumpton letters. (No.2)*
27. *The Paston letters.* Ed. James Gairdner.
28. *The Paston letters. (No. 24)*
29. *The Paston letters. (No.710)*
30. *The Paston letters. (No.721)*
31. Brethele or brethelyng signifies a worthless person.
32. Lynda Telford. *Tudor Victims of the Reformation.*
33. The Dukedom of Norfolk had been confiscated by Henry VII after Bosworth due to Howard having fought for Richard III. It was eventually restored.
34. Previously married to Anne Plantagenet, the fifth daughter of King Edward IV. Anne died in 1511.
35. 1533 was the year Henry VIII married Anne Boleyn. Their daughter, the future Queen Elizabeth I, was born in September of the same year.
36. It was usual for Henry VIII to buy support with bribes of land and offices. Whenever a person of standing was due to be executed, there would be a rush among courtiers who hoped to beg for his estates.
37. Elizabeth Holland was later to become part of Queen Anne Boleyn's household. It was probably done as a service to Anne's uncle, the Duke of Norfolk, but made the duchess even more vituperative about the queen.

38. At the time of her marriage, Elizabeth Stafford was described as being 'passably pretty'. Her father had given her an annuity of 500 marks on her marriage, and Thomas Howard received a further 2,500 marks in dowry with her. She must have been a perfectly pleasant young woman, the termagant came later, with dissatisfaction.
39. Barbara Harris. *Marriage Sixteenth Century Style.*
40. Ibid.

CHAPTER 10

1. National Coalition against Domestic Violence. 2014.
2. Office of National Statistics. 2015.
3. Peter G. Jaffe. *Children of Battered Women.*
4. *Cause paper E. 221 (1394)* Nesfield and Nesfield.
5. Frederik Pedersen. *Marriage Disputes in Medieval England.*
6. Ibid.
7. Alison McRae Spencer. *Putting Women in their Place.*
8. *Court Rolls of the manor of Wakefield.*
9. *Cause paper E. 257. (1348–1349)* Scot and Devoine.
10. Richard A. Helmholz. *Marriage Litigation in Medieval England.*
11. Alison McRae Spencer. *Putting Women in their Place.*
12. Chaucer. *The Canterbury Tales.*
13. Keith Moxey. *Peasants, Warriors and Wives.*
14. Ibid.
15. St Boniface. *The Letters.*
16. Theodore of Tarsus. (602–690) became Archbishop of Canterbury in 668. He was a famous reformer of the Church, and his *Poenitentiale Theodori* is strict and severe in relation to women.
17. Michael Lapidge. *Archbishop Theodore: Commemorative Studies of his Life.*
18. Henrietta Leyser. *Medieval Women.*
19. A personal observation from years of animal breeding, and incidentally, friendships with both veterinary surgeons and nuns.
20. Henrietta Leyser. *Medieval Women.*

21. St Cuthbert (634–687). Probably of Scottish origin, Cuthbert was a monk and bishop of the Northumbrian Church. He became one of the most important medieval saints, with a cult centred on his tomb at Durham Cathedral.
22. Henrietta Leyser. *Medieval Women.*
23. Regine Pernauld. *Eleanor of Aquitaine.*
24. Simon Armitage. *Sir Gawain and the Green Knight.*
25. Christine de Pisan (1364–1430).
26. Karen Pratt. *Woman Defamed and Woman Defended.*
27. A corrody is an agreement between a religious house and a retired person, whereby the retiree may live in the religious house for payment of a one-off fee. Many houses were tempted into agreeing to corrodies but found when the money was gone, they were still left with a permanent guest.
28. Barbara A. Hanawalt. *The Ties that Bound.*
29. *Bedfordshire Coroner's Rolls.*
30. Barbara A. Hanawalt. *The Ties that Bound.*
31. *Bedfordshire Coroner's Rolls.*
32. *The Book of Margery Kempe.* Folio Society.
33. Patricia Bell. Trans. *Bedfordshire Wills (1480–1519).*
34. J. Howell. *Epistolae Ho-Elianae.* Ed. J. Jacobs. (1890)

BIBLIOGRAPHY

Articles

BAILDON W.P. 'Feet of fines for the county of York from 1347 to 1377 – Edward III.' Yorkshire Archaeological Society (1915).

BARROW J. 'A 12th century bishop and literary patron, William de Vere' in: Vitiator XVIII. *Journal of the Centre for Medieval and Renaissance Studies*. Oxford (1987).

BENNETT, Judith. 'Medieval peasant marriage.' An examination of marriage licence fines in the 'Liber Gersumarum' of Romsey Abbey. *In Pathways to medieval peasants*, ed. J.A. Raftis. Toronto (1981).

BROWN Sandra. 'The Peculiar Jurisdiction of York Minster during the Middle Ages.' Unpublished Ph.D. thesis, University of York. (1980).

BRUNDAGE. James A. 'Carnal delight. Canonistic Theories of Sexuality.' In: *Proceedings of the fifth International Congress of Medieval Canon Law*, Salamanca. 21–25 September 1976. *Monumemta Iuris Canonici Series C. Subs. Vol.6* Vatican City (1980).

BRYSON Sarah. 'Childbirth in Medieval and Tudor Times' (thetudorsociety.com)

CHENEY C.R. 'Rules for the observance of feast days in medieval England.' In *Bulletin of the Institute of Historical Research. No 34 1982.*

CLARKE Elaine. 'Some aspects of social security in medieval England.' In *Journal of Family History 7*. (1982).

COURT ROLLS OF THE MANOR OF WAKEFIELD. *(Oct 1350 to Sept 1352)* Eds. Moira Habberjam, Mary O'Regan, and Brian Hale. *Wakefield Court Rolls Series, vol 6*. Yorkshire Archaeological Society.

COLLUM P.H. 'And hir name was charite'. Charitable giving by and for women in late medieval Yorkshire. In: *Woman is a Worthy Wite – Women in English Society 1200–1500* Ed. P.J.P. Goldberg.

DODD Sandra. 'Women and Work in the Middle Ages' (sandradodd.com)

ELLIOTT Dyan. 'Dress as mediator between inner and outer self.' (The pious matron of the high and later middle ages.) In: *Medieval studies 53*. (1991).

'English wills Proved at the Prerogative Court at York (1477 1499)'. Eds: Heather Falvey, Lesley Boatwright, and Peter Hammond. These refer to eighty-nine wills, wholly or partly in English with translations of any Latin sections. Richard III Society.

FIRTH C.B. 'Benefit of clergy in the time of Edward IV' in *English Historical Review No. 32*.

GILBERT Rosalie. 'Rosalie's Medieval Women' (rosaliegilbert.com)

HARRIS Barbara. 'Marriage Sixteenth century style, Elizabeth Stafford and the Third Duke of Norfolk.' In: *Journal of Social History, Vol 15 Issue 3*. (1982).

HELMHOLZ Richard A. 'Bastardy litigation in medieval England.' In: *American Journal of Legal History. No. 13*. (1969).

HOLLYWOOD. Amy. 'Feminist studies' In: *Blackwell's Companion to Christian Spirituality*. (2005).

HOWELL Cicely. 'Peasant inheritance customs in the Midlands 1280–1700' in: *Family and Inheritance, Rural Society in Western Europe*. Eds. Jack Goody, Joan Thirsk, and E.P. Thompson. 1976.

JEWELL. Helen. 'Women at the courts in the Manor of Wakefield. (1348–1350) in: *Northern History vol. XXVI* (1990).

JONES E.D. 'The medieval leyrwite' a historical note on female fornication. In: *English Historical Review. 107.* (1992).

LEWIS Michael R. Article on 'King's Evil' (medscape.com)

McRAE-SPENCER Alison. 'Putting women in their place – social and legal attitudes towards violence in marriage in late medieval England' (Article based on M.A. Dissertation)

MILLER E. 'Medieval York.' In: *Victoria County History – City of York.* Ed. P.M. Tillott (1961).

MORTON David. 'Sex in the middle ages' Blog d.martin.ca

MOUNT Toni. 'Aspects of Fifteenth Century Life – Whores and Winchester Geese – the Oldest Profession' In: *Ricardian Bulletin 2016* from talk given at York Research Weekend, April 2016.

MURRAY Jacqueline. 'On the origins and role of wise women in causes for annulment on the grounds of male impotence.' In: *Journal of Medieval History No. 16.* (1990).

OLSEN T.J. 'Edward the Confessor's promise of the throne to William of Normandy' In: *English Historical Review. LXXII.* (1957).

RENDFIELD Kim. 'Medieval childbirth' (unusualhistoricals.blogspot)

ROSENTHAL Joel. 'Fifteenth century widows and widowhood, bereavement, reintegration and life choices' in: *Wife and Widow in Medieval England.* Ed. Sue Sheridan Walker. University of Michigan. (1993).

ROSS Margaret C. 'Concubinage in Anglo-Saxon England'. *In Past and Present No.108* (1983)

SAWKINS Anna. Internet article regarding antibiotics, their uses, side-effects and superbugs. Alhealth.co.uk.

SHEEHAN Michael. 'Theory and practice – marriage of the unfree and the poor in medieval society.' In: *Medieval Studies No.50.* (1988) Journal of Pontifical Institute of Medieval Studies.

SHEEHAN Michael. 'The formation and stability of marriage in fourteenth century England – evidence of an Ely register.' In: *Medieval Studies No.33* (1971) Journal of Pontifical Institute of Medieval Studies.

SPUFFORD Margaret. 'Peasant inheritance customs and land distribution in Cambridgeshire from the sixteenth to the eighteenth centuries.' In: *Family and Inheritance in rural society in Western Europe 1200–1800.* (1976) Eds. Jack Goody, Joan Thirsk, and E.P. Thompson.

Wiltshire Archaeological Magazine Vol V.

WYNNE-DAVIES. Lesley. 'To my wife, her own clothes.' In *Ricardian Bulletin,* (Richard III Society) (2005).

WYNNE-DAVIES. Lesley. 'The case of Agnes Blacston' In: *Buckinghamshire Inquests and Indictments' Bucks.* Record Society. (1994). (Also under her maiden name of Lesley Boatwright.)

Primary Sources

ALAN of LILLE *De Planctu Naturae* ed. Nikolaus M. Haring. Spoleto. (1978).

ANGLO-SAXON CHRONICLES. Translated by G.N. Garmonsway. London (1953).

Corrected in 1960. Sections A–F as follows: A – Winchester; B and C – Abingdon; D – Worcester; E – Peterborough; F – English/Latin made at Canterbury after the Conquest. (The 'E' version, known as the Laud of Peterborough, was copied in the twelfth century from the Kentish Chronicle, which is now lost.)

ST.AUGUSTINE *Treatises on Marriage and Other Subjects* ed. R.J. Deffarari. Vol.27 New York (1955).

BEDE *Ecclesiastical History of the English People* Oxford University Press. (2008)

BEDFORDSHIRE CORONER'S ROLLS Translated by R.F. Hunnisett. Bedfordshire Historical Record Society. (41) (1961).

BEDFORDSHIRE HISTORICAL RECORD SOCIETY XIII. 1913.

BEDFORDSHIRE WILLS (1480–1519) Translated Patricia Bell. Bedfordshire Historical Record Society (45) (1966).

ST BERNARD OF CLAIRVAUX Sermon 65 'On the Song of Songs' translated by Wakefield and Evans, in *Heresies of the High Middle Ages. C6 and C4.*

ST BERNARD OF CLAIRVAUX *Sermons on the Song of Songs Vols. 1–4* English/Latin translation by Cistercian Publications. (1971).

ST BONIFACE. *The Letters* edited and translated by Ephraim Emerton. Columbia University Press (2000).

BORTHWICK INSTITUTE OF HISTORICAL RESEARCH. University of York. *Cause Papers of the York Consistory Court, CP, E, F, G, Various.* Plus *Cause Papers of the Dean and Chapter D/C, CP, Various.*

BRITISH INSTITUTE OF HISTORICAL RESEARCH. *Probate Registry 2, fo.278*

BRITISH LIBRARY. *Harleian Manuscript 1288. Fo.35v*

BROMYARD John of Summa *Praedicantum, Parts 1 and 2* printed Venice (1586).

CALENDAR OF LONDON COURT ROLLS

Mayor's Court Roll. (CLCR/MCR) G-M13, m14d. edited A.H. Thomas. 'Calendar of early Mayor's Court Rolls preserved in archives of City of London at the Guildhall.' Cambridge University Press. (1924).

CLCR-L-BL Folio189v

CLCR-Rep.3 fol.40R

CLCR-L-B.B fol.3R

CARPENTARIUS Alexander. *Destructorium Vitiorum* Cologne (1485).

CELY PAPERS edited Henry Eliot Malden. (Camden Society) (1900).

CHALGROVE MANOR COURT ROLLS. (1278–1313) Vols.28 and 37. Edited Marian K. Dale for Bedfordshire Historical Record Society (1956).

CHAUCER Geoffrey. *The Canterbury Tales* translated Neville Coghill. Penguin. 2003

CHERTSEY ABBEY COURT ROLLS. (Abstract). Translated Elsie Toms. Surrey Record Society. Vol. 21.

CHOBHAM Thomas of *Summa Confessorum* edited F. Broomfield. (*Analecta Medievalia Namurencia 25.*) Louvain (1968).

COURT ROLLS OF THE MANOR OF HALES.(1272–1307) edited J. Amplett and others. Worcester Historical Society (1910).

COURT ROLLS OF THE MANOR OF WAKEFIELD. Editors : W.P. Baildon, J.P. Walker, John Lister and others. Translated Sue Sheridan Walker. Series 109. (1945 and 1982). Yorkshire Archaeological Society Record Series 29, 36, 57, 78, 109 and 111.

DURHAM HALMOTE ROLLS IX. *Halmota Prioratus Dunelmensis (1296–1384)* Edited W.H.D. Longstaffe and J. Booth. Surtees Society, Durham. (1889).

FABYAN Robert. *The Great Chronicle of London. (Known as Fabyan's Chronicle).* Edited Arthur Hermann Thomas and Isobel Dorothy Thornley. Pub. G.W. Jones, London, (1938).

GLOSSA ORDINARIA (or *Biblia Latina cum Glossa Ordinaria) 4 Vols.* Introduction by Karlfried Froelich and Margaret Gibson. (Facsimile reprint of the first edition) Turnhout Brepols 1992.

GRATIAN JOHANNES *The Decretum Gratiani (Also known as Concordia Discordantium Canonum)* Bologna (1140).

HENLEY Walter of *Le Dite de Hosebondrie* translated Elizabeth Lamond, edited William Cunningham. 1890. Royal Historical Society.

HUGH of St Victor. *De Sacramentis (or Sacraments of the Christian Faith).* Translated by Roy J. Defarari. Published by Medieval Academy of America (1951).

HUGUCCIO '*Theories on the formation of marriage*' edited J. Roman 1903. *(Summa d'Huguccio sus le Decret de Gratien d'apres le manuscrit 3891). Bibliothèque* Nationale, Causa 27, Questo 2.

INNOCENT III *On the misery of the human condition* or *De Miseria Condicionis Humanae* edited and translated Robert E. Lewis, Chauver Library, Athens, Ga. (1978).

KEMPE Margery. *The Book of Margery Kempe* Introduced and edited by B.A. Windeatt. Folio Society. London (2004).

LAWS OF AETHELSTAN – Clause 31
LAWS OF ALFRED – Clause 42
LAWS OF CNUT II – Clause 53.
LETTERS AND PAPERS HENRY VIII. Vols. 7 and 8. (1534 to July 1535)
LISLE LETTERS. Secker and Warburg. (1983).
LOGGE REGISTER OF PCC WILLS (1479–1486) 2 vols. Editors Lesley Boatwright, Moira Habberjam and Peter Hammond. The transcriptions and translations of the 379 wills and testaments recorded in Latin or English in the Register of the Prerogative Court of Canterbury. Known as 'Logge' after the first of the wills, that of John Logge.
Richard III Society.
LOMBARD Peter. *Sententiae in IV Libris Distinctiae. 2 Vols.* Edited by The Fathers of the College of St Bonaventure. Rome. (1971–1981)

MACHYN Henry. *The Diary of Henry Machyn.* Edited by John Gough Nichols. Camden Society. (1848).

OVID. *Ars Amatoria Amores*

PASTON LETTERS Edited by James Gairdner. Alan Sutton Publishing. (1988).
PENAFORT. St Raymond of. *Summa on Marriage* introduced and translated by Pierre Payer. Medieval Sources in Translation, Pontifical Institute of Medieval Studies, (2005).

PETER THE CHANTER. *Summade Sacramentis et Animae Consiliis* edited by Jean Albert Duguaquier. (Three parts in five volumes.) *Analecra Medievalia Namurcensia.* Louvain and Lille. (1954–1963).

PISAN Christine de. *The Book of the Citie of Ladies* Penguin. (2004).

PLUMPTON CORRESPONDENCE. Edited by Thomas Stapleton. (Camden Society 1893)

PREROGATIVE COURT OF YORK – English Wills 1477–1499. Editors Heather Falvey, Lesley Boatwright, Peter Hammond. Being 89 wills written wholly or partly in English (with translations). Richard III Society,

PROME. (Parliamentary Rolls of Medieval England). 1275–1504. (Rotuli Parliamentarum CD edn. 2005).

PUBLIC RECORD OFFICE SC2/191/56m2m2d. 'King's Lynn'

RYPON Robert of. *Sermons of Robert of Rypon* British Library *Harleian Manuscript 4894. Fol. 176v.*

SALISBURY John of. *Historia Pontificalis* edited and translated by M. Chibnall. Oxford Medieval Texts, Oxford. (1986).

SALISBURY John of. *Letters of John of Salisbury* edited and translated by W.J. Millar, H.E. Butter, and C.N.L. Brooke. 2 Vols. NMT Edinburgh (1955). (Reprinted Oxford Medieval Texts, Oxford. (1986).

SHILLINGFORD John. *Letters and papers of John Shillingford* ed. Stuart A. Moore. Camden Society. (1871).

STONOR LETTERS AND PAPERS. (2 Vols) Edited by C.L. Kingsford. Camden Society, (1919).

TERTULLIAN. Quintus Septimus Florens Tertullian. *Apologeticus* (Approx. 196 AD)

YORK MEMORANDUM BOOK (2 Vols) Surtees Society. 120 and 125. Edited by M. Sellars, (1912–1915).

Secondary Sources

ABBOTT Elizabeth. *A History of Celibacy*. Da Capo Press. (2001).

ADAMSON Margot R. *A Treasury of Middle English Verse Selected and Rendered into Modern English*. London (1930).

AMT Emilie. *Women's Lives in Medieval Europe*. Psychology Press. (1993).

ANGLO-SAXON CHRONICLES. Translated by Michael A. Swanton. Phoenix. (2000).

ARMITAGE. Simon. *Sir Gawain and the Green Knight*. Faber. (2009).

ARMSTRONG. Catherine. *William Marshall, Earl of Pembroke*. Amstrong-Walker. (2007)

ASHDOWN-HILL. John. *The Private Life of Edward IV*. Amberley. (2016).

D'AVRAY. David. *Medieval Marriage – Symbolism and Society*. Oxford University Press. (2004).

BAGLEY J.J. *Life in Medieval England*. Batsford. (1960).

BALSDON. J.P.V.D. *Roman Women*. Bodley Head. (1962).

BALSDON. J.P.V.D. *Life and leisure in ancient Rome*. Bodley Head. (1969).

BALDWIN SMITH. Lacey. *A Tudor Tragedy*. Jonathan Cape. (1961).

BARNES. P.M. *The Anstey Case. A Medieval Miscellany for Doris Mary Stenton*. Edited P.M. Barnes and C.F. Slade. Pipe Roll Society. Lxxvi. London (1962).

BENNETT. H.S. *Life on the English Manor*. Cambridge University Press. (1967).

BENNETT. H.S. *The Pastons and their England*. Cambridge University Press. (1968)

BERESFORD Maurice and HURST J.G. *Deserted Medieval Villages*. Sutton. (1989).

BINDOFF. S.T. *Tudor England*. Pelican. (1964).

BLAIR John. *The Anglo-Saxon Age: A Very Short Introduction*. Oxford University Press. (2000).

BROWN. Gabrielle. *The New Celibacy: A Journey to Love, Intimacy and Good Health*. McGraw-Hill. (1989).

BROOKE. Christopher. *The Medieval Idea of Marriage.* Oxford University Press. (1989)

BROOKS. Richard. *The Knight who saved England.* Osprey. (2014).

DINCHIN-BUCHMAN. Dian. *Herbal Medicine: The Natural Way to Get Well and Stay Well.* Wings Books. 1999.

CAMPBELL. James. *The Anglo-Saxons.* Penguin. (1991).

CAWTHORNE. Nigel. *The Curious Cures of Old England.* Piatkus. (2006).

CHAUCER. Geoffrey. *The Canterbury Tales.* Penguin classics. (2005).

CHIBNALL. A.C. Sherington: *Fiefs and Fields of a Buckinghamshire Village.* Cambridge University Press. (1965).

COULTON. G.G. *Life in the Middle Ages.* Cambridge University Press. (1967).

COSS. Peter R. *The Lady in Medieval England – 1000–1500* Sutton. (1998).

CRAWFORD. Anne. *Letters of Medieval Women.* Sutton. (2002).

DAVIS. Natalie Zemon. *The Return of Martin Guerre.* Penguin. (1983).

DYER. Christopher. *Making a living in the Middle Ages (People of Britain 850–1520)*
Yale University Press. (2002).

EDWARDS. Robert. *The Oulde Dance.* State University of New York. (1991).

EDWARDS. Robert. *Matrons and Marginal Women in Medieval Society.* Boydell and Brewer. (1995).

ELLIOTT. Dyan. *Spiritual Marriage. (Sexual Abstinence in Medieval Wedlock)* Princeton University Press. (1993).

EMMISON. F.G. *Elizabethan Life – Disorder.* Essex Sessions and Assize Records, Essex County Council. (1970).

EMMISON. F.G. *Elizabethan Life II – Morals and the Church Courts.* Essex Record Office Publications. No.63 vol.2. (1973).

FARMER. David Hugh. *Oxford Dictionary of Saints*. Clarendon Press. Oxford. (1978).

FELL. Christine. *Women in Anglo-Saxon England*. Blackwell. (1984).

GASQUET. F.A. *The Great Pestilence. (AD 1348–9)* Simpkin, Marshall, Hamilton, Kent and Co. (1893).

GIES. Frances and Joseph. *Life in a Medieval Village*. Harper Perennial. (1990).

GOLDBERG. P.J.P. *Women, Work and Life Cycle in a Medieval Economy – Women in York and Yorkshire 1300–1500* Oxford University Press. (1992).

GRONBERGER. Sven Magnus. *St Bridget of Sweden: A Chapter of Medieval Church History*. Forgotten Books. (2017).

HAMILTON. J.S. *The Character of Edward II – the Letters of Edward of Caernarfen Reconsidered*. Woodbridge. (2006).

HANAWALT. Barbara A. 'The ties that bind – peasant families in medieval England.' Oxford University Press. 1989.

HASSALL. W.O. 'How they lived – an anthology of original accounts written before 1485' New York. 1962.

HELMHOLZ. Richard A. *Marriage Litigation in Medieval England*. Cambridge University Press reprint.(2007).

HILL. Paul. *The Age of Aethelstan – Britain's Forgotten History* Tempus. 2004.

HILTON. R.H. *The English Peasantry in the Later Middle Ages*. (In: Ford Lectures for 1973.) Oxford University Press (1975).

HISTORY OF THE COUNTY OF YORK. *Houses of Cistercian Monks*. Vol.3. (1974).

HOFFMAN. David. *Complete Herbal*. Element Books. (1996).

HOUGH. Carol. *Marriage and Divorce*. (In Wiley-Blackwell Encyclopaedia of Anglo-Saxon England.) (2008).

HOWELL. J. *Epistolae Ho-Elinae*. London (1890).

JACKSON. J.C. *Chartulary of Rievaulx Abbey*. Surtees Society. (1887).

JAFFE. Peter G. (with David Wolfe and Susan K. Wilson) *Children of Battered Women*. Sage Publications. (1990).

JEWELL. Helen. *Women in Medieval England*. Manchester. (1996).

JONES Michael K. and UNDERWOOD Malcolm G. *The King's Mother: Lady Margaret Beaufort, Countess of Richmond and Derby*. Cambridge University Press. (1992).

JONES. Terry. *Terry Jones' Medieval Lives*. BBC Books. (2005).

KARRAS. Ruth Mazo. *Common Women: Prostitution and Sexuality in Medieval England*. Oxford University Press. (1996).

KARRAS. Ruth Mazo. *Sexuality in Medieval Europe: Doing unto Others*. University of Pennsylvania Press. (2005). (Reprinted Routledge.)

KARRAS. Ruth Mazo. *Unmarriages: Women, Men and Sexual Unions in the Middle Ages*. University of Pennsylvania Press. (2012).

KENDALL. Paul Murray. *The Yorkist Age*. Allen and Unwin. (1962).

LAPIDGE. Michael. *Archbishop Theodore: Commemorative Studies of his Life and Influence*. Cambridge University Press. (1995).

LAPIDGE. Michael. Ed. *Wiley-Blackwell Encyclopaedia of Anglo-Saxon England*. Wiley-Blackwell. 2008.

LAURENCE. Anne. *Women in England. 1500–1760. (A social history)*. Phoenix. 1994.

LEYSER. Henrietta. *Medieval Women. (A social history of women in England, 450–1500)*. Phoenix. (1996).

LOFTS. Norah. *Domestic Life in England*. Weidenfeld and Nicolson. (1976).

MARTIN. Sean. *The Cathars: Rise and Fall of the Great Heresy*. Oldcastle Books. (2014).

MATTINGLY. Garrett. *Catherine of Aragon*. Jonathan Cape. 1944.

MAZZUCHELLI. Mario. *The Nun of Monza. (Translated by Evelyn Gendal.)* Hamish Hamilton. (1963).

McLAREN. Angus. *A History of Contraception, from Antiquity to the Present Day*. Wiley-Blackwell. (1992).

McLAREN. Angus. *Impotence: A Cultural History*. University of Chicago Press. (2007).

McSHEFFEREY. Shannon. *Medieval Marriage*. University of Pennsylvania Press. (2004).

McSHEFFEREY. Shannon. *Gender and Heresy 1420–1530*. University of Pennsylvania Press. (1995).

MORTIMER. Ian. *The Greatest Traitor: The Life of Sir Roger Mortimer, Ruler of England, 1327–1330*. Pimlico. (2004).

MORTIMER. Ian. *Time Traveller's Guide to Medieval England*. Vintage. (2009).

MOXEY. Keith. *Peasants, Warriors and Wives: Popular Imagery in the Reformation*. Chicago. (1989).

MUIR. Richard. *Old Yorkshire*. Michael Joseph. (1987).

MYERS. A.R. *England in the Late Middle Ages*. Pelican. (1963).

MYRC. John. *Instructions for Parish Priests*. Edward Peacock. EETS. o.s. 209. London (1940).

OTIS. Leah Lydia. *Prostitution in Medieval Society – the History of an Urban Institution in the Languedoc*. University of Chicago Press. (2009).

O'REGAN. Mary. *The Medieval Manor Court of Wakefield*. Rosalba Press. (Richard III Society, Yorkshire). (1994).

PEDERSEN. Frederik. *Marriage Disputes in Medieval England*. Hambledon. (2000).

PERNAUD. Regine. *Eleanor of Aquitaine. (Translated by Peter Wiles)*. Collins. (1967).

PLATT. Colin. *The English Medieval Town*. Secker and Warburg. (1976).

PLATT. Colin. *Medieval England*. Routledge. (1978).

PLATT. Karen. *Woman Defamed and Woman Defended*. Oxford University Press. (1996).

PODLECH. Dieter. *Herbs and Healing Plants of Britain and Europe*. Collins. (1996).

POWER. Eileen. *Medieval Women*. Cambridge University Press. (2008).

PRATCHETT. Terry. *Mort*. Corgi Books. (1988).

PUBLIC RECORD OFFICE SC2/191/56 m2m2d *The Making of King's Lynn.*
(PRO Publications)

RIDDLE. John M. *Contraception and Abortion from the Ancient World to the Renaissance.* Harvard University Press. (1992).

ROGERS. J. Thorold. *A History of Agriculture and Prices in England. Vol.I. Oxford.* (1866).

ROSENTHAL. Joel. *Fifteenth Century Widows and Widowhood – Bereavement, Reintegration and Life Choices.* University of Michigan Press. (1993).

ROSSIAUD. Jacques. *Medieval prostitution.* Wiley-Blackwell. (1995).

RUSSELL. Jesse. *Walkington Wolds Burials.* VSD (2012).

SHUFFELTON. George. Ed. 'How the wise man taught his son' in: *A Compilation of Middle English Verse.* (2008).

SMITH. Lesley. *The Glossa Ordinaria – the Making of a Medieval Bible Commentary.* Brill Academic Publications. (2009).

SPENCE. Joan and Bill. *Medieval monasteries of Yorkshire.* Ambo. (1981).

SPUFFORD. *Margaret. Contrasting Communities – English Villagers in the Sixteenth and Seventeenth Centuries.* Cambridge University Press. (1974).

STENTON. Doris Mary. *English Society in the Early Middle Ages : 1066–1307.* Pelican. 1962.

STEVENSON. K.W. *NuptialBblessings – A study of Christian Marriage Rituals.* London. (1982).

TELFORD Lynda. *Tudor Victims of the Reformation.* Pen and Sword. (2016).

TREVALYAN. G.M. *English Social History.* London. (1942).

WHITE. Hugh. *Ancrene Wyse.* Penguin. (1993).

WHITTOCK. Martyn. *A Brief History of Life in the Middle Ages.* Running Press. (2009).

WISE. Terence. *1066 – Year of Destiny*. Osprey. (1979).

WOOLGAR. C.M. *The Great Household in Late Medieval England*. Yale University Press, (1999).

WOOLGAR. C.M. *The Senses in Late Medieval England*. Yale University Press. (2006).

WOOLLEY. Benjamin. *The Queen's Conjuror – the Science and Magic of John Dee*. Flamingo. (2002).

ZIEGLER. Philip. *The Black Death*. Collins. (1969).

INDEX